AUTHORS OF THE BIBLE

WHO, WHEN, WHERE WHAT, AND WHY

FRED GLYNN

SF RG PRESS
San Francisco

SFRG PRESS

For information, address:
SFRG Press
Post Office Box 15007
San Francisco, California 94115
www.authorsofthebible.com

ISBN 0-915210-02-9

Glynn, Fred

Authors of the Bible: Who, When, Where, What, and Why

Includes bibliographic references and index

Cover design by Dale Murphy, Nuts-n-Bolts Graphics
Photo copyright Neil Bromfield

Manufactured in the United States of America

Regretfully we are returning your . . .

Readers' Report

Anonymous, *The Bible*

I must say that the first few hundred pages of this manuscript really hooked me. Action-packed, they have everything today's reader wants in a good story. Sex (lots of it, including adultery, sodomy, incest), also murder, war, massacres, and so on.

The Sodom and Gomorrah chapter, with the transvestites putting the make on the angels, is worthy of Rabelais; the Noah stories are pure Jules Verne; the escape from Egypt cries out to be turned into a major motion picture … In other words, a real blockbuster, very well structured, with plenty of twists, full of invention, with just the right amount of piety, and never lapsing into tragedy.

But, as I kept on reading, I realized that this is actually an anthology, involving several writers, with many—too many stretches of poetry, and passages that are downright mawkish and boring, and jeremiads that make no sense.

The end result is a monster omnibus. It seems to have something for everybody, but ends up appealing to nobody. And acquiring the rights from all these different authors will mean big headaches, unless the editor takes care of that himself. The editor's name, by the way, doesn't appear anywhere on the manuscript, not even in the table of contents. Is there some reason for keeping his identity a secret?

I'd suggest trying to get the rights only to the first five chapters. We're on sure ground there. Also come up with a better title. How about *The Red Sea Desperadoes*?

—Umberto Eco[1]

1 Eco, Umberto, Misreadings, Harcourt, Inc., Orlando, Florida, 1993, pages 33-4

CONTENTS

CONTENTS

INTRODUCTION

Besides identifying, as clearly as possible, the two dozen men and women who wrote the *Bible*, *Authors of the Bible* also describes the varying circumstances that caused those authors to write what they did. By *Bible* we mean the *Hebrew Bible* or *Old Testament*—the *Bible* that Jesus, centuries later, would have come to know.

Although it has lately become fashionable to read the *Bible* as "literature"—which it certainly is—it is a great deal more than that. It contains far more history than is generally realized. Since the biblical authors dealt with topics that were too politically sensitive to write about openly, much of the *Bible* was written in the form of allegories. *Authors of the Bible* discusses the history that probably lay behind the allegories.

The *Bible* is a book about power. How power is acquired. How power is kept. How power is lost. More is to be learned about power from a thoughtful reading of the *Bible* than from modern works such as Niccolo Macchiavelli's *The Prince* or Eric Hoffer's *The True Believer*.

The *Bible* gives a history of the struggle for power within the two monarchies, Israel and Judah, as well as the ongoing struggle between the two after Solomon's death. The *Bible* also gives a history of the struggle for power between the monarchy and the two priestly factions—one claiming descent from Moses, the other, from Aaron.

AUTHORS OF THE BIBLE

The first of the *Bible*'s authors was, almost certainly, the legendary—but very real—King David who began the writing of the *Book of Jashar* at Ziklag, a small settlement in the Negev desert, around 1005 BCE when he dictated an elegy lamenting the deaths of King Saul and Saul's son, Jonathan. Probably never intended to be a "sacred" book, the *Book of Jashar* grew when David and his scribe created alibis for the dozen or so murders that had helped put David on Saul's throne. Although the *Book of Jashar* served David as an effective spin-piece throughout his long career, only a few fragments have survived.[1]

Soon after David and his scribe finished writing, a second author added material borrowed from David's book to eyewitness accounts of events at King David's court and other material, thus creating most of what we know today as *Book of Samuel*. Around thirty years later, a third author borrowed still more material from David's book and used it, along with a wide range of material, including myths, songs and legends, not all of which had been written down before—to create several new books: *Genesis*, *Exodus*, *Joshua*, *Judges*, and a new beginning to the *Book of Samuel*.

At this point much of the *Book of Jashar* had been rewritten and what remained seems to have been set aside and eventually lost. Later, other authors—including prophets such as Isaiah, Jeremiah, Ezekiel, and others—added their own books. Later, editors modified the surviving, earlier books, inserting their own points of view and laws that enhanced and perpetuated their power. And even later, in Alexandria in the mid-third century BCE, other authors added primarily literary works such as the *Song of Songs* and *Ecclesiastes* which had been rather directly inspired by Greek literature and philosophy.

The result is a mosaic, a composite of pieces of all sizes where sometimes even a single verse will contain material from three or four authors. Identifying who wrote what and when and why is the subject of this book. It is a task that has occupied many scholars since 1651 CE and most archaeologists of the last half century.

READING THE BIBLE

Why hadn't the search for the authors' identities begun earlier? There are several reasons. For the first sixteen hundred years after the *Hebrew Bible* had been completed around 140 BCE until the mid-fifteenth century CE, there were very few copies since they all had to be copied by hand. Second, because they were written in languages understood only by the very educated—Hebrew, Greek, and Latin. And many of those who had copies or had access to copies may not have been interested in learning more about its origins since it served their purposes just fine as it was.

All this changed when Johannes Gutenberg developed movable type and printed copies of a Latin version of the *Bible* in Germany in the mid-fifteenth century CE. While this greatly increased the number of bibles—and the number of people who would read it—it was still inaccessible to the great mass of people because they could not read Latin.

In the early sixteenth century, Martin Luther challenged the Church in Rome to debate principles which were central to its authority, thus beginning the Reformation. So that lay people could understand the issues, Luther translated the *New Testament* into German and published it in 1522 followed by the *Old Testament* that he published in 1534.

William Tyndale, an Oxford-educated scholar, was among those whom Luther convinced that the Church was in need of reformation. Since Tyndale had noticed that priests were claiming biblical authority for various policies of the Church for which there was no biblical basis, the remedy was obvious. Translated into languages that ordinary people actually spoke, the *Bible* itself would make it impossible for the Church to misuse it.

Despite enormous difficulties Tyndale translated large portions of the *Bible* into English. Before his translation was complete, the Church realized how dangerous an English *Bible* could be. Tyndale was arrested while in Belgium, tried for heresy, convicted and sentenced to death. The sentence was carried out at Villevorde Castle, about six miles from Brussels, on the morning of October 6, 1536. Tyndale was tied to a stake surrounded by straw and wood, accorded the very real privilege of being strangled first, and then burned. Even before his death there was great interest in his translations and numerous anonymously printed copies were sold clandestinely.

After the deaths of King Henry VIII and Elizabeth I, James, the son of Mary Queen of Scots, became king. James commissioned the translation of the *Bible* into English. The king's translators worked quickly, borrowing much from Tyndale's translations. The result was the Authorized King James Version of 1611.

Widely distributed—James had ordered a copy chained to every pulpit throughout the realm to enable public inspection—the Authorized King James Version had an immense impact on the English people. It produced a more literate public. It standardized the English language. It was Tyndale's English, after all, that Shakespeare used so effectively. And it was King James' *Bible* that widened the gulf between Canterbury and Rome, thus strengthening the power of the English monarchy.

But, as the *Bible* became more widely available, people began to ask who had written it.

In 1651 Thomas Hobbes published *The Leviathan*, a book on the optimal, rational design of government. Although Hobbes allowed that Moses might have written some of the first five books of the *Bible*, he denied that Moses could have written those books in their entirety. With this observation, Hobbes touched off a three hundred and fifty year inquiry into the authorship of the *Bible*.

In 1655 Isaac de la Peyrere, French explorer and diplomat (Ambassador to Denmark), a Calvinist from Bordeaux, published *Prae Adamitae (Men Before Adam)* in Belgium. de la Peyrere expressed his belief that while Adam may have been the first Jew, there were other humans, non-Jews, living elsewhere in the world whose ancestors were of far more ancient origin than Adam. de la Peyrere's book had a profound effect. The Church felt threatened and would have had de la Peyrere charged with heresy, tried, and executed but for the fact that de la Peyrere came from a wealthy and influential family. de la Peyrere was allowed to save himself by agreeing to enter a monastery and never write again.[2]

In 1670 the *Tractatus Theologico-Politicus* was published anonymously, bearing the name of a fictitious printer at Hamburg. Its author was the philosopher Benedict Spinoza, an excommunicated Dutch Jew, who had written the book in Latin lest it disturb the faith of the uneducated masses. In the *Tractatus Theologico-Politicus* Spinoza went further than Hobbes in identifying who had not written the *Bible*: Spinoza stated flatly that it was "clearer than the sun at noonday that the Pentateuch was not written by Moses, but by someone who lived long after Moses."[3]

Just over a hundred years after Hobbes had pointed out various problems that impeded identifying the author or authors of the Bible, Jean Astruc, a physician at the court of Louis XV in Paris, published *Conjectures sur les Memoires Originaux* anonymously in Brussels in 1753. Astruc noted that the author of some passages in *Genesis* referred to God as Yahweh in Hebrew ("Dieu" in French) while the author of other passages referred to God as "Elohim" in Hebrew ("l'Eternel Dieu"). Although Astruc was primarily concerned with two authors who used different names to refer to God, he showed how Moses might have used four initial source documents—to which Astruc referred as "A," "B," "C," and "D"—to create the *Book of Genesis*.

In 1780, Johann Eichorn lent his support to Astruc's attribution of the Pentateuch to two principal authors; instead of "A" and "B," Eichorn referred to them as "E" (for those portions of the text which referred to God as "Elohim") and "J" (for those that referred to God as Yahweh or, in German, "Jahweh") respectively.

In 1798, Karl David Ilgen stated that the E document was the product of not one author, but two. Part of the original E document retained its designation as E, but part of it would become known as P, the Priestly Source. Because of certain problems with Ilgen's analysis, his attribution of the original E document to two authors would be largely ignored for the next 55 years.

In 1805, William de Wette, noting that the language in the *Book of Deuteronomy* was, as Richard Elliott Friedman puts it, "strikingly different from the four books that had preceded it," suggested that there had been a fourth author involved in the writing of the Pentateuch. de Wette noticed that the law codes in Deuteronomy happened to coincide with the details of a religious reform described in the *Bible*, led by the young King Josiah of Judah. Since the impetus for Josiah's reform was said to be the discovery of a scroll in the Temple of Yahweh in Jerusalem, de Wette's conclusion was that Josiah's new scroll was none other than the *Book of Deuteronomy*, penned shortly before its "discovery" and passed off as an ancient law code.

In 1853 Herman Hupfeld popularized Ilgen's theory that a Priestly writer had written a separate work, "P" which was now incorporated into the Pentateuch. This fourfold division, generally accepted by bible scholars today, is not altogether convincing. For example, the assignment of the opening of *Genesis*, *Genesis* 1:1-2:4, to P seems to make less sense, stylistically, than to attribute it to E. And portions presently attributed to E would make more sense attributed to P.

Since the hypothetical sources separated by scholars had reasonable narrative continuity when read separately, it was hypothesized that they were originally independent documents which had been spliced together by the work of a later redactor (an editor-author), who was dubbed "R."

Then, in 1876, a German bible scholar, Julius Wellhausen, published *Prolegomena to the History of Israel*. Wellhausen's principal original contribution was a thorough examination of the evolution of the forms of worship of the Israelites and their successors, the Jews. This he combined with a comprehensive and authoritative summary of the work of previous scholars. Wellhausen's view of how the *Bible* was written is generally referred to as the Documentary Hypothesis. It remains the basis of the understanding of most mainstream bible scholars on the subject of the authorship of the *Bible*.

In the past the tendency has been to analyze the authorship of the Bible on a book-by-book basis beginning with *Genesis*. This is true of Emil Kautzsch's *An Outline of the History of the Literature of the Old Testament* (1898) and the Revised Edition of S. R. Driver's *An Introduction to the Literature of the Old Testament* (1913), two of the most valuable sources on the subject. Both books contain a great deal of useful information.

The most forceful recent advocate of the Documentary Hypothesis is Richard Elliott Friedman. His 1987 book, *Who Wrote The Bible?* is at once thoroughly scholarly and exceptionally readable, and has done much to revive public interest in the Hypothesis.

More recently, in *The Hidden Book In The Bible*, Friedman set forth the interesting hypothesis that the Pentateuchal source "J" continues intermittently up through the end of the second chapter of *I Kings*. The author of this source thus created the world's first prose masterpiece, covering the creation of the world through the ascension of Solomon to the throne of Israel.

The archaeological discoveries of the past ninety years have already led to changes in the way we envision the origin and history of the people who wrote the *Bible*. And those changes are, in turn, leading to a new, more detailed picture of how, when, where, why, and by whom it was written.

Fred Glynn, June 2006

ENDNOTES

1. There are certain individual works such as *Jacob's Blessing*, *The Blessing of Moses*, *The Song of Deborah*, *The Song of the Sea*, etc., works with archaic linguistic features that are widely—though possibly erroneously—accepted as predating the *Book of Samuel* and the Pentateuch. For a possible list of fragments from the *Book of Jashar*, see Appendix 2, *An Outline of the Book of Jashar*.

2. Copies of de la Peyrere's book survived and unauthorized copies were apparently widely sold. Its effects were widespread since it raised the question of why Yahweh had created the native Americans. It also seems to have been the inspiration for Samuel Spaulding's early nineteenth century novel, *The Manuscript Found*, about adventures of the so-called "lost tribes of Israel" settling in the New World after the fall of Israel in 722 BCE. Some believe that Spaulding's novel was the basis for Joseph Smith's *The Book of Mormon* published in Palmyra, New York, in 1830.

3. de Spinoza, Benedict, *A Theologico-Political Treatise*, a reprint of the G. Bell & Sons edition of 1883, Dover Publications, Inc. New York, 1951, page 124.

Chapter 1

In the Beginning...

The Settlement of Canaan

Around 10,000 years ago, in the Fertile Crescent between the Tigris and Euphrates rivers, an agricultural revolution began when semi-nomadic hunter-gatherers began to corral the herds of animals with whom they had previously wandered from place to place, seeking out plants in places where they were known to grow and settled down, raising animals and plants in defensible places such as hillsides or hilltops that had, or were close to, adequate soil and water.[1] Gradually they increased the complexity of their spoken language so that they could communicate with each other about things other than those in the immediate present and, as a result began to work more closely together for their mutual benefit. Trade, developed through specialization of individual and tribal skills, led to a need to record the details of their agreements—a need solved by the making of marks on various materials close at hand, such as clay.

Around 3500 BCE, in what archaeologists call the Early Bronze Age, a sizeable number of people established almost 100 villages and larger towns throughout the central ridge in the highlands to the east of the coastal plain at the eastern end of the Mediterranean Sea, south of the Beth-Shean and Jezreel valleys, and west of the Jordan valley.[2]

By 2200 BCE, however, most of those settlements had been abandoned and remained so until shortly after 2000 BCE, when a second wave of settlement began with the establishment of small, scattered villages that gradually grew into a complex network of about 220 settlements. These settlements ranged from villages to towns to fortified regional centers—including Hebron, Jerusalem, Bethel, Shiloh, and Shechem—and had a total population estimated at about 40,000.[3]

Around 1720 BCE, Egypt was attacked by the Hyskos—sometimes called "the shepherd kings"—who established their capital at Avaris, proclaimed their own line of kings, and ruled northern (Lower) Egypt. southern (Upper) Egypt was ruled by kings at Thebes.

Upper and Lower Egypt had been at peace for more than a hundred years when, around 1574 BCE, a group of noisy hippopotami escaped from their pampered existence in the Sacred Pool east of Thebes into the canal which connected the pool with the Nile. A deliberately provocative complaint on their behalf soon arrived from the Hyskos king, Apepi I, in Avaris. Condescendingly addressed to "the Prince of the southern city" rather than to Sequenenre Tao, king of Thebes, Apepi complained that he could not sleep, so loud were the cries of the hippopotami.

Of course Apepi could not hear them—500 miles separated Avaris and Thebes—but Seth, the god whom Apepi worshipped, to whom hippopotami were sacred, could hear them and wanted something done immediately. When Seqenenre Tao read Apepi's letter to his army officers all seem to have agreed that Apepi's letter was a declaration of war. Early in the thirty-year war that followed, Seqenenre Tao was hacked to death by at least two men, one of whom wielded a Hyskos axe.

Sequenenre's son Kamose failed to achieve victory over the Hyskos during his five year reign. Midway through the twenty-four year reign of Kamose' brother Ahmose I war resumed and by around 1558 BCE, the Egyptians had taken Avaris and had succeeded not only in driving the Hyskos out of Egypt but in bringing the region along the eastern end of the Mediterranean Sea under Egyptian control-as far north as Ugarit, and as far east as the Jordan and Orontes rivers.

Ahmose I was succeeded by Amenhotep I (1551-1524 BCE), Tuthmosis I (1524-1518 BCE), Tuthmosis II (1518-1504) and Tuthmosis III (1504-1450). Due to Tuthmosis III's extreme youth, his mother, the strong-willed Hatshepsut, became co-regent in 1498 BCE and, with the support of key members of King Tuthmosis II's court, reigned as Queen Hatshepsut until her death in 1483 BCE.

Toward the end of her reign, Egyptian control of Canaan (which had become only sparsely populated and would remain so for the next three centuries[4]) seems to have weakened. Three cities—Gaza, Yehem, and Megiddo—chose this time to rebel. After Hatshepsut's death, Tuthmosis III, now in the twenty-first year of his "reign," became the sole king of Egypt. Two years later, in a brilliantly planned and daringly executed campaign—a classic in the history of warfare—he suppressed the rebellion.

In 1442 BCE Tuthmosis III's successor, Pharaoh Amenhotep II (1453-1419 BCE), then in the ninth year of his reign, campaigned in Palestine strengthening Egyptian control there as well as keeping Canaan firmly under Egyptian control. Peace in the region characterized the final twenty-five years of Amenhotep II's reign and the entire thirty-three years of his successor, Tuthmosis IV (1419-1386 BCE). There seems to have been no successful uprising within nor any significant invasion of Canaan during this period.

Thus Egypt's well documented history clashes irreconcilably with *I Kings* 6:1 which implies a date of 1441 BCE for the exodus of the Hebrew slaves from Egypt—an exodus which included a forty-year sojourn in the Sinai desert. Egypt's well documented history also clashes irreconcilably with *Exodus* 1:11 which vividly portrays Hebrew slaves fleeing from the building of the cities of Pithom and Rameses, something that could not have happened until some time after Rameses II, the nominal builder of the latter city, had begun his sixty-seven year reign in 1279 BCE.

Around the time that Rameses II died in 1212 BCE, a third, major wave of settlement in Canaan began with an initial population of 45,000 in 250 sites. Still firmly under Egyptian control, these would gradually develop into a mature network of large cities, medium-sized market centers, and small villages. The Canaanites may have begun to press for more autonomy about this time because five years later Rameses II's successor, Merenptah (1212-1202 BCE), suppressed an insurrection in Canaan and erected a stele at Thebes that boasts, in part, that:

> Canaan is captive with all woe, Askelon is captured, Gezer seized, Yanoam made non-existent, Israel is wasted, bare of seed.[5]

It is the first known reference to Israel though whether Israel had been a village or a tribe is not known. It is clear, however, that Israel had not, at that point, conquered Canaan.

Seven more rulers would succeed Merenptah before Rameses V began a six year reign[6] in 1147 BCE. By 1143 BCE he was apparently living in seclusion, his face disfigured from smallpox, when his brother, Nebmaatre Meryamum, became co-regent, ruling under the name Rameses VI.

When, as a result of smallpox, murder or suicide,[7] Rameses V died in 1141 BCE, Rameses VI, now ruling on his own, withdrew Egyptian troops from Canaan and Midian to quell a civil war in Egypt. With the exodus of the Egyptian troops, nearly four hundred years of Egyptian domination of Canaan and Midian came to an end.

In Canaan, the departure of the Egyptians led to a relatively peaceful peasant revolt against the Canaanite elite who had served as administrators for the Egyptians. The peasants' goals were modest—like those of the biblical Adam and Eve: They wished to keep a larger share of what they produced and they wanted an opportunity for their children to become better educated.[8]

In *The Bible Unearthed*, Israel Finkelstein reports that:

> the villagers of Canaan were forced to concentrate on local subsistence and no longer produced a significant surplus of grain over and above what they needed for themselves. Thus the highland and desert-fringe pastoralists had to adapt to the new conditions and produce their own grain. Soon, the requirements of farming would cause a reduction in the range of seasonal migrations. Flocks would then have to be reduced as the period of migrations grew shorter, and with more and more effort invested in agriculture, a permanent shift to sedentarization occurred.[9]

In Egypt there were shortages of grain (consistent with the reduced production in Canaan) and other foodstuffs. Rampant inflation and political unrest ensued.

In Midian, the departure of the Egyptians from the copper mines at Timna in 1141 BCE had been followed by the miners' destruction of the Temple of Hathor near the mines and the toppling and defacing of some of Hathor's statues.[10] Then the miners carved holes to support poles and erected a red and yellow tent made of wool and flax and began the worship of Yahweh.

The miners also revered "a gilded copper image of a snake."[11] Venomous snakes were—and still are—common in this region and were a persistent threat to the miners working in the poorly lit mines. The purpose of the serpent's image seems to have been to assure those who had been bitten by poisonous snakes that by looking upon the image they could be cured.[12]

In Canaan, at the time, the Canaanites, like many of the other people in the region, worshipped a pantheon of gods who ruled the actions of the sun, moon, wind, rain and other natural phenomena, gods whose wishes had to be respected with regard to the time to sow and the time to reap. Soon—within three or four generations—the Canaanite peasants added the God of the Midianites to their pantheon and took on a new identity as Israelites.

In the third edition of *A History of Israel*, historian John Bright concedes that the artifacts found at Timna argue "that some connection existed between Israel's religion and that of the Midianites."[13] But, what was that connection?

According to *I Samuel* 14:35, it was Moses—portrayed as the son-in-law of a Midianite priest, Jethro—who had introduced the worship of Yahweh, to the Israelites. Given what we know about the Midianites at Timna, the story of Moses introducing the worship of the Midianite's god after escaping from slavery under the Egyptians is not surprising. But, just when were the Israelites—or proto-Israelites—introduced to the Midianites' god, Yahweh? Since there is no evidence at Timna of the Midianites worshipping Yahweh before the destruction of the temple of Hathor at Timna in 1141 BCE, it would probably have been somewhat later—not at the time of the biblical exodus, but closer to the beginning of the reign of Israel's first king, Saul around 1025 BCE.

Because the archaeological record at Timna, in the Sinai generally, and in Canaan where the Israelites were supposed to have been involved in a violent conquest, conflicts with the biblical account, a look at the searches—in the late nineteenth and twentieth century—for hard evidence of the Israelites' forty-year, seven-hundred mile trek through the wilderness and their legendary subsequent conquest of Canaan may help shed some light on what actually happened three thousand years ago.

THE SEARCH FOR KADESH-BARNEA

Oddly, it was during the period of Egyptian domination of Canaan that the exodus is said to have occurred. According to *I Kings* 6:1, the exodus took place four hundred and eighty years before Solomon's construction of the temple in Jerusalem. If Solomon built his temple in the fourth year of his reign, i.e., 961 BCE, then a date of 1441 is clearly implied. On the other hand, *Exodus* 1:11 states that the exodus took place during the building of the cities of Pithom and Rameses, which implies a date of around 1263-2 BCE for the exodus.[14] While the discrepancy of nearly two hundred years in the implied biblical dates is significant, the archaeological evidence—what the Hebrews or Israelites did or did not leave behind at Kadesh-Barnea as well as any signs of a violent conquest in Canaan—has more bearing on the credibility of the biblical account.

Said to be—or to have been—located somewhere between the Wilderness of Paran and the Wilderness of Zin, Kadesh-Barnea was the oasis where Moses caused water to flow by striking a rock with his staff. It was here that 603,550 able-bodied men plus their wives and children, estimated at between two and a half and three million people altogether, were said to have stayed for an extended period—possibly as long as thirty-eight years—during their flight from Egypt over three thousand years before. Thus perhaps no site has more potential for establishing the historicity of the Torah, the five books of Moses—or for denying it.

In 1838 an American, Edward Robinson,[15] was among the first, in modern times, to seek the site of the biblical Kadesh-Barnea. Robinson was followed by Edward Henry Palmer[16] in February 1870 and by an American evangelist, H. Clay Trumbull in 1881[17] both of whom believed Ain Qadeis to be the site. In 1905, a German archaeologist, Nathaniel Schmidt, suggested that Ain Quaiderat was a more likely site.

Until 1914 no excavations had been made at any of the three proposed sites. Then, in the months immediately preceding World War I, the London-based Palestine Exploration Fund asked Turkish government—which had control of the Sinai—for permission to search for archaeological evidence of the Israelites' forty-year trek from the Egyptian delta to Canaan. Funding for the project was said to have come from an anonymous donor. The Palestine Exploration Fund then commissioned Charles Leonard Wooley, 32, Thomas Edward Lawrence, 25—who would later become known as "Lawrence of Arabia,"—and Lawrence's young Arab servant, Salem 'Dahoum' Ahmed, 16, who set out on December 29, 1913 to join the Fund's expedition in the northern Sinai.

Dahoum and Lawrence had met three years earlier, when Dahoum was given the task of caring for Lawrence who was recovering from an illness—thought to be typhoid fever—in Carchemish. They soon became close friends.[18, 19]

Their mission, as they would learn from instructions addressed to Wooley that they received, en route, at Aleppo, was to make "an examination from the archaeological point of view, as there are many remains of great interest to the Bible student, and it is for this part of the work that the Committee are desirous of enlisting the services of yourself and Mr. Lawrence."[20]

Indeed, it was through the continuing support of Dr. David Hogarth, who had been the most influential of Lawrence's mentors at Oxford, that Wooley, Lawrence, and Dahoum (upon Lawrence's insistence) had been chosen to examine whatever physical evidence remained of the Israelites' forty-year, seven-hundred mile trek through the northern Sinai. While Lawrence and Wooley had been trained as archaeologists, historians, and classicists, Dahoum had been given a 'crash-course' in photography and the making of impressions of artifacts too large to move. He had also been enrolled as a British Intelligence agent.[21]

On their arrival at Ain Qadeis, however, Wooley and Lawrence found not the oasis of verdure and beauty that Trumbull had described as "adequate for the whole host of Israel,"[22] but two pools of brackish water, one a foot and a half deep, hardly fit for the few dozen workmen that had accompanied them. Furthermore, after establishing that Ain Qadeis could not have been the biblical Kadesh-Barnea, Wooley and Lawrence jovially observed in their report, *The Wilderness of Zin*, published the following year, that it spoke "wonders for the Children of Israel that they left Moses alive after he brought them to a place like that."[23]

But, if Ain Qadeis were not the site of the biblical Kadesh-Barnea, what was?

Following up Schmidt's suggestion, Wooley and Lawrence decided to make a brief excavation at Ain Quaiderat, four miles northwest of Ain Qadeis. After three days of excavation Lawrence and Wooley concluded that the site had probably been fortified in the seventh century BC by the Judahites during the reign of King Josiah (639-609 BCE)[24]—and destroyed in 609 BCE by the Pharaoh Neccho who was en route to wage war against the Assyrians.

Within a few months of their arriving in the Sinai, Wooley and Lawrence concluded that there was "almost nothing that related to the Biblical period in which the Palestine Exploration Fund was interested" and that while the "Jews may have spent forty years in this wilderness during the Exodus… their passage had left no recognizable signs."[25]

As for the roles that he, Wooley and Dahoum were really playing, Lawrence explained, in a letter to his parents, that they were serving as "red herrings, to give an archaeological color to a political job."[26] It was not Lawrence's first experience as a spy—his Oxford thesis, *Crusader Castles*, having already supplied useful information on fortifications that the French and Syrians were constructing for the forthcoming war—nor would it be his last.

A major war was in the making and, if England were to retain control of its recently constructed Suez Canal and the western Mediterranean, maps of the Sinai were necessary to facilitate the movement of English troops as well as to stymie the control that the Germans and Turks had in the area.

Thus Wooley and Lawrence were ordered to produce—as rapidly as possible—a report which would attempt to dispel any suspicions that the Turkish and German governments might have about the Palestine Exploration Fund's expedition being a cover for an espionage operation. Unfortunately that could not be done quickly enough.

World War I—the so-called "Great War" or "War That Will End War"—broke out in August 1914 and Wooley and Lawrence's report was not published until the following year. Over forty years would go by before the search for the route of the biblical exodus would resume.

It wasn't until later expeditions—notably those of Moshe Dothan in 1956 and of Rudolf Cohen between 1976 and 1982—that the full significance of Wooley and Lawrence's discovery of the site of the biblical Kadesh-Barnea was revealed.

Dothan's excavations uncovered the remains of a fortress built during the reign of King Uzziah (785-733 BCE)[27] and a 10th century BC fortress which may have been built by King Solomon (965-928 BCE)[28] and destroyed by Pharaoh Shishak in 925 BCE.[29] Cohen's excavations revealed that there had been no activity there from the sixteenth to twelfth centuries BCE. In other words, the exodus, as described in *Exodus, Leviticus, Numbers* and *Deuteronomy*, had not—and could not have—taken place.

Israeli archaeologist Amahai Mazar, writing in 1990, put it this way:

> Archaeological research at the oasis of Kadesh-Barnea did not reveal even one shred from the Late Bronze Age or Iron Age I. The place was only populated during the third millennium BCE and in the time of the Israelite Monarchy, when a royal fortress was established.

To which Mazar added:

> There is nothing in the archaeological record to suggest that the settlers came from outside the land of Israel, as stated in the biblical tradition.[30]

THE ORIGIN OF THE ISRAELITES

If the exodus from Egypt had not taken place as described in *Exodus, Leviticus, Numbers* and *Deuteronomy*, then where had the Israelites come from—and when—and under whose leadership?

In an article, *The Hebrew Conquest of Palestine*,[31] published in 1962, George Mendenhall suggested that instead of a bloody conquest of Canaan by Israelites from outside of Canaan, what had probably occurred was a relatively peaceful revolt of indigenous Canaanite peasants.

Mendenhall's concept of a peasant revolt is shared by Finkelstein who states that:

> Most of the people who formed early Israel were local people—the same people whom we see in the highlands throughout the Bronze and Iron Ages. The early Israelites were—irony of ironies—themselves originally Canaanites.[32]

The archaeological evidence shows that the Canaanites who became Israelites were different from the Canaanites who did not. According to Finkelstein, what set the Canaanites who became Israelites apart from their neighbors was that while:

> people demonstrate their ethnicity in many different ways: in language, religion, customs of dress, burial practices, and elaborate dietary taboos" the distinguishing difference in the third wave of 'settlement' was that "pigs were not cooked and eaten, or even raised in the highlands. Comparative data from the coastal Philistine settlements of the same period—Iron Age I—show a surprisingly large number of pigs represented among the recovered animal bones. Though the early Israelites did not eat pork, the Philistines clearly did, as did (as best we can tell from the sketchier data) the Ammonites and Moabites east of the Jordan.[33]

Finkelstein speculates that perhaps:

> the proto-Israelites stopped eating pork merely because the

> surrounding peoples—their adversaries—did eat it, and they had begun to see themselves as different. Distinctive culinary practices and dietary customs are two of the ways in which ethnic boundaries are formed... half a millennium before the composition of the biblical text, with its detailed laws and dietary regulations, the Israelites chose—for reasons that are not entirely clear—not to eat pork...[34]

If there had been no captivity in Egypt and no exodus, then who was Moses—and what did he do?

In *The Original Torah, The Political Intent of the Bible's Writers*, S. David Sperling suggests that the Bible's Moses is an allegorical figure[35] representing King Saul who is said to have reigned from 1025 to 1005 BCE.[36]

Why did the biblical authors feel the need for allegory? According to Sperling "allegories often arose out of the need for an author to be indirect and to stay out of harm's way."[37] At the time the story of Moses was first written, David's successor, Solomon, was very concerned, just as David had been, lest any remnant of the House of Saul try to regain control of Israel and/or Judah.

I Samuel's portrait of King Saul, Israel's first king, is extremely negative and seems to have been deliberately designed to discredit the House of Saul. In *I Samuel*, Saul is portrayed as paranoid and subject to violent mood-swings. For reasons that are obscure, even Yahweh is portrayed as having withdrawn his support of Saul—or so the prophet-judge-seer Samuel, then Yahweh's voice on earth, is reported to have said.

If we accept Sperling's concept that the fictional character Moses in *Exodus* is an allegorical description of King Saul, we may, by asking ourselves questions about Saul and Moses, be able to learn something about the history and real character of Israel's first king as we reread the biblical account.

Is the biblical account of Moses having married into a Midianite family headed by Jethro, a priest, to be taken as meaning that Saul had married into a Midianite family? If so, what would Saul's motive have been? To establish a trade alliance which would exchange Canaanite olive oil, wine, figs, grain, and other produce for Midianite copper and iron? Would the Canaanites' adoption of the Midianite god, Yahweh, have served to further strengthen that relationship? How had Saul become involved with the Midianites in the first place? And how might the biblical description of Moses apply to Saul?

In his massively annotated, impressively scholarly, and wonderfully readable translation of the first five books of the *Bible*, *The Five Books of Moses*, Robert Alter describes Moses thusly:

> what is of interest about the character of Moses is what bears on his qualities as a leader—his impassioned sense of justice, his easily ignited temper, his selfless compassion, his feelings of personal inadequacy. Alone of biblical characters, he is assigned an oddly generic epithet, "the man Moses." There may be some theological motive for this designation, in order to remind us of his plainly human status, to ward off any inclination to deify the founding leader of the Israelite people...[38]

If the biblical Moses is an allegorical figure, then Alter's description of Moses may be giving us a far more detailed, far more accurate picture of the historical Saul than survives in *I Samuel.*

Indeed, the picture of Saul in *I Samuel* shows signs of having been rendered nonsensical either by scribal error or deliberate tampering. For example, when the Masoretic text of *I Samuel* 13:1 is translated, literally, into English, it reads:

> Saul was a year old and two years he reigned.[39]

Considering that Saul had been out looking for lost cattle,[40] that he stood a head taller than any of his subjects when he was chosen to be king,[41] and that he won a major battle over the Philistines after he had become king,[42] he would have had to have been, if we view the text as inerrant, a precocious child indeed...

Setting aside the question of Saul's age when he became king and the length of his reign, the stories of Moses and Saul have much in common. For example, Sperling observes that:

> numerous Bible scholars have called attention to the linguistic resemblance between Yahweh's words to the prophet Samuel about Saul and Yahweh's first address to Moses:
>
> Tomorrow about this time I will send to you a man from the land of Benjamin, and you shall anoint him to be prince over my people Israel. He shall save my people from the hand of the Philistines, for I have seen the affliction of my people because their cry has come to me. (*I Samuel* 9:16)
>
> Just as Yahweh designated Saul to save his people because he had heard their cry and attended to their sufferings, so did he designate Moses:
>
> Then Yahweh said, "I have observed the misery of my people who are in Egypt; I have heard their cry on account of their taskmasters. Indeed, I know their sufferings. (*Exodus* 3:7)
>
> In like manner, both heroes were called on to destroy Amalek, an ancient enemy of Israel. Just as Yahweh designated Saul to wipe out Amalek in *I Samuel* 15, so Moses was called on to eradicate Amalek in *Exodus* 17 and *Deuteronomy* 25. Both Saul and Moses acted as prophets and both men presided over the Yahweh cult.[43]

When Samuel anointed Saul as king, he did so with extreme reluctance. He warned the Israelites that they would lose their freedom and that their taxes would increase. Appearing to bow to popular demand, Samuel "expounded to the people the rules of the monarchy, and recorded them in a document which he deposited before the Lord."[44]

Samuel also warned the people that if they failed to "revere the Lord, worship Him, and obey Him,"[45] they would suffer. Since Samuel was the Lord's voice, it is clear that Samuel was relinquishing none of his power to Saul who would serve as a sort of Constitutional monarch. Samuel promised to continue to instruct the people "in the practice of what is good and right."[46]

Prior to King Saul, "there was no king in Israel, everyone did as he pleased."[47] From this we might infer that one of Saul's innovations was the establishment of some sort of legal code, possibly something as simple and understandable as some (but not all) of the Ten Commandments which introduced the exclusive worship of Yahweh. But whether Saul caused anything to be written about a legal code or what he accomplished during his reign is not known.

Saul's reign ended soon after Achish, the Philistine king of Gath, had declared David his "vassal forever"[48] and his "bodyguard for life."[49] Soon thereafter, Saul and three of his sons were killed by Philistine or Amelekite soldiers[50] in the battle of—or in an ambush at—Mount Gilboa in 1005 BCE.[51]

ENDNOTES

1. Dawkins, Richard, *The Ancestor's Tale, A Pilgrimage to the Dawn of Evolution*, Mariner Books, an imprint of Houghton Mifflin Company, New York, 2004, p. 27
2. Finkelstein, Israel and Silberman, Asher, *The Bible Unearthed*, Touchstone, an imprint of Simon and Schuster, New York, 2001, pp 113-4
3. Finkelstein, op cit., p 55
4. Finkelstein, op cit., p 115
5. Sperling, S. David, *The Original Torah, The Political Intent of the Bible's Writers*, New York University Press, New York 1998 p 53
6. Shaw, Ian, editor, *The Oxford History of Ancient Egypt*, Oxford University Press, Oxford, England, 2000, p. 307
7. Clayton, Peter, *Chronicles of the Pharaohs*, Thames & Hudson, London, 1994, p 167
8. Kennedy, James, *Peasants in Revolt: Political Allegory in Genesis 2-3*, Journal for the Study of the Old Testament (JSOT) 47, 3-14. With Kennedy's concept of *Genesis* 2-3 as an allegory of a peasant revolt and Sperling's concept of the Moses story being an allegory about Israel's first king, Saul, it becomes an interesting exercise to read not only *Genesis* 2-3 as an allegory but all of the original *Genesis* 1:1 through *Judges* 21: 25 (i.e., those portions written by the Yahwist and the Elohist) as an allegory about the origin and history of the

Israelite people between 1141 and 1025 BCE.

9. Finkelstein, op cit., p 118

10. Bright, *A History of Israel*, Westminster Press, Philadelphia, 1981, p. 127

11. Rothenberg, Beno, *Were These King Solomon's Mines?*, Thames & Hudson, London, 1972, pp 125-179

12. *II Kings* 18:4. See also *Numbers* 21:6-9 which states: "The Lord sent seraph serpents against the people. They bit the people and many of the Israelites died. The people came to Moses and said, 'We sinned by speaking against the Lord and against you. Intercede with the Lord to take away the serpents from us!' And Moses interceded for the people. Then the Lord said to Moses, 'Make a seraph figure and mount it on a standard. And if anyone who is bitten looks at it, he shall recover.' Moses made a copper serpent and mounted it on a standard; and when anyone was bitten by a serpent, he would look at the copper serpent and recover."

    The Timna Valley where the Midianites operated the copper mine was infested with many venomous snakes and remains so to this day. The snakes were quite reasonably feared by the miners at Timna which explains the purpose of the gilded copper snake found by Beno Rothenberg during his excavations at the mine in the 1960s. Though we may question the efficacy of a supposedly magical copper serpent in enabling snakebite victims to recover, we would have to concede that, absent modern anti-venom vaccines, it would, at least, give snakebite victims some very much needed—and possibly effective—hope!

13. Clayton, Peter, op cit., p. 155

14. Bright, op cit., p 127

15. Robinson, Edward, *Biblical Researches in Palestine*, Volumes 1-4, 1860. The very rare Volume 4 is a very slim book containing several maps bound in.

16. Palmer, Edward Henry, *The Desert of the Exodus*, Deighton, Bell & Co., Cambridge, England, 1871, pp 349-358. He was undoubtedly England's foremost expert on Arab affairs and the geography of the Sinai. A passionate Christian, Palmer's hatred of and contempt for the Bedouin and Arabs generally, are repeatedly and violently expressed in *Biblical Researches in Palestine*. See pages Volume 2, pp 296-297 where he advocates genocide. The Bedouin must have sensed Palmer's feelings. On August 11th, just four days after his forty-second birthday, he was murdered by Bedouin while on a military expedition in the Sinai.

17. Trumbull, H. Clayton, *Kadesh-Barnea, Its Importance and Probable Site*, Hodder-Stoughton, London, 1884. A charming and fascinating account of Trumbull's search.

18. It was to Selim "Dahoum" Ahmed, sometimes referred to as "Sheikh Ahmed," who had died in September 1918 that Lawrence dedicated his masterpiece, *The Seven Pillars Of Wisdom*, thusly:

    To S.A.

    I loved you, so I drew these tides of men into my hands
    and wrote my will across the sky in stars
    To earn you Freedom, the seven-pillared worthy house
    that your eyes might be shining for me
    When we came.

Death seemed my servant on the road, till we were near
and saw you waiting:
When you smiled, and in sorrowful envy he outran me
and took you apart:
Into his quietness.

Love, the way-weary, groped to your body, our brief wage
ours for the moment.
Before earth's soft hand explored your shape, and the blind
worms grew fat upon
Your substance.

Men prayed me that I set our work, the inviolate house,
as a memory of you.
But for fit monument I shattered it, unfinished: and now
The little things creep out to patch themselves hovels
in the marred shadow
Of your gift.

It is curious that upon such singular, individual passions the fates of nations often depend.

19. Yardley, Michael, *T. E. Lawrence, A Biography*, Stein & Day, New York, 1985
20. Wooley and Lawrence, *The Wilderness of Zin*, Palestine Exploration Fund, London 1915
21. Stewart, Desmond, *T. E. Lawrence, A New Biography*, Harper & Row, New York, 1977, pp. 104, 272
22. Trumbull, op cit., pp. 237-321
23. Wooley and Lawrence, op cit.
24. Akenson, Donald Harmon, *Surpassing Wonder, The Invention of the Bible and the Talmuds*, Harcourt Brace & Co., New York, 1994, p 521
25. Wooley and Lawrence, op cit.
26. Lawrence, M. R., *The Home Letters of T. E. Lawrence and his Brothers*, Blackwell, Oxford, 1954, p. 280
27. Akenson, op cit, p 521
28. Akenson, op cit., p 521
29. Clayton, Peter, op cit., p 185
30. Mazar, Amahai, *Archaeology of the Land of the Bible, 10,000-586 BCE*, Doubleday, New York, 1990, pp 329-330
31. Mendenhall, George, *The Hebrew Conquest of Palestine*, Archaeological Review, XXV/3, 1962, pp 66-87
32. Finkelstein, op cit., p 118
33. Finkelstein, op cit., p 119
34. Finkelstein, op cit., p 119

35. Sperling, op cit., p 38

36. Akenson, op cit., p 521

37. Sperling, op cit., pp 122-123

38. Alter, Robert, *The Five Books of Moses*, pp 301-302

39. Alter, Robert, *The David Story, A Translation With Commentary of 1 and 2 Samuel*, W. W. Norton, New York, 1999, p 70. Alter notes that most translators observe the custom when translating *I Samuel* 13:1 which is to leave blank both the age at which Saul became king and the length of his reign. Furthermore, the use of the formula "X was Y years old when he became king and reigned Z years over (name of kingdom)," as is the case in the *Book of Kings* and the *Book of Chronicles*, indicates that *I Samuel* 13:1 was inserted at a relatively late date either during the time of the seventh century BCE Deuteronomist or the Redactor in the fifth or fourth century BCE.

40. *I Samuel* 9:3-10:24

41. *I Samuel* 9:2

42. *I Samuel* 14:22-23a

43. Sperling, op cit

44. *I Samuel* 10:25

45. *I Samuel* 12:14

46. *I Samuel* 1:23

47. *Judges* 21:25

48. *I Samuel* 27:12b

49 *I Samuel* 28:2b

50. The account in *I Samuel* 31:1-6 of a cowardly, fearful but as yet unwounded, Saul asking his even more frightened armor bearer—unsuccessfully—to kill him lest he die a painful, humiliating death at the hands of the Philistines. This conflicts, of course, with the account at *II Samuel* 1:8 which states that a brave, mortally wounded Saul had asked an Amelekite at the battle of Mount Gilboa to "finish me off." The latter account raises the question of what an Amelekite, even a non-combatant resident alien Amelekite, would have been doing on the battlefield—let alone, risking his life poaching on the Philistines' looting of the dead and wounded Israelites. The absence of Saul's general, Abner when Saul and his sons Jonathan, Ishi and Malkishua were killed at Mount Gilboa raises the question of whether the encounter was an ambush involving only a few Philistines and/or Amelekites, rather than a battle involving hundreds or even thousands of troops. It is hard to imagine a battle without Abner being present. Ishbaal, another of Saul's sons, seems to have been left behind for reasons—such as youth or incompetence—which have gone unstated.

51. Akenson, op cit., p 521

CHAPTER 2

DAVID, ABIATHAR AND THE BOOK OF JASHAR

David and his six hundred warriors—mercenaries we would call them today—were at Ziklag, a small village in the Negev desert, in 1005 BCE when an Amelekite courier brought him the news that Israel's first king, Saul, and three of Saul's sons had been killed at Mount Gilboa by warriors under the command of the man for whom David worked, the Philistine king, Achish of Gath.[1]

In the days immediately preceding that news, David and his men had raided an Amelekite village in the Negev and had looted it. Supposedly they had killed all the Amelekite men—except for four hundred young men who escaped on camels—leaving their wives and mothers and property to the untender mercies of David and his men.[2]

The courier also brought David Saul's crown and armband—the symbols of Saul's kingship. The biblical account of what happened during and after the battle—or ambush—is confused. The Amelekite courier's account was given as follows:

> I just chanced to be on Mount Gilboa, and look, Saul was leaning on his spear, and look, chariots and horsemen had overtaken him. And he turned round behind him and saw me and called to me, and I said 'Here I am.' And he said to me, 'Who are you?' and I said to him, 'I am an Amelekite.' And he said to me, 'Pray stand over me and finish me off, for the fainting spell has seized me, for while life is still within me.'

> And I stood over him and finished him off, for I knew that he could not live after having fallen. And I took the diadem that was on his head and the band that was on his arm, and I have brought them here to my lord.'[3]

The Amelekite who told David that he "just chanced to be on Mount Gilboa" was probably not the only Amelekite there because Achish may have hired Amelekites to replace David and his six-hundred men who had been turned away from the battle at the last minute, supposedly at the request of the four other Philistine kings.

In quick succession, David made five strategic moves. First he had his men kill the Amelekite courier who may have been expecting a handsome reward for having brought news that he may reasonably have expected David to welcome.[4] Since it is unlikely that the Philistines would have allowed a stray Amelekite to loot the body of the dead or dying Saul, we might reasonably infer that Achish had given the diadem and armband to the Amelekite with instructions to give it to David. If such was the case—and we cannot know that it was—then the gift of Saul's diadem and armband would have been Achish's way of giving David Saul's kingdom—provided David could get the Israelites to accept him as their king. Presumably David would remain Achish's vassal and there would be peace between Gath and Israel.

Second, David composed an elegy lamenting the deaths of Saul and Saul's oldest son, Jonathan:

> "The splendor, O Israel, on your heights lies slain,
> How have the warriors fallen!
> Tell it not in Gath,
> proclaim not in Ashkelon's streets,
> Lest the Philistine daughters rejoice,
> lest the daughters of the uncircumcised gloat.
> O hills of Gilboa — no dew
> and no rain upon you, O lofty fields
> For there the warriors' shield was besmirched,

the shield of Saul unfurnished with oil.
From the blood of the slain,
from the warriors' fat—
Jonathan's bow did not retreat
and the sword of Saul never turned away empty.
Saul and Jonathan, beloved and dear,
in their life and their death they were not parted.
They were swifter than eagles,
and stronger than lions.
O daughters of Israel, weep over Saul,
who clothed you in scarlet and bangles.
who studded your garments with jewelry of gold.
How have the warriors fallen
in the midst of the battle.
Jonathan, upon your heights slain!
Very dear you were to me.
More wondrous your love to me
than the love of women.
How have the warriors fallen,
and the gear of battle is lost."[5]

David's admonition to "tell it not in Gath... lest the Philistine daughters gloat" was hypocritical. As David would have been well aware, everyone in Gath would have already been informed of Saul and Jonathan's deaths upon King Achish's return from the battlefield. The purpose of the elegy seems to have been to make it seem—to Saul's subjects—that David was not in any way responsible for the deaths of Saul and Saul's heir apparent, Jonathan. David's sorrow concerning Jonathan seems insincere since David—who knew of the impending battle well in advance—did nothing, according to the biblical account, to warn Jonathan. It was strikingly ungrateful since Jonathan is said to have warned David on a number of occasions when David's life was in danger.

Nevertheless, the inclusion of David's elegy in the *Book of Jashar*—

even though it is a single example—suggests that David was responsible for the writing of that now long-lost book. David's writing of the elegy would have been the beginning of the writing of the *Book of Jashar*. The purpose of the *Book of Jashar* was to portray David in the most favorable possible light. It was, perhaps, coincidental that it was the beginning of the *writing*[6] of the *Bible*.

Next, as a third step, David sent some of the booty he had taken from the sack of the Amelekite village:

> and he sent from the booty to the elders of Judah, to his friends, saying, 'Here is a gift for you from the booty of the Lord's enemies,' to those in Bethel, and to those in Ramoth-negeb, and to those in Jattir, and to those in Aroer, and to those in Siphmoth, and to those in Eshtomea, and to those in Facal, and to those in the towns of the Jerahmeelite, and to those in the towns of the Kenite, and to those in Hormah, and to those in Bor-ashan, and to those in Athach, and to those in Hebron and in all the places where David, with his men, had moved about.[7]

It was clearly a move designed to soothe whatever hard feelings remained from David's years living off the land. The mention of Hebron is significant because David's fourth step was to consult with Abiathar, the sole surviving priest from the shrine at Nob.[8] When escaping from Nob, Abiathar had taken an ephod with him—a device which was thought to permit direct communication with Yahweh.

While the *Bible* is silent as to whether copies of David's elegy[9] on the deaths of Saul and Jonathan accompanied the gifts David sent to the elders of Judah and Israel as well, it would have been a shrewd move on his part.

The only other reference to the *Book of Jashar* occurs in the *Book of Joshua* where Joshua is said to have persuaded the Lord to make the sun to stand still:

> Then spake Joshua to the Lord in the day when the Lord delivered up the Amorites before the children of Israel and he said

> in the sight of Israel, Sun, stand thou still upon Gibeon, and thou Moon, in the valley of Ajalon. And the sun stood still, and the moon stayed, until the people had avenged themselves upon their enemies. Is not this written in the book of Jasher? So the sun stood still in the midst of heaven, and hasted not to go down about a whole day.[10]

The inclusion of the story about Joshua suggests that David may have caused stories portraying the various tribal heroes favorably to be included in the *Book of Jashar* thus flattering the elders of the various tribes he sought to rule.

Since the *Book of Jashar* contained David's elegy, it had to have been completed either during David's time or later. Now, if the original *Book of Samuel* (which makes reference to it) were written during the early years of David's successor, King Solomon,[11] then it is fairly reasonable to assume that the *Book of Jashar* had been written, in its entirety, during David's reign. Lastly, the only client likely to have commissioned such a work during David's reign would have been David himself, making David the first of all the biblical authors.

We are told nothing about David's ongoing relationship with King Achish after David assumed the role of King of Judah at Hebron. Did he continue to serve Achish as his vassal? When David and his men fought the Philistines after David had become king, did they do so to assist Achish in his struggles against the four other Philistine kings? We really do not *know*.

While the text of the *Book of Jashar*, except for the two excerpts just cited, has long since been lost, there are a few clues as to what it originally contained. In *An Outline of the Literature of the Old Testament*, Emil Kautzsch attributes the text of David's elegy on Saul and Jonathan to a source he calls "Da," or the David Source.[12] We might infer that other material attributed to the Da source by Kautzsch may have been included in the *Book of Jashar* but there is no way to be certain of that at this late date. *Appendix 2, An Outline of the Book of Jashar*, outlines what the original *Book of Jashar* may have contained.

As a fifth step in promoting his position David, in an apparently uncharacteristic moment of piety, asked Abiathar to consult the ephod as to what he should do:

> And it happened afterward that David inquired of the Lord, saying, 'Shall I go up into one of the towns of Judah?' And the Lord said to him, 'Go up.' And David said, 'where shall I go up?' And He said, 'To Hebron.' And David went up there, and his two wives as well, Ahinoam the Jezreelite and Abigail wife of Nabal the Carmelite. And his men who were with him David brought up, each man and his household, and they settled in Hebron. And the men of Judah came and anointed David there as king over the house of Judah.[13]

As Robert Alter observes:

> It is a little odd for a single tribe to have a "king," but the act is deliberately presumptive on David's part—first the king of Judah, eventually of all the tribes. Saul's son Ish-bosheth, by contrast becomes king of an alliance of northern tribes. The text is silent as to the Philistines' view of David's move to the kingship in Hebron, but one can assume that they countenanced it as a reasonable act on the part of their vassal opposing the house of Saul.[14]

Although David would remain at Hebron as king of Judah for seven years, his ambitions far exceeded that.

He waged a continuous war with his fellow Israelites:

> And the fighting between the house of Saul and the house of David went on a long time, and David grew stronger and stronger and the house of Saul weaker and weaker.[15]

A falling out between Ishbosheth and Abner, the head of Ishbosheth's army, over one of Saul's concubines led Abner to offer Israel's crown to David:

> And Abner sent messengers to David in his stead, saying, 'To whom should the land belong? Make a pact with me and, look, my hand will be with you to bring round to you all Israel.'[16]

While David was quick to accept, Joab, the head of David's army, quite possibly concerned that David had promised Joab's job to Abner, killed Abner. Again, a politically expedient public display of grief was called for:

> And David said to Joab and to all the troops who were with him, 'Tear your garments and gird on sackcloth and keen for Abner.' And King David was walking behind the bier. And they buried Abner in Hebron. And the king raised his voice and wept over the grave of Abner, and all the people wept. And the king lamented over Abner and said,
>
> Like the death of the base
> should Abner have died?
> Your hands—never bound,
> Your feet never placed in fetters!
> As one falls before scoundrels you fell.'[17]

Only one man and a boy were left blocking David's path to Israel's throne—Saul's son Ishbosheth and Jonathan's crippled twelve-year old son, Mephibosheth. Ishbosheth was the first to go:

> And the sons of Rimmon the Beerothite, Rechab and Baanah went and came in the heat of the day to the house of Ish-bosheth as he was taking his midday rest. And, look, the woman who kept the gate had been gleaning wheat, and nodded and fell asleep. And they came into the house as he was lying in his bed in his bedchamber, and they struck him and killed him and cut off his head and took his head and went off through the Arabah all night long. And they brought Ishbosheth's head to David in Hebron and said to the king, 'Here is the head of Ishbosheth son of Saul your enemy, who sought your life.[18]

If Rechab and Baanah had been expecting any promised—or merely anticipated—reward money, they were mistaken. To do so would have undermined any pretense on David's part that he had not been involved for him to have shown them any gratitude for removing the last major obstacle to his seizure of Israel's throne. The two men were summarily put to death. Once again, David deplored the death of men who had stood in his way. Dead, Rechab and Baanah would never reveal why they had killed Ishbosheth.[19]

In 965 BC, after ruling Judah for forty years, and Israel for thirty-three, an ailing, shivering David, 70, found himself a virtual prisoner in his own palace. His servants, anxious to do all that they could to make him comfortable, sought out a girl and found Abishag, a Shunamite, reputed to be the most beautiful virgin in all of David's kingdom, to help David keep warm.[20] Joseph Heller, in *God Knows*, his 1984 novel of David's life, vividly describes the scene, told from the point-of-view of a dying King David:

> Abishag the Shunamite washes her hands, powders her arms, removes her robe, and approaches my bed to lie down on top of me. I know even as she takes gentle possession of me with her small arms and legs and with her tiny plump belly and fragrant mouth that it will do no good. My shivering will continue, and she will fear she has failed me again. The chills that rack me grow from within. Abishag is beautiful. They tell me the child is a virgin… Abishag will try her best without succeeding, and when she rises from my bed, I will be just as cold as before, and just as forlorn.
>
> All day long the light in my room is dreary, as though densely clouded with too many invisible motes. The flames in my oil lamps flicker dimly. My eyes often close without my sensing that I am again drifting off into another brief sleep. They usually feel gritty, inflamed.
>
> "Are my eyes red?" I will inquire of Abishag.

> She tells me they are very red and soothes them with trickles of cool water and glycerin squeezed from strips of white wool. The weirdest silence prevails under my roof and outside my windows in the streets and seems to hold and muffle all the jarring noises of the city in a deadening grip. About my halls, my watchmen and servants go on tiptoe and speculate in whispers. Perhaps they are making bets. Jerusalem is prospering as never before, but the populace is astir with rumors and alarming expectations. The atmosphere is rife with suspense and increasing dread, with mounting displays of ambition, deceit, and hungering opportunism.[21]

Outside the palace, a couple of miles away, at the far end of the garden, one of David's oldest surviving sons, Adonijah, was hosting a feast, consolidating the political support of nearly all of the most powerful men of David's court. As it happened, he was celebrating, somewhat prematurely, his imminent rise to his father's throne. Robert Alter's translation, in *The David Story*, tells the story this way in *I Kings* 1:

> And Adonijah, son of Haggith was giving himself airs, saying, 'I shall be king!' And he made himself a chariot and horsemen with fifty men running before him... And he parlayed with Joab, son of Zeruiah and with Abiathar the priest, and they lent their support to Adonijah.[22]

Inside the palace, Nathan the prophet and Shimei and Rei and David's warriors and Benaiah, head of the palace guard, and Zadok the priest and Bathsheba, possibly David's favorite wife, and Bathsheba's son, Solomon, then around 20—none of them having been invited to Adonijah's feast—discussed what to do.

> And Nathan said to Bathsheba, Solomon's mother, saying, 'Have you not heard that Adonijah son of Haggith has become king, and our lord David knows it not?" And now, come let me give you counsel that you may save your own life and the life of your son Solomon. Go and get you to King David and

> say to him, 'Has not my lord the king sworn to your servant, saying: Solomon your son shall be king after me, and he shall sit on my throne. And why has Adonijah become king?' Look, while you are still speaking there, I shall come after you and fill in your words."[23]

Bathsheba did as Nathan had suggested, and was pointing out that after David's death, Adonijah would treat her and her son, Solomon, badly, when David's servants interrupted:

> And they told the king, saying, 'Here is Nathan the prophet.'[24]

Whereupon, Bathsheba left the room and Nathan entered:

> And he came before the king and bowed to the king, his face to the ground. And Nathan said, 'My lord the king, have you yourself said, 'Adonijah shall be king after me and he shall sit on my throne?' For he has gone down today and made a sacrificial feast of oxen and fatlings and sheep in abundance and he has invited all the king's sons and the commanders of the army and Abiathar the priest, and there they are eating and drinking before him, and they have said, 'Long live King Adonijah!' But me—your servant—and Zadok the priest and Benaiah son of Jehoida and Solomon your servant he did not invite."[25]

According to *I Kings*, Bathsheba delivered the speech that Nathan had coached her to give, Nathan confirmed it, and David granted Bathsheba's request:[26]

> And King David answered and said, 'Call me Bathsheba.' And she came before the king and stood before the king. And the king swore and said, 'As the Lord lives Who rescued me from every strait, as I swore to you by the Lord God of Israel, saying, 'Solomon, your son, shall be king after me, and he shall sit on my throne in my stead,' even so will I do this day." And Bathsheba did obeisance, her face to the ground and bowed to

> the king and said, 'May my lord King David live forever."[27]

All that seemed left to do was to anoint Solomon king:

> And Zadok the priest, with Nathan the prophet and Benaiah son of Jehoida and the Cherethites and the Pelethites[28] went down and mounted Solomon on King David's mule and led him to Gihon. And Zadok the priest took the horn of oil from the Tent and anointed Solomon, and they blew the ram's horn and all the people said, "Long live King Solomon!"[29]

A bloodbath ridding Solomon of potential enemies was about to begin. So, too, was a campaign to legitimize King Solomon's right to the throne. That campaign would lead to the rewriting or cannibalization of the *Book of Jashar* which had undoubtedly grown over the course of David's forty year reign. It would not long survive David.

ENDNOTES

1. *II Samuel* 2-9
2. *I Samuel* 30:16-17
3. *II Samuel* 1:6-10
4. *II Samuel* 1:15
5. *II Samuel* 1:17-27
6. There were undoubtedly some oral traditions about the heroes of the dozen or so tribes which Saul had united to form Israel but the *Book of Jashar* seems to have been the first book, of what would later become the *Bible*, to have been written. The priest, Abiathar, that David took in after the massacre at Nob may have served as David's scribe.
7. *I Samuel* 30:26-31
8. *I Samuel* 22:20-21
9. *II Samuel* 1:18
10. *Joshua* 10:12-13
11. Bright, John, *A History of Israel*, Westminster Press, Philadelphia 1981, p 219 which states, in relevant part, "Outstanding in this class is the matchless Court History of David (*II Samuel*, chs. 9-20; *I Kings*, chs. 1:2), of which we have spoken, certainly written during Solomon's reign."
12. Kautzsch, Emil, *An Outline of the Literature of the Old Testament*, Williams and Norgate,

London, 1898, pp 233, 239

13. *II Samuel* 2:1-2

14. Alter, Robert, *The David Story, A Translation with Commentary on 1 and 2 Samuel*, W. W. Norton, New York, 1999, p. 202

15. *II Samuel* 3:1

16. *II Samuel* 3:12

17. *II Samuel* 3:31-34

18. *II Samuel* 4:5-8

19. *II Samuel* 4:12

20. *I Kings* 1:1-4

21. Heller, Joseph, *God Knows*, Alfred A. Knopf, New York, 1984, p. 3

22. *I Kings* 1:5-7

23. *I Kings* 1:11-14

24. *I Kings* 1:23

25. *I Kings* 1:24-36

26. See Baruch Halpern's comments in *David's Secret Demons* regarding the role that Solomon's mother, Bathsheba, may have played in the palace coup described in *I Kings* 1-2.

27. *I Kings* 1:28-30

28. Alter, op cit., p 370. Alter describes the Cherethites and the Pelethites as "members of the palace guard of Philistine origin" whose function here was to "provide a show of arms for the act of anointing Solomon."

29. *I Kings* 1:38-39

CHAPTER 3

SOLOMON AND HIS COURT HISTORIAN

In 965 BCE Bathsheba's son Solomon, 25,[1] became king of Judah and Israel—thanks to David's sudden, unexpected abdication. However, as Solomon probably already knew, gaining power is one thing and keeping it is another. In David's time, no one knew this better than the priest Abiathar who had served David for over forty years. And now Abiathar, having made the mistake (as it turned out) of supporting David's legitimate heir, Adonijah, had been banished to Anathoth, a small village a few miles from Jerusalem. Abiathar's place had been taken, in Solomon's administration, by Zadok, the priest, assisted by Jehoshophat, the recorder, and the scribes, Elihoreph and Ahiah.

One of the serious problems facing Solomon, there may have been a suspicion that Solomon was Uriah's son, not David's[2] and thus not a legitimate heir to the throne. Another may have been that Solomon may not have been as well known or as well liked as David's legitimate heir, the handsome Adonijah.[3] An even more important concern was that Solomon needed to distance himself from the bloodbath involved in eliminating those whom he had reason to fear.[4]

Just as David had found it expedient to have a book written as a public relations device, so, too, did Solomon. He hired a Court Historian[5] to establish, beyond any doubt, that David had been his biological father; that although he was not well known, he had a rare kind of wisdom; and that the bloodbath which he had the misfortune to oversee was his father, David's idea, not his.

At the time of Solomon's accession to David's throne, and for months or years thereafter, Jerusalem would have been filled with gossip about the details of the coup and so it would be necessary to be fairly frank as to how Solomon had become king. Although some of the details in *I Kings* 1-2 seem to have been reversed[6]—the idea for reminding David of a promise to make Solomon king in his stead probably came from Bathsheba rather than Nathan—much of it resembled what the people of Jerusalem had already heard. Solomon's Court Historian's account is masterfully terse—a total of just under a hundred verses divided between two chapters.[7]

Next his Court Historian buried any questions there may have been about whether Uriah had been Solomon's father in two chapters in a biography of David that begins at *I Samuel* 16:1 and ends, for all practical purposes, at *II Samuel* 24:25. The two chapters that identify David as Solomon's father are, of course, *II Samuel* 10-11 which tell the story of David's seduction of Uriah's wife, Bathsheba. Those two chapters make wonderfully racy reading—and have been turned into several major motion pictures[8]—but should not be taken for fact.

According to Emil Kautzsch, Professor of Theology at Halle, in his *An Outline of the Literature of the Old Testament*, London, 1898, Chapters 9, 10, and 11 of *II Samuel* were the work of a "Jerusalem Source, an old history of David, written most probably in Jerusalem, in any case in Judah, dating from the time of Solomon or Rehoboam."[9]

The story is worth a very close look. Robert Alter's very beautiful translation of *II Samuel*: 11 begins:

> And it happened at the turn of the year, at the time the kings sally forth, that David sent out Joab and his servants with him and all Israel, and they ravaged the Ammonites and besieged Rabbah. And David was sitting in Jerusalem.
>
> And it happened at eventide that David arose from his bed and walked about on the roof of the king's house, and he saw from

> the roof a woman bathing, and the woman was very beautiful. And David sent and inquired after the woman, and the one he sent said, 'Why this is Bathsheba daughter of Eliam wife of Uriah the Hittite.'
>
> And David sent messengers and fetched her and she came to him...[10]

Since Bathsheba's father, Eliam, was one of 'The Thirty'[11]—that is one of David's top thirty-seven army officers, as was Uriah—it is difficult to believe that David had never seen Bathsheba before. David had probably known her since she was a child; she had probably been born a year or two after David had first become king at Hebron; he had probably watched her grow up; he had probably been present at her marriage to Uriah. So when David looked down from his roof and saw her bathing, knowing her husband was away, fighting at Rabbah-Ammon, it is more likely that his interest was of a fatherly, rather than of a lustful, nature. It's possible, if there is any truth to the story, that David may have called her to the palace to advise her that displaying herself publicly, as she had, was inappropriate.

Still, the biblical account accuses David of having an affair with her. So, where could the Court Historian have obtained the following information?

> ...and he lay with her, she having just cleansed herself of her impurity, and she returned unto her house. And the woman became pregnant and sent and told David and said, "I am pregnant."[12]

At the time Solomon's Court Historian was gathering his information, Uriah was dead. David was either dead or dying. Realistically, only Bathsheba could have come up with such a story—and she had two powerful motives. She wished to survive and she wanted her son, Solomon, to become king. Halpern's extensive analysis as to who Solomon's father was more likely to have been is well worth reading.[13]

Solomon's legendary wisdom, about which the people of Jerusalem were told to offset Adonijah's short-lived popularity, depends upon two marvelously inventive tales.[14] Of the two, the story of Solomon's dream is perhaps the more revealing. Thanks to Solomon's Court Historian's elegant economy it reads well in *I Kings* 3:4-15 though somewhat less so in the Chronicler's expurgated version in *II Chronicles* 1:6-12.

But, it is in Stefan Heym's modern telling, in his novel, *The King David Report*, where we are given a hypothetical context for Solomon's dream, that we see the story for the self-serving account that it really is. Solomon is interviewing Ethan of Ezrah for the post of Court Historian. Since Ethan is regarded as the wisest man in all Israel—other than Solomon[15]—Solomon decides to give Ethan a sample of his, Solomon's, wisdom:

> I hear it being said from Dan even unto Beer-sheba, Ethan, that you are one of the wisest men in Israel?
>
> But I replied, "Who may claim to be wiser than the Wisest of Kings, Solomon?"
>
> At which his delicate lips curled peevishly, and he said, "I will tell you a dream, Ethan, which I had the other night after sacrificing and burning incense in the high place at Gibeon." And to Elihoreph and Ahiah, the scribes, and to Jehoshaphat ben Ahilud, the recorder, "Mark this dream, for I want it entered into the annals."
>
> Whereupon Elihoreph and Ahiah took from their gowns stylus and tablets of wax, and waited to take down the royal words. And this is the dream of King Solomon.
>
> "In Gibeon. Yahveh appeared to me by night, and Yahveh said, Ask what I shall give you. And I said, You have shown unto Your servant David, my father great mercy, according as he walked before You in truth, and in righteousness, and in uprightness of heart; and You have kept for him this great kindness, that You have given him a son to sit on his throne, as it

is this day."

The King stopped toying with the noses of the Cherubim, and shoved forward his feet which were encased in red sandals of fine goatskin.

"And now, O Lord my God, I said to Yahveh, you have made your servant king instead of my father; and I am but a little child; I know not how to go out or come in. And your servant is in the midst of Your people which You have chosen, a great people that cannot be numbered nor counted for multitude."

The King straightened, and the light from the window glistened on the gold-embroidered cap he wore on his dark, thinning hair.

"Therefore, O Lord my God, I said to Yahveh, give to your servant an understanding heart to judge your people, that I may discern between good and bad; for who is able to judge so great a people as yours? And Lord Yahveh said unto me, Because you have asked for this thing, and not for yourself long life, nor riches, nor the perdition of your enemies, behold, I have given you a wise and understanding heart, so there was none like you before you, neither after you shall any arise like you."

And the King rose and quickly scanned the faces of his ministers, and he saws their devout seriousness. Satisfied, he concluded, "And I shall also give you that which you have not asked. Lord Yahveh told me, to wit, both riches and honour, so that there shall not be any among the kings like you all your days. And if you will walk in my ways, to keep my statutes and my commandments, as your father did walk, then I will lengthen your days."

Whereupon Zadok the priest and Nathan the prophet delightedly clapped their hands, while Elihoreph and Ahiah, the scribes, cast up their eyes in admiration. And Jehoshaphat ben

> Ahilud, the recorder, exclaimed that never in his day had he heard of a dream more pithy, or more apt to impress the hearts and minds of the people. But Benaiah ben Jehoiada stayed silent, moving his efficient-looking jaw as though he were chewing bitter cud. And King Solomon stepped down from his throne and approached me and laid his short-fingered hand upon my shoulder and said, "Eh?"
>
> I said that I considered the royal dream a jewel of its kind, of extraordinary beauty, powerful in wording and imagination, and proof of a deep personal feeling on the part of the King for our Lord Yahveh and for Yahveh's unfathomable intent and purposes.
>
> "That's as a poet," said the King. "But as a historian? I understand from my district officer in Ezrah that you are working on a History of the People of Israel."
>
> "A dream, O Wisest of Kings," I bowed, "can be as much of a historical force as a flood or a host of men or a curse of God—especially a dream as well told and documented as yours."
>
> King Solomon gazed at me again, less certain than before; then his mouth broadened into a grin, and he said, "I have seen men swallowing knives and others eating fire, but never have I seen a more agile dance on the edge of a sword. What is your opinion, Benaiah ben Jehoiada?"
>
> "Words," grunted Benaiah. "How many words have I heard mouthed in the days of your father, King David: and where are those from whose lips they spouted?"[16]

A good question, from a busy man.

Mystery shrouds the last years of Solomon's thirty-five year reign.[17] Resentment had been growing among the elders of Israel's ten tribes over their having to bear a disproportionate share of the labor involved in Solomon's grandiose projects as well as being forced to pay excessive tribute to Jerusalem—much of which involved fortifying Judah's southern borders to protect Judah against a prospective attack from Egypt on the south with whom relations had soured.[18]

Relations had soured with Assyria as well, exposing Israel to the danger of attack from the north where Solomon had failed to adequately fortify the borders. Furthermore, Solomon had been only partially successful in settling the huge foreign trade deficit. Solomon had given King Hiram of Tyre twenty villages as payment for help building his palace, temple, and Judah's merchant marine. Even so, Hiram was unhappy because the twenty villages[19] generated so little revenue while Israel's tribal elders were unhappy at the erosion of their sovereignty. In spite of Hiram's unhappiness Solomon proved himself a master of diplomacy because we are told immediately thereafter that:

> Hiram sent the king one hundred and twenty talents of gold.[20]

What was an already bad situation in the northern kingdom was made even worse when Ahijah, a prophet from the shrine at Shiloh in the northern kingdom, acting—it is said—on behalf of the elders of Israel's ten tribes, approached Solomon's corvée (forced labor) master, Jeroboam, offering him Israel's crown.[21]

Jeroboam accepted Ahijah's offer but Solomon quickly suppressed the rebellion. Jeroboam fled to Egypt where he, his family and supporters lived in luxurious exile as the guests of Pharaoh Sheshonq.[22]

While we do not know the name of Solomon's Court Historian, the many clues as to its author's complex purposes places the time when the author began his work in the early years of King Solomon's reign, sometime after 965 BCE. For a number of reasons it is possible—perhaps even likely—that Solomon's Court Historian served as a mentor to the next of the Bible's authors.

ENDNOTES

1. See Halpern, Baruch, *David's Secret Demons: Messiah, Murderer, Traitor, King*, William B. Eerdmans Publishing Company, Grand Rapids, 2001, page 240 where Halpern states that (David Noel) "Freedman suggests that Solomon was about 25 years old when he came to the throne…"
2. Halpern, op. cit., pp 404-405. According to Halpern, Solomon "was named for Uriah, "his replacement." His name, Adonijah's failure to invite him, and his grandfather's politics all indicate that he was not David's son. Only Yahweh and Solomon's supporter, Nathan, in the apology in Samuel penetrate this surface presentation. Even if Solomon were the product of a liaison between David and Bathsheba, his name would imply that Bathsheba and David presented him as a boy that Uriah had fathered. In other words, there was considerable doubt as to his royal ancestry—because he had none. Ironically, in Matthew, as distinct from Luke, Jesus' lineage descends through Solomon, the beneficiary of Yahweh's dynastic promise to David in *II Samuel* 7. A cloud on Solomon's paternity affects Jesus' genealogical claim to be the Davidic messiah."
3. *I Kings* 1:5-40
4. *I Kings* 2:1-9
5. Halpern, op cit., p 96, note 4. After expressing the opinion that *II Samuel* is an apology which some, notably Hayim Tadmor, have attributed to David, Halpern notes that "Far more likely is Stefan Heym's intuition, in *The King David Report* (New York: Putnam, 1973), that the apology is Solomon's work.
6. Halpern, op cit., p 396
7. *I Kings* 1:1-53 plus *I Kings* 2:1-46
8. Two major motion pictures titled *"David and Bathsheba"* have been made. One, in 1951, starred Gregory Peck as David; the other, in 1985, starred Richard Gere.
9. Kautzsch, Emil, *An Outline of the History of the Literature of the Old Testament*, Williams & Norgate, London, 1898
10. Alter, Robert, *The David Story: A Translation of 1 and 2 Samuel with Commentary*, W. W. Norton & Company, New York, 1999, p 214-215, i.e., *II Samuel* 11:2-3
11. *II Samuel* 23:39
12. *II Samuel* 11:4-5, Alter's translation
13. Halpern, Baruch, op cit., pp 34-39
14. The first is the famous story of Solomon's Dream wherein when Yahweh asks what wish Solomon would like to have him grant, Solomon modestly asks for wisdom—which Yahweh gives him, adding riches and long life as a reward for his modesty. The second story is the one in which Solomon settles a dispute between two prostitutes over which one's baby lived and which one's died. When he rules that the baby is to be cut into two equal halves and that one half is to be given to each of the two women claiming to be the baby's mother, one woman begs the king to reconsider and expresses a willingness to forgo her claim. Solomon then rules that the woman who was willing to give up her claim so that the baby might live should be regarded as the baby's mother and so gives the baby to her.
15. As to Ethan's wisdom, compared to Solomon's—or the reverse—*I Kings* 4:30-31 states that

"And Solomon's wisdom excelled the wisdom of all the children of the east country, and all the wisdom of Egypt. For he was wiser than all men; than Ethan the Ezrahite, and Heman, and Chalcol, and Darda, the sons of Mahol: and his fame was in all nations round about." As far as we know, to date, none of those nations put their alleged high regard for Solomon into writing. Ethan of Ezrah is credited with the writing of one psalm, *Psalm 89*.

16. Heym, Stefan, *The King David Report*, G. P. Putnam's Sons, New York, 1973, pp 5-7

17. Even the length of Solomon's reign is in doubt. *I Kings* 14:25 puts Sheshonq's siege of Jerusalem—and Rehoboam's ransom of it—in the fifth year of Rehoboam's reign. Peter Clayton's *Chronicles of the Pharaohs* dates Sheshonq's siege of Jerusalem at 925 BCE. Thus Solomon's reign, said by Akenson to have begun in 965 BCE, would have extended from 965 BCE to 930 BCE. Thus, our calculation of 35 years.

18. *I Kings* 26-40 describes Solomon's problems with his corvee-master, Jeroboam. That Solomon's relations with Egypt had soured despite his marriage to Pharaoh's daughter—and his having built a sumptuous mansion for her on the Millo—is implied by Egypt's having given sanctuary to a fugitive Jeroboam.

19. See *I Kings* 9:11-13

20. *I Kings* 9:14

21. *I Kings* 11:29-31

22. *I Kings* 11:40

CHAPTER 4

REHOBOAM, J, E, AND THE TORAH

Around 931 BCE Solomon, 56, died. Like David's, Solomon's death occurs curiously off-stage. Just how he came to die we are not told nor are we told precisely where he was buried. Instead, we are simply told that:

> Solomon slept with his fathers and was buried in the city of his father David; and his son Rehoboam succeeded him as king.[1]

Even the length of Solomon's reign, a formulaic "forty," implying little more than "many," is in doubt. A thirty-five year reign seems more probable.[2]

Solomon's death presented what seems like an ideal opportunity for his son and successor, Rehoboam, to smooth over the differences between the two kingdoms, to reassert fiscal prudence, and to take a more rational approach to the nations' internal and external problems. Unfortunately Rehoboam inherited neither David's skill as a leader and warrior nor his father's ability to finesse difficult situations.

After Solomon's death, Israel's leaders, with Jeroboam, recently arrived from Egypt, already at their head, met with Rehoboam at Shechem. They offered him Israel's crown in exchange for reductions in taxes and forced labor. Rehoboam promised to think about it; he asked them to return in three days for his decision.

He then consulted his courtiers. The older ones, the taking of whose advice had given his father a reputation for wisdom, urged him to grant the requests of Israel's tribal elders. The younger ones advised taking a hard line.[3] Unfortunately, Rehoboam decided to take the advice of the latter. Three days later he met with Jeroboam and Israel's tribal leaders and angrily promised, not to decrease, but to increase Israel's tax and labor burdens:

> My father made your yoke heavy, but I will add to your yoke; my father flogged you with whips but I will flog you with scorpions.[4]

Israel anointed Jeroboam instead as their king; Rehoboam escaped Schechem with his life. The breakup of the two kingdoms resulted in neither kingdom having the critical mass to withstand attack from its neighbors thus presenting Jeroboam's former host, Pharaoh Sheshonq, with an extraordinary opportunity which he may well have anticipated.

Around 925 BCE Sheshonq attacked Judah[5] and demanded an enormous tribute from King Rehoboam. The now-timid Rehoboam saw the wisdom of paying quickly.[6] Shattering whatever illusions Jeroboam may have had about his former host's previous generosity, Sheshonq attacked Jeroboam and Israel even more savagely.

The reasons for Sheshonq's harsher treatment of Jeroboam and Israel remain obscure. Though they had given Jeroboam Israel's crown, Israel's tribal leaders—or, more likely, the chief priests at Israel's various sacred shrines—had, quite likely, kept Israel's financial control for themselves, leaving Jeroboam I with little or no money with which to bargain with Sheshonq. It appears that in order to obtain the tribute he deemed necessary, Sheshonq had to deal directly—and severely—with the leaders of Israel's cities and villages.

> Pharaoh then turned his attention to Israel, pursuing his earlier protégé Jeroboam, who fled over the Jordan. Finally, Sheshonq halted at Megiddo, the scene of Tuthmosis III's victory 500

> years before, and erected a suitable victory stele in the manner of his predecessors.[7]

It is against this background that we see the beginnings of the work of the third major biblical author known to us—because of the use of the word "Jahweh" to indicate God, as "J".

In 1987, bible scholar Richard Elliott Friedman,[8] citing Jo Ann Hackett's *Women's Studies and the Hebrew Bible*[9] was among the first to suggest that we at least consider the possibility that J was a woman:

> Originating at, or at least reflecting the interests of—the Judaean court, it came from a circle in which both men and women had a certain status. That is, even in a male-led society, women of the noble class may have more power, privileges, and education than males of a lower class.[10]

Three years later, in 1990, literary critic Harold Bloom suggested that J was almost certainly a woman.[11] As Bloom put it:

> I have admitted that to identify J as a woman is a fiction, but so, of course, is the usual easy assumption that J was a man. I now elaborate upon the sublime fiction that J was either a princess of the Davidic royal house or else the daughter or wife of a court personage...[12]

Bloom also noted that J:

> had no heroes, only heroines. Sarai and Rachel are wholly admirable, and Tamar, in proportion to the narrative space she occupies, is very much the most vivid portrait in J. But Abram, Jacob, and Moses receive a remarkably mixed treatment from J. If she had a male hero, then it was David the King, who is not an overt part of her story, though Joseph, his surrogate is.[13]

Like Joseph, David was the youngest son of many. Like Joseph, David rises to a place of power. If Abigail were Saul's wife, rather than Nabal's[14] and had pursued David as the Egyptian vizier's wife had pursued Joseph, there would be an additional parallel. The possibilities of those and other possible parallels are tantalizing, but they are still far from certain.

That J's account universally portrays women favorably, the argument that J was a woman is both strong and reasonable.

In addition to certain similarities in the writing of J and Solomon's Court Historian, it is interesting to note that J did not tamper with Solomon's Court Historian's biography of David[15]—possibly out of respect for the man who may have been her mentor.

As to who would have been king when J wrote her account—certainly one way to place a date on her work—Bloom goes on to add that J's:

> anagrammatic references to Rehoboam (J, as we shall see, has a way of punning ironically on Rehoboam's name) and the many unfavorable allusions to Jeroboam indicate Rehoboam's reign in the curtailed kingdom of Judah as a likely time and place…[16]

Whereas Solomon's Court Historian wrote to validate Solomon's succession to David's throne, J wrote, partly to provide Judah with a history and partly to bring about a reconciliation and reunification of the kingdoms of Judah and Israel—under the control of the House of David. For someone close to, or a member of, the House of David, this would have been a very natural thing to do.

What J was writing was neither fiction nor a scholarly history. Instead, it seems more like an allegory about the creation of Israel between 1141 BCE and 1005 BCE—with real history hidden behind it. Some of J's account, which begins at *Genesis* 2:4, may have been designed—like the stories of human mortality and the flood—to provide the Israelites with a mythic history much like that of their neighbors, the Babylonians. Some—such as the allegorical story of Saul concealing an historical Saul—would have been taboo at the time of J's writing.[17,18] Most of what J was writing about, however, had probably happened less than two hundred years prior to her writing.

According to James Kennedy, writing in the *Journal for the Study of the Old Testament* in 1990, J provided us with an ironic, allegorical commentary on the relationship between the Canaanite peasants and the monarchy:

> The creation account of *Genesis* 2-3 describes a basic social contradiction facing the Judahite royal elite, namely, the struggle between royal social and economic interests and the peasant class. The narrator solves this social contradiction in favour of the royal elite by portraying the first couple as peasants who must submit to the royal centralized authority of the state represented in the character of Yahweh. The narrative of the couple's revolt against Yahweh is a literary expression of the social threat of peasant unrest and rebellion. By couching the social symbolic equivalent of peasant rebellion in a cosmogony, the narrator portrays peasant unrest as natural and endemic to the rural setting. Peasants are thus painted as a constant threat calling for strong measures of elitist control.[19]

Kennedy's hypothesis about *Genesis* 2-3 being an allegory applicable to the Judahite monarchy may be a little off the mark. It is more likely that *Genesis* 2-3 is an allegory about the peasant revolt that put Saul on Israel's throne—which was, after all, the beginning of Israel as a people.

Embedded within an ingenious story line—though not in strict chronological order nor forming a single continuous allegory—J's allegories continue through the end of the *Book of Judges* and seem to have been designed to form a prequel to the original *Book of Samuel*.

The greatest of all of J's allegories dealt with the history of Israel's first king, Saul—as told in the original *Book of Exodus*. Since the story of Saul's downfall (at David's hands) would have been taboo at the time of J's writing—J hid her comments about Saul behind a well-imagined story of a heroic figure who had led the Israelite people out of Egyptian bondage.

But the place where the Israelite people had been held in bondage was Canaan, not Egypt. Thus when we go back and reread *Exodus* we may get a better insight into how indigenous Canaanites staged the relatively peaceful peasant revolt suggested by George Mendenhall.[20] If we read it, as Sperling suggests, as an allegory about the reign, policies, accomplishments, and legitimacy of King Saul,[21] it is one which King Jeroboam I's subjects would have been glad to see included in the canon.

Thus from what J wrote, in *Exodus*, about Moses building the first altar for the worship of Jahweh, we may infer that J was confirming the Court Historian's story in *I Samuel* 14:35 which describes Saul building his first altar for the worship of Jahweh.[22]

The stories about Joseph and his brothers and their adventures in Egypt—ultimately as Pharoah's guests—have also been described as allegorical, based on Israel's King Jeroboam I. This suggests that J's writing (or at least a significant part of it) could only have occurred after the death of King Solomon in or around 930 BCE.

Similarly, J's stories about Aaron form an allegory either about Jeroboam I[23] or about a chief priest—possibly Ahijah—under Jeroboam I.

In yet other allegories, J's Abraham may represent David, while Melchizedek may represent Zadok, one of David's two high priests.[24]

David's *Book of Jashar*, judging by the material borrowed by Solomon's Court Historian, portrayed King Saul as rejected not only by Samuel, but also by Jahweh. In *I Samuel* Saul is portrayed as mentally unstable, given to homicidal fits—fits during which he pursues a blameless David… The Saul who exists today only behind J's allegorical Moses is a far more stable, far stronger leader than portrayed by David and Solomon's Court Historian.

It is generally thought that someone, writing somewhat later, set about adding material favorable to the northern kingdom. That person (and the text that he or she wrote) is generally referred to as "E" because of that author's use of the word "Elohim" to indicate God.

There are various theories about who had written the E account, when that person had lived and written, and what the original E document looked like. The prevailing view is that E had been written by a Levite priest or scribe who had written an account similar to J's, but with a different point of view. Whereas the J document had presented a point of view favorable to the southern kingdom, Judah, the E document had presented a point of view which would be appreciated in the northern kingdom, Israel.

The two principal views as to how the J and E documents had come to be combined are that there had either been (a) a redactor who had combined the J and E accounts into a document called "RJE" or (b) that a redactor in the fifth century had selected pieces of the original J, E, P, and D texts and had edited and amended them and had combined it all into a composite resembling the first five books of the *Bible* as we now have them.

Robert Coote, Professor of Old Testament at the San Francisco Theological Seminary, describes a somewhat different point of view. According to Coote, after the J account had been completed, a second writer, sympathetic to the interests of the northern kingdom, Israel, made certain insertions in the J text:

> E was written by a scribe who studied the scroll of J, planned the insertions carefully, and then rewrote the scroll with the additions planned. E's supplements made J's narrative about a third longer.[25]

Coote notes that:

> The view that E once existed independent of J is still widely held and taught, especially in the United States, largely because of the continuing influence of two important German scholars, Martin Noth and Hans Walter Wolff, and now of

> Alan W. Jenks in the United States. Nevertheless, like most of the composite writings in the Bible, JE was in fact composed by supplementation rather than by the editing of two similar documents.[26]

Since in a number of cases the E texts deal with the same subjects that the J texts deal with, there are what appear to be contradictory tellings of the same story.

For example, the story of how the Israelites acquired land at Shechem is told twice. In the first telling, the author of E tells us that the Israelites purchased the land from the Shechemites:

> Jacob arrived safe in the city of Shechem which is in the land of Canaan—having come thus from Paddan-aram—and he encamped before the city. The parcel of land where he pitched his tent he purchased from the children of Hamor, Shechem's father, for a hundred kesitahs. He set up an altar there, and called it El-elohe-yisrael.[27]

In the second telling, the author of J tells us that the Israelites acquired land from the Shechemites by deceit. According to J, Dinah had gone into the city of Shechem and had met Hamor's favorite son, Shechem, who, after he had forced himself upon her, asked his father to ask for Dinah's hand in marriage. This Hamor did, offering to pay whatever Jacob asked. Jacob's sons responded to Hamor's request by saying that Dinah could only marry Shechem if the Shechemites circumcised themselves so as to conform to the Israelites' customs. Then, after all the Shechemite males had been circumcised:

> On the third day, when they were in pain, Simeon and Levi, two of Jacob's sons, brothers of Dinah, took each his sword and came upon the city unmolested and slew all of the male… The other sons of Jacob came upon the slain and plundered the town… They seized their flocks and herds and asses, and all that was inside the town and outside, all their wealth, all their children, and their wives, all that was in the houses, they

> took of captives and booty... [28]

But, why have the two contradictory accounts been left intact?

The answer may be that whoever had thus combined the northern and southern traditions as to the status of the ownership of Shechem into one reflecting both was setting the stage for unifying their political and religious structures as well. Given that J was, most likely, a member of the court at Jerusalem,[29] interested in the reconciliation and reunification of the two kingdoms, it is possible that J wrote the E account as well.

Professor Coote has noted that:

> In addition, there are places where E makes use of J phrases but gives them a distinctive E meaning.[30]

Coote also points out that:

> E was a product of the court. Apparent duplications result from the writer's imitating J or reproducing J in his own version.[31]

In *The Bible With Sources Revealed*, Friedman observes that:

> The Hebrew of J and E comes from the earliest stage of biblical Hebrew.[32]

Judging by the similarities of their styles, J may have learned the craft of writing from Solomon's Court Historian. But, if not, J had certainly been influenced by his style. And she was familiar with ancient Mesopotamian creation stories such as Enuma Elish[33]—which she used as a model for the beginning of her *Genesis*.

She was familiar with the myths of kings such as Sargon of Akkade—which she used to tell the story of Moses' birth, of his being placed in a little floating basket, and of his rescue by Pharaoh's daughter. She also knew of the serpent's theft of human immortality, or renewal, in the Epic of Gilgamesh,[34] which she cleverly wove into her *Genesis*.

Genesis was one thing, *Exodus*, another. But, if there had been no captivity in Egypt and no exodus,[35] the question then arises as to what it was that J was trying to tell us with the story of Moses. Was she trying to tell us something about King Saul? But, if so, why would J feel she had to resort to such a subterfuge?

In *The Original Torah, The Political Intent Of The Bible's Writers*, S. David Sperling states that:

> if Moses was not a historical figure but an allegory from which later Israel could "derive sanctions and values," we must attempt to find the model, or models, for the allegory. There is one thread that runs through all the different Moses traditions. Moses is the prophet who unites the people of Israel under the banner of the god Yahweh. He is also a royal or quasi-royal figure who stands above every Israelite institution. This means that Moses is an allegorical representation of the royal historical figure who united Israel under the banner of Yahweh and who claimed sovereignty over all competing institutions. The prime candidate for the figure who stands behind the creation of the allegorical figure Moses is Saul, the first king of Israel.[36]

Additionally, however, J seems to have used the telling of the tribal stories to comment upon David, Solomon, and Jeroboam. For example, as S. David Sperling observes:

> the career of Jeroboam I also provides the background of the novella of Joseph, to which thirteen chapters in the *Book of Genesis* are devoted. In the Bible, Joseph, son of Jacob, is the eponymous ancestor of the northern kingdom, which, among its other names, was known as the House of Joseph or, simply, Joseph. Modern scholarship of a generation ago attempted to seek a historical background for the story of Joseph in the Hyskos period. 'Hyskos' is based on an Egyptian phrase meaning 'rulers of foreign lands,' that is, rulers of alien origin, who reigned over portions of lower Egypt as the fifteenth dy-

nasty in the first half of the second millennium BCE. Most of the Hyskos names appear to be linguistically close to Hebrew, including one that contains the element Ykb, 'Jacob.' Inasmuch as Jacob was a good Hyskos name, it appeared plausible that the biblical Joseph's rise to power had been facilitated by friendly relatives. Indeed, in 1965, the prominent Egyptologist John Wilson wrote: 'It is possible that Joseph served a Hyskos pharaoh in the seventeenth century.'

Contemporary scholarship has abandoned that avenue for a number of reasons, not the least of which is that a Hyskos background completely negates the fundamental premise of the story, that Joseph and his brothers are foreigners whose 'Hebrew' origin visibly distinguishes them from their native Egyptian hosts. They differ not only in language but also in dietary customs and permissible occupations. In addition, the Egyptian names in the story are not found together in the same historical period before the twenty-first dynasty (circa 1069-945 BCE). At the other chronological extreme, there are no compelling linguistic or historical reasons to date the story later than the ninth to eighth century of the first millennium BCE. The tradition of Joseph in Egypt was known to the writer of the early northern *Psalm 82*. In addition, the story of Joseph is the necessary bridge to the traditions of descent into Egypt and subsequent exodus, which originally were northern Israelite traditions. It is of great interest, therefore, to compare the central elements of the Joseph story with the narrative about Jeroboam.

In *Genesis* 37, Joseph dreams that the sheaves of his brothers bow down to his sheaf. The brothers' reaction is one of alarm: "Will you rule over us as king? Will you have complete dominion of us?"

As a result of this dream and one that follows, his brothers

> plot to kill Joseph. He finds sanctuary in Egypt, where he is protected and elevated by Pharaoh. According to *I Kings* 11, Jeroboam, 'corvee master of the House of Joseph,' was told by the prophet Ahijah that he would be 'king over Israel.' Upon hearing Ahijah's prophecy, Solomon attempted to kill Jeroboam but Jeroboam arose and fled to Egypt where Pharaoh Sheshonq gave him sanctuary. (*I Kings* 11:40)
>
> Scholars are unanimous in identifying Shishak, the earliest-named pharaoh in the Bible, with Shoshenq I, the Libyan who founded the twenty-second Egyptian dynasty. In keeping with his policy of undermining strong rulers in Asia, Sheshonq provides a haven for Jeroboam. Thanks to Sheshonq's sponsorship, Ahijah's prophecy was fulfilled with Jeroboam establishing an independent northern kingdom.
>
> What we have here in the Joseph story is a thinly veiled allegory. The prophecy that Jeroboam receives corresponds to Joseph's dream, and Shishak corresponds to Joseph's anonymous pharaoh. The development of the allegory of Joseph may now be confidently reconstructed. By the tenth century, the allegory of Israel in Egypt already existed; likewise available were entertaining tales about the rejected brother who rises to power outside his homeland and then returns in triumph.[37]

Unfortunately, despite the best efforts of J, the two kingdoms did not reunite and continued on separately, being attacked almost constantly by their various neighbors as well as each other. Jeroboam I was probably glad to see J's conciliatory efforts fail—better to be the king of one kingdom than none at all. The priesthoods in the two kingdoms, with their vastly different agendas, may also have been glad to see J's reunification efforts fail—the weakening and collapse of the monarchy would usher in a new period when they would once again, as Samuel had, rule the land.

ENDNOTES

1. *I Kings* 11:43
2. See Endnote 1, above
3. *I Kings* 12:6-11
4. *I Kings* 12:12-19. The word "scorpions" refers to particularly barbaric whips with sharp iron barbs built into them for the purpose of tearing chunks of flesh off the victim. Their use was often fatal.
5. Clayton, Peter, *Chronicles of the Pharaohs*, Thames & Hudson, London, 1994, p 185
6. *I Kings* 14:25-26
7. Clayton, op cit, p 185
8. One of the world's foremost bible scholars, Friedman is Professor of Hebrew and Comparative Literature and holder of the Katzin Chair at the University of California at San Diego. He received his doctorate at Harvard and was a visiting fellow at Oxford and Cambridge.
9. Friedman, Richard Elliott and Williamson, H. G. M., editors, *The Future of Biblical Studies: The Hebrew Scriptures, Semeia Studies*, Scholars Press, Decatur, Georgia, 1986
10. Friedman, Richard Elliott, *Who Wrote The Bible?*, Summit Books, New York, 1987, p 86
11. Bloom, Harold, *The Book of J*, Vintage Books, New York, 1990, p 34
12. Bloom, op cit, p 36
13. Bloom, op cit, p 32
14. Nabal was the name of Abigail's husband. The name Nabal, as Robert Alter tells us in *The David Story*, p 152, means "base fellow," "churl," or "fool." Reversing the letters in Nabal's name yields the name of Joseph's grandfather, Laban, a notoriously treacherous man. Some sort of word game is going on here but what truth lay behind the stories is probably beyond our current reach.
15. Kautzsch, Emil, *An Outline of the Literature of the Old Testament*, Williams and Norgate, London, 1898, p 236-243
16. Bloom, op cit, p 36. If Bloom is right, this would seem to date J's writing as having occurred during the reign of King Rehoboam.
17. Sperling, S. David, *The Original Torah, The Political Intent of the Bible's Writers*, New York University Press, New York 1998, p. 122
18. Sperling, op cit., pp 75-134
19. Kennedy, James, *Peasants in Revolt: Political Allegory in Genesis 2-3*, Journal for the Study of the Old Testament, 47, pp 3-14
20. Mendenhall, George, *The Hebrew Conquest of Palestine*, Biblical Archaeologist, XXV/3, 1962, pp. 66-87
21. Sperling, op cit, pp 121-134
22. *I Samuel* 14:35. See also Sperling, op cit., pp 129-130

23. Sperling, op cit., p 98

24. Sperling, op cit., pp 85-86

25. Coote, Robert, *In Defense of Revolution*, Fortress Press, Minneapolis, 1991, p 14

26. Coote, op cit., p 14

27. *Genesis* 33:18-20

28. *Genesis* 34:1-31

29. Bloom, op cit., p 9

30. Coote, op cit., p 15

31. Coote, op cit., p 15

32. Friedman, Richard Elliott, *The Bible With Sources Revealed*, HarperSanFrancisco, San Francisco, 2003, p 13

33. See Kramer, Noah, *History Begins at Sumer*

34. Kovacs, Renee Gallery, *The Epic of Gilgamesh*, Stanford University Press, Stanford, 1989, p 107

35. Sperling, op cit., p 43

36. Sperling, op cit., p 122

37. Sperling, op cit., p 98-99

CHAPTER 5

KING UZZIAH AND THE PROPHETS

After King Rehoboam died in 911 BCE, Abijam became king and ruled until 908 BCE. He was followed by three kings, co-regents, whose reigns overlapped: Asa (908-867 BCE), Jehoshaphat (870-846 BCE) and Jehoram (851-843 BCE). They were followed by Ahaziah (843-842 BCE), Athaliah (842-836 BCE), and Joash (835-798 BCE).

Then, in 798 BCE, Amaziah became king of Judah. Amaziah, 39, interested in expanding Judah by conquest, mustered a large force[1] consisting of every able-bodied male of Judah over the age of 20 (except those who, for one reason or another, were eligible for exemption). In addition, according to the Chronicler, writing in the mid-fourth century BC, Amazaiah hired 100,000 mercenaries from Israel for 100,000 silver talents.[2]

Appalled by the expense, one of the Temple priests advised King Amaziah "O King! Do not let the army of Israel go with you, for the Lord is not with Israel—all these Ephraimites. But go by yourself and do it; take courage for battle, (else) God will make you fall before the enemy. For in God there is power to help one or make one fall!"[3]

When King Amaziah inquired as to what he was to do about the 100,000 talents he had committed to the war, the priest replied that "The Lord has the means to give you much more than that."[4]

And so, as the Chronicler would write hundreds of years later, "Amaziah detached the force that came to him from Ephraim," and ordered them to "go back to their place," the Ephraimites were "greatly enraged."[5] Small wonder.

Whether Israel's King Joash had received—and kept—the 100,000 silver talents King Amaziah had promised or not is not clear. What *is* clear is that the 100,000 mercenaries who had anticipated participating in sharing the loot after the various battles got nothing. Understandably, as they returned home to Israel, they looted and pillaged along the way.[6]

After King Amaziah and his men won battles at Mount Seir and Sela (Petra), in each of which they killed 10,000 men, Israel's King Joash and his men "made forays against the towns of Judah from Samaria to Beth-horon, killing "3,000… and taking much booty."[7] King Joash of Israel also led his men against Jerusalem where they made a 600 foot breach in the wall and took all of the treasure from the Temple and the king's palace.

Understandably angered by the priests' disastrously bad advice, King Amaziah turned against the priests in Jerusalem. The priests, not to be outdone, formed a conspiracy against him. He was murdered at Lachish in 779 BC and his sixteen year old son, Uzziah, became king.[8]

Although we do not know who taught young King Uzziah the craft of kingship, he ran his kingdom for forty years with great success. Under Uzziah, Judah was more prosperous than it had ever been before—even more prosperous than under David and Solomon. He may have, for a long time, avoided antagonizing the Temple priests, by sending the prophet Amos to meddle in the affairs of King Jeroboam II.

The prophet Amos was from "a settlement of shepherds who had their home at Tekoa, in Judah, and who… reared a special breed of sheep, of small and stunted growth, but prized on account of their wool." He "had under his charge herds of larger cattle as well… and was employed in the cultivation of sycamore trees."[9] Amos' job was to puncture the figs to cause them to ripen faster.

Although it was a time of extraordinary prosperity in both kingdoms, there was a widening gap between the rich and the poor, of whom there were a great many. There was also a good deal of social injustice. Israel's poor and weak found a champion in Amos who championed their cause; railing against the ruling elite in both Judah and Israel, Amos 'prophesied,'

> They hate the arbiter in the gate. And detest him whose cause is just. Assuredly, because you impose a tax on the poor and exact from him a levy of grain, You have built houses of hewn stone. But you shall not live in them.[10]

Despite Amos' championing of their cause, the poor seem not to have benefited from it at all. On the contrary, the chief priest at the shrine at Bethel, Amaziah (not to be confused with Uzziah's father who had the same name), seems to have regarded Amos as a spy in the employ of King Uzziah. Amaziah complained to Israel's King Jeroboam II:

> "Amos is conspiring against you within the House of Israel. The country cannot endure the things he is saying. For Amos has said, 'Jeroboam shall die by the sword, and Israel shall be exiled from its soil." Apparently with Jeroboam II's approval, Amaziah ordered Amos to leave, "Seer, off with you to the land of Judah! Earn your living there, and do your prophesying there. But don't ever prophesy again at Bethel, for it is a king's sanctuary and a royal palace."[11]

Amos left Israel, angrily advising Amaziah that the Lord had said (of Amaziah) that "Your wife shall play the harlot in the town, your sons and daughters shall fall by the sword, and your land shall be divided up with a measuring line. And you yourself shall die on unclean soil for Israel will be exiled from its soil."[12]

Returning to Judah, Amos went on to write the *Book of Amos* which consists of nine chapters of prophecies—oracles against foreign nations and Israel, oracles of indictment against Israel for her sins and injustices, and visions and words of judgment.

Amos' only ally in Israel (other than the poor who may have found the social aspects of Amos' message appealing) seems to have been the prophet Hosea who, like Amos, was a champion of social justice.

The *Book of Hosea* is a collection of dark oracles, composed and arranged by Hosea and his disciples. Its opening is strangely reminiscent of Amos' parting words to Amaziah, the chief priest of Israel. After Amos stated unequivocally that he was neither a prophet nor a prophet's disciple, he compared Amaziah's wife to a harlot.

Unlike Amos, Uzziah—at least at first—avoided religious controversy. He concentrated on building up his infrastructure. He built up strong defenses, "towers in Jerusalem on the Corner Gate and the Valley Gate and on the Angle, and fortified them" with what the *Bible* calls "clever devices… set on the towers and the corners, for shooting arrows and large stones."[13] The nature of these weapons is unknown as no examples have survived.

Uzziah also built towers in the wilderness and he built up a large army of warriors—a battle-ready force who were mustered by Jeiel the scribe and Massechiah, the adjutant under Hananiah, one of the king's officers. Although the *Bible* credits him with a total of 2,600 clan chiefs and a trained army of 307,500 (the latter figure probably greater than the entire populations of Israel and Judah combined)—all of them, nevertheless, were probably well equipped, armed with shields and spears and helmets and mail and bows and slingstones—we may assume that it was, at least, a large army, capable not only of defense, but, when necessary, of waging an offensive war.[14]

The Chronicler tells us that Uzziah went forth to fight the Philistines, and breached the wall of Gath, the wall of Jabneh and the wall of Ashdod. God, we are told, helped him against the Philistines, against the Arabs who lived in Gur-baal, and against the Meunites. The Ammonites paid tribute to Uzziah—probably to offset some of his military expenses from which they, too, benefited. Uzziah's fame was said to have spread to the approaches of Egypt and Judah grew exceedingly strong.

It is also said that Uzziah applied himself to the worship of God—keeping in mind, no doubt, his late father's fate—during the time of Zechariah, instructor in the visions of God. In any case, during this time he made a public display of worshipping the Lord, the consequence of which, we are told is that God made him prosper.

In addition to building towers in the wilderness, he also set his men to the hewing out of many cisterns, for he had much cattle, and farmers in the foothills and on the plain and vine dressers in the mountains and on the fertile lands, for he loved the soil.[15]

At 56, having ruled for forty years, Uzziah decided that the time had come to curtail the power of the Aaronid priesthood. Although the Aaronid priests had not yet made their legal code public—possibly because it was, as yet, incomplete—they seem to have begun to promote the offering of sacrifices on a large scale, sacrifices which benefited them financially. The Aaronid legal code, Leviticus, was probably first codified during Hezekiah's reign but neither completed nor published until around the time of Ezekiel.

Uzziah may have come to believe in the message of social justice and true religious reform promoted by Amos and Hosea. Uzziah may also have been listening to his nephew, Isaiah (who would find his calling to be a prophet in the last years of Uzziah's reign) to promote religious reform in Judah that is, to reform the Aaronid priesthood that controlled the Temple. The need for genuine reform was great. As Isaiah would later put it, with words that recall Amos' earlier ones (*Amos* 5:21-24):

> What need have I of all your sacrifices?
> Says the LORD.
> I am sated with burnt offerings of rams,
> And suet of fatlings,
> And blood of bulls;
> And I have no delight
> In lambs and he-goats.

That you come to appear before Me
Who asked that of you?
Trample My courts no more;
Bringing oblations is futile,
Incense is offensive to Me.
New moon and sabbath,
Proclaiming of solemnities,
Assemblies with iniquity,
I cannot abide.
Your new moons and fixed seasons
Fill me with loathing,
They are become a burden to Me,
I cannot endure them.
And when you lift up your hands,
I will turn My eyes away from you;
Though you pray at length,
I will not listen
Your hands are stained with crime
Wash yourselves clean;
Put your evil doings
Away from My sight
Cease to do evil;
Learn to do good.
Devote yourselves to justice;
Aid the wronged.
Uphold the rights of the orphan;
Defend the cause of the widow…[16]

Isaiah's motives for reforming the religious establishment may have been based more upon practical considerations than upon theological speculation. Not only were the priests blatantly corrupt, selling 'justice' off to the highest bidder, they were siphoning off far too much of the national resources, only to squander their riches on luxurious waste. Isaiah must have also seen that the day would come, not too far off, when the nation would need the help of those who now being victimized, who would then be unwilling.

> To whom will you flee for help,
> And how will you save your carcasses...[17]

Around 739 BC, Uzziah seems to have decided to break the priests' monopoly in communicating with God—no longer would people have to pay the priests to offer incense to God; they could do it for themselves, as he would show them by example.

And so King Uzziah entered the Temple, presumably by himself, to offer incense on the incense altar. He was almost immediately confronted by the high priest, Azariah, who, together with eighty other priests, followed him into the Temple and told him that it was not for him "to offer incense to the Lord, but for the Aaronite priests, who have been consecrated, to offer incense"—and ordered him out of the Sanctuary.[18]

Instead of leaving the Sanctuary, however, Uzziah, holding the censer and ready to burn incense, got angry with the priests. What happened next is unclear. According to the priests' account,

> leprosy broke out on his forehead in front of the priests in the House of the Lord beside the incense altar.[19]

A far more reasonable explanation is that either Uzziah's incense or the censer had been tampered with, causing flames to leap up from the censer and burn his forehead—it is a scene reminiscent of the one in *Exodus* where the Korahites supposedly burned to death while attempting to burn incense. The Aaronid priests seem to have been expert with pyrotechnics for quite some time. That he was still, at 56, fleet of foot may explain how he escaped with his life despite being pursued by "eighty brave priests."[20]

What afflicted Uzziah could hardly have been leprosy, a disease that is slow in developing. Far more probable is that he suffered from burns when flames leapt up from the censer.

There is no mention of the priests attempting to treat Uzziah's illness. Presumably they had not yet discovered the technique for diagnosis and treating leprosy described in Leviticus 13-14.

Regardless of the cause, however, the priests—making a very rapid diagnosis indeed, pronounced Uzziah to be a leper and so, leprous or not, he was banished—to a palace south of Jerusalem where he lived for the next eleven years while his son, Jotham, acted as the Prince Regent of Judah.

According to Josephus, when Uzziah died (in 727 BC) he was buried alone in his garden. According to the *Second Book of Chronicles* he was buried in the burial field of the kings, which would have necessitated a move. At that point, his grave was marked with a stone with the following inscription in Aramaic of the late Second Temple period:

> Hither were brought the bones of Uzziah, King of Judah, and do not open.[21]

The battle for power between the monarchy and the priesthood was about to reach a climax.

ENDNOTES

1. Astruc, Jean, *Conjectures sur la Genese, Editions Noesis*, Paris, 1999, originally published in Brussels, 1753, pp 131-148
2. *II Chronicles* 25:6
3. See Driver, S. R., *An Introduction to the Literature of the Old Testament*, Scribners', New York, 1913, Kautzsch, Emil, *An Outline of the History of the Literature of the Old Testament*, Williams & Norgate, London, 1898
4. *II Chronicles* 25:9-10. There is, naturally enough, no mention of a divine bequest of 100,000 talents in Amaziah's favor.
5. *II Chronicles* 25:10
6. *II Chronicles* 25:13a
7. *II Chronicles* 25:13b
8. *II Chronicles* 25:23-24

9. *II Chronicles* 25:27-26:1
10. *Amos* 7:14
11. *Amos* 5:10-11a
12. *Amos* 7:10-13
13. *Amos* 7:16b-17
14. *II Chronicles* 26:15
15. *II Chronicles*
16. *Isaiah* 1:13-17
17. *Isaiah* 10:3b
18. *II Chronicles* 26:18
19. *II Chronicles* 26:19
20. *II Chronicles* 26:20
21. Keller, Werner, *The Bible As History*, Wm. Morrow & Co., New York, 1964, page 221

CHAPTER 6

KING HEZEKIAH AND THE PRIESTLY CODE

When Hezekiah became king at 25, on the death of his father, Ahaz, he had probably had as good an education in the art of kingship as any of the kings of Judah. He was born in Jerusalem in 751 BCE, around the time that his great-grandfather, King Uzziah was deposed by the Temple priesthood and banished, supposedly as a leper, to live out his remaining eleven years in a luxurious villa two and a half miles south of Jerusalem at Ramat Rahel while his son, Jotham, reigned in his place, as regent.

He was four years old when the king of Israel, Jeroboam II, died and was succeeded as king by Zechariah and then Shallum and then Menahem, all within the course of a year.

He was five years old when Israel's King Jeroboam died and Zechariah became king; six when Zechariah died and Shallum became king, followed only a few months later by Menahem; fourteen when Menahem died and Pekahiah became king; fifteen when Pekahiah died and Pekah became king; nineteen when Damascus was taken by the Assyrian king, Tiglath-Pileser; twenty-two when King Pekah was deposed and slain and Hoshea became King of Israel. All things considered, quite a childhood education for a future king…

And he was eight years old when his father, Ahaz, 20, became king and ruled for sixteen years. Ahaz bought peace by taking gold and silver from the temple in Jerusalem and gave it, as tribute, to the Assyrian king, Tiglath-Pileser, to forestall Tiglath-Pileser's attack on Jerusalem. Tiglath-Pileser then advanced on Damascus which had been threatening Jerusalem, and captured it.[1]

Invited to Tiglath-Pileser's victory celebration in Damascus, Ahaz was so impressed with the temple there that he had the temple in Jerusalem modified—with the help of a priest named Uriah—and asserted his right to officiate at the sacrifices offered at the temple.[2]

Ahaz seems not to have been well liked by the priesthood for they later began their summary of his reign thusly:

> Twenty years old was Ahaz when he began to reign and reigned sixteen years in Jerusalem and did not that which was right in the sight of the Lord, his God, like David his father. But he walked in the ways of the kings of Israel… and he sacrificed and burnt incense in the high places, and on the hills, and under every green tree.[3]

In the twelfth year of Ahaz's reign, when Hezekiah was 20, Hoshea, son of Elah, became king of Israel in Samaria for nine years. When the Assyrian king, Shalmaneser, discovered that Hoshea had sent envoys to King So[4] of Egypt, he marched against Israel, conquered it, deported many of the Israelites to Assyria before sending many of them elsewhere.

Thus, at 25, Hezekiah had seen a great deal of history made. His father, Ahaz, and grandfather, Amon, had probably appraised him of the delicate state of affairs between the monarchy and the priestly factions.

Although the priesthood and the monarchy had become mortal enemies, the twenty-five-year old Hezekiah wisely decided to mend fences with the priestly factions by repairing the Temple,[5] enhancing the power of the Aaronid priests, while biding his time and concentrating upon strengthening the infrastructure of his kingdom.

To do this, he relied heavily, as his great-grandfather, Uzziah, had done before him, upon advanced technology. Just where he got the technical expertise is not known but the construction, in the early years of his reign, of the Siloam Tunnel, an underground tunnel to supply water in the event of an extended siege was an engineering marvel. And so, under Hezekiah's relatively enlightened rule Judah prospered.

In 722 BCE, the fourth year of Hezekiah's reign, the northern kingdom was conquered by the Assyrian king, Shalmaneser V, putting to an end, for all time, Israel's attempt to escape from under the Assyrian yoke. There would be no more Israel. Only Judah would survive.

The fall of Samaria, as Israel was then called, resulted in a massive influx of refugees into Jerusalem. Not only must Hezekiah have been concerned with the influx of so many former members of Israel's royal families coming into Jerusalem, the Aaronid priesthood at Jerusalem's Temple must have been concerned with the presence of so many out-of-work Levite priests. If given jobs at the Temple they would soon outnumber the Aaronid priests—particularly if they were given any of the better positions—and an unwanted change of power would occur; if they did not, the Levites would intrigue against them and against Judah's royal family and an unwanted change of power would occur.

The solution seems to have been to draw up a new constitution. Just whose idea it was is not known for certain but the prophet, Isaiah, then around twenty-nine years old, is a prime candidate. Judah would become a constitutional monarchy. The name of the constitution? Leviticus. In Leviticus, Hezekiah is given credit for restructuring the priesthood:

> Hezekiah reconstituted the divisions of the priests and Levites, each man of the priests and Levites according to his office, for the burnt offerings, the offerings of well-being, to minister, and to sing hymns and praises in the gates of the courts of the Lord; also the king's portion, from his property, for the burnt offerings—the morning and evening burnt offering, and the burnt offerings for Sabbaths, and new moons, and festivals as prescribed in the Teaching of the Lord.[7]

Whether Hezekiah was acting on his own or had been urged on by the Aaronid priests when he decided to destroy one of the Levite priests' chief religious symbols, Neshutan,[8] is not known. Neshutan was a bronze snake, mounted on a rod, that the Lord was supposed to have ordered Moses to make as an aid to saving the lives of, and curing, those who had been bitten by venomous snakes. Because the Israelite people had complained about Moses' failure to provide food and water:

> The Lord sent seraph serpents against the people. They bit the people and many of the Israelites died. The people came to Moses and said, "We sinned by speaking against the Lord and against you. Intercede with the Lord to take away the serpents from us!" And Moses interceded for the people. Then the Lord said to Moses," Make a seraph figure and mount it on a standard. And if anyone who is bitten looks at it, he shall recover. Moses made a copper serpent and mounted it on a standard; and when anyone was bitten by a serpent, he would look at the copper serpent and recover.[9]

The account of Hezekiah's destruction of a symbol sacred to the Levites shows the depth of the division between the Aaronids and the Levites.

> Now it came to pass… that Hezekiah the son of Ahaz king of Judah began to reign. Twenty and five years old was he when he began to reign; and he reigned twenty and nine years in Jerusalem. His mother's name also was Ahi the daughter of Zachariah. And he did that which was right in the sight of the Lord, according to all that David his father did. He removed the high places, and brake the images and cut down the groves and brake in pieces the brazen serpent that Moses had made: for unto those days the children of Israel did burn incense to it: and he called it Nehushtan.[10]

Although it would seem that Hezekiah's destruction of Neshutan would have been contrary to the wishes of the Lord as expressed in *Numbers* 21:6-9, it would seem designed to bring him into favor with the Aaronid priests who would later write, or rewrite, their account of his elevation to Judah's throne.

One of the consequences of the instability in the northern kingdom was that refugees began to flee southward from the northern kingdom into Jerusalem. At first there were probably only a few—wealthy families who had chosen the wrong side in the struggle for Israel's throne, priests who had similarly allied themselves with the "wrong" side and now, having found themselves out of work, had to subsist on whatever their former patrons were willing to give them.

That Hezekiah

> trusted only in the Lord the God of Israel; there was none like him among all the kings of Judah after him, nor among those before him[11]

would tend to indicate that the author of this portion of *II Kings* was writing some time after the fall of the monarchy in Judah. That Hezekiah

> clung to the Lord; he did not turn away from following Him, but kept the commandments that the Lord had given to Moses[12]

would seem to indicate that the writer was of the priestly class.

S. R. Driver, in *Introduction to the Literature of the Old Testament*, observes that the account of King Hezekiah which begins at *II Kings* 18:

> includes a prophecy, Chapter 19:21-31, attributed to Isaiah, and unquestionably his; but there is no ground for supposing that the narrative as a whole, though it stands also (together with Chapter 20:1-9) in the *Book of Isaiah* (Chapters 36-39), is from Isaiah's hand... There are reasons for concluding it to be the work of a prophet writing in the subsequent generation,

> which was incorporated, with slight additions, in his work by the compiler of Kings.[13]

To which Driver added that:

> As the narrative approaches the time in which the compiler himself lived (Chapter 21 ff)... the rest is the comment of the compiler... Which is not assigned to any individual prophet, though it agrees remarkably with parts of Jeremiah.[14]

When the kingdom of Israel fell in 722 BC, a time of great political turmoil began. Refugees fled into Judah from the north, bringing with them religious customs which were unacceptable to the Temple priesthood in Jerusalem. Prophets such as Micah and Hosea were struggling to be heard, the Aaronid priests were struggling for power, not only against the Levites but also against the monarchy—as they had been in the time of King Uzziah—and King Hezekiah had the Assyrians to worry about.

Although the author of *II Kings*' account of King Hezekiah concedes that Hezekiah did "what was right in the sight of the Lord God of Israel," Hezekiah suffered a number of setbacks, including the loss of a number of cities to the Assyrians and having to pay a huge tribute to the Assyrian emperor, Sennacherib.

It is during the reign of King Hezekiah, or perhaps a bit later, that Richard Elliott Friedman places the early work of the Priestly Source. He marshals a number of strong arguments to support his claim among which is that the Deuteronomist, writing somewhat later, around the time of King Josiah, was familiar with the Priestly law code, the centralization of worship that occurred during King Hezekiah's reign, the separation of the priesthood into Aaronid and Levitical factions:

> And Hezekiah appointed the courses of the priests and the Levites after their courses, every man according to his service, the priests and Levites for burnt offerings and for peace offerings, to minister, and to give thanks, and to praise in the gates of the tents of the Lord.[15]

In *Who Wrote The Bible?* Richard Elliott Friedman points out that the

> laws and stories of P reflect the interests, the actions, the politics, and the spirit of the age of Hezekiah the way that D reflects the age of Josiah.[16]

There seems to be no evidence that any of the original Priestly document—that is, any of the first fourteen chapters of the *Book of Leviticus*—had been made public prior to the reign of King Josiah although its existence may well have been known by both the Aaronid and Levite priests from the time of King Hezekiah. There was, after all, the problem of how to explain the sudden appearance of a document supposedly written by Moses some five or six hundred years earlier—the very kind of problem that the Levites would, around 621 BCE, solve so well with their temple renovation story which was further confirmed by Josiah's order to return the Ark to the temple.

Similarly persuasive evidence points to a second Priestly source working after the reign of King Josiah, during the exile, prior to the sending of Ezra to Jerusalem. Unlike the work of the Court Historian, the Jahwist, the Elohist, and the Deuteronomist, this Priestly document may have remained separate from the earlier work until the time of the Redactor. It's possible that whatever had been in the temple archives prior to the time the Levites acquired control may not have survived while identical, or nearly identical, documents kept by others elsewhere may have survived.

When Hezekiah died around 797 BC, his son Manasseh became king and began a fifty-five year reign. Manasseh relaxed some of the religious policies imposed on the population by Hezekiah, for which Manasseh would later be described as having "done evil in the sight of the Lord." When Manasseh died, his son, Amon, reigned for two years before being murdered, probably as the result of a Temple conspiracy which involved Judah's militia (the "people of the land"), whereupon Amon's son, Josiah, 8, became king aided by an anonymous Regent, possibly the high priest, Hilkiah, himself...

ENDNOTES

1. *II Kings* 15:13
2. *II Kings* 16:7-9
3. *II Kings* 16:10-18
4. See Clayton, Peter, *Chronicles of the Pharaohs*, Thames & Hudson, London, 1994, pp 182-192. Just who "King So," to whom *II Kings* 17:4 refers, was is not clear. In 731 BCE the pharaoh at Tanis would have been either Sheshonq V or Osorkon IV, at Leontopolis, the pharaoh would have been Iuput, while in Nubia, it would have been Piankhi.
5. *II Kings* 18:3
6. Finkelstein, Israel, and Silberman, Asher, *The Bible Unearthed*, HarperSanFrancisco, San Francisco, 2002
7. *II Chronicles* 31:2-3
8. See Rothenberg, Beno, *Were These King Solomon's Mines?*, Stein and Day, New York, 1972 pp 152, 173
9. *Numbers* 21:6-9
10. *II Kings* 18:1-4
11. *II Kings* 18:5
12. *II Kings* 18:6
13. Driver, S. R., *An Introduction to the Literature of the Old Testament*, p 197
14. Driver, op cit., p 197
15. *II Kings* 31:2
16. Friedman, Richard Elliott, *Who Wrote The Bible?*, HarperSanFrancisco, San Francisco, 1987, p 211

CHAPTER 7

KING JOSIAH AND THE DEUTERONOMIST

At 45, King Manasseh of Judah was in the thirty-third of his fifty-five year reign in 665 BCE when his first son, Amon, was born. Manasseh was 52 when a son, Jeremiah, was born to a priest named Hilkiah in the small town of Anathoth, a suburb of Jerusalem. Whether or not Jeremiah's father, Hilkiah, was the same Hilkiah who later became the chief priest in the temple in Jerusalem is uncertain. Since the text does not distinguish between them, perhaps neither should we.

Manasseh was 61 in 649 BCE when the wife of his sixteen-year old son, Amon, gave birth to a son, Josiah. King Manasseh would rule for another six years, dying in 643 BCE. His son, Amon, 22, then became king. Jeremiah, who was already fifteen years old, would later become one of Judah's most prolific and powerful prophets.

Like his father, Manasseh, Amon was regarded by the *Bible*'s authors as a wicked king. As the *Bible* puts it, Amon

> did what was displeasing to the Lord, as his father, Manasseh had done. He walked in all the ways of his father, worshiping the fetishes which his father had worshiped and bowing down to them. He forsook the Lord, the God of his fathers, and did not follow the way of the Lord.[1]

That Amon followed his father's religious policies should not be surprising.

When Amon became king the Israelite people were still far from being unanimously monotheistic. Even the priests seem not to have denied the existence of other gods, they only disputed the right of other gods to be worshipped—they were monolatrous, not monotheistic. And a good segment of the Israelite people were not very in tune with the "Yahweh-only" movement—as the popularity of the other gods indicates.[2]

The situation was understandable. A hundred years earlier, during King Hezekiah's reign, there had been a huge influx of refugees in Judah after the fall of the northern kingdom in 722 BCE. This was, perhaps, the most significant factor in the increase of the number of people in Judah who worshipped gods other than Yahweh. Not only that, there were growing numbers of foreign businessmen in Jerusalem who worshipped gods other than Yahweh. And even among Israelites who worshipped more than one god there was, by no means, a consensus as to which of the gods from the former Canaanite pantheon should be considered "Israelite" gods.

For two years the priests of the Yahweh-only faction in Jerusalem continued to watch in anger as King Amon worshipped and bowed down to idols, just as they had watched for fifty-five years as his father had previously done.

Then, in 640 BCE, as the *Bible* puts it, "Amon's courtiers conspired against him, and they killed the king in his palace."[3] The *Bible* does not tell us who those courtiers were nor does it tell us what the assassins' motives were. The text tells us that rough justice was not long in coming:

> the people of the land put to death all who had conspired against King Amon, and the people of the land made his son Josiah king in his stead.[4]

The phrase 'the people of the land' does not refer to an ad hoc mob—it refers to the members of the volunteer army—men who could be called up by the scribe of the commander of the army.[5] Thus Amon's courtiers—and, perhaps, even Amon himself—were killed by army volunteers who had been summoned for that purpose. That the author of the account—who was, as we shall see, a priest himself—did not disapprove of the militia's action when writing his account of Amon's death. Indeed, the account quietly suggests that the priests and the army reservists had conspired against King Amon.

The *Bible* does not identify Amon's assassins by name nor does it attribute any motive for Amon's murder. One of the purposes of the Deuteronomist's text seems to have been to exonerate the Yahweh-only priests who were the chief beneficiaries of Amon's murder. According to the text, the priests had no part in either Amon's death or in the slaughter of the alleged assassins. After all, the alleged assassins were said to be members of Amon's court. If, as was likely, they shared Amon's religious views, religious differences would seem to be ruled out as a motive for Amon's murder—that is, if we accept the notion that it was Amon's courtiers who were guilty of his murder.

For some reason, however, the assassins spared the life of King Amon's eight-year old son, Josiah—who was the key to the Yahweh-only priests gaining control of the government of Judah. Had Josiah been kidnapped? And, if so, by whom? And, why? The text does not say. Although the text is silent as to motive, the facts presented in the text do suggest a very powerful motive, power—and the shift of power at least points a finger of suspicion at the priests.

Since Josiah came to share the views of the Yahweh-only priests—and would do that which the priests have said

> was pleasing to the Lord,[6]

it would be reasonable to infer that those priests had undertaken his education though we know little of Josiah's childhood and education. Those who were responsible for his care seem not to have neglected his social life—he was thirteen years old when he married Hamutal who bore him a son, Eliakim, and fourteen when he married Zebuda who, a year later, bore him a second son, Jehoahaz.

The text is silent as to who ruled Judah during Josiah's early years. Some sort of regency may have existed and it's possible that the high priest, Hilkiah, took that task upon himself. Unfortunately, we simply do not know.

Josiah seems to have expanded the territory under Judah's control, with the construction of forts along its southern border—including one at Kadesh-Barnea—and forays into the territory to the north which had once been Israel.

Josiah seems to have given his first recorded order at twenty-six when he told the scribe Shaphan to go

> to the high priest Hilkiah and let him weigh the silver that has been deposited… which the guards of the threshold have collected from the people.[7]

To this Josiah added,

> And let it be delivered to the overseers of the work who are in charge at the House of the Lord, that they in turn may pay it out to the workmen that are in the House of the Lord, for the repair of the House: to the carpenters, the laborers, and the masons, and for the purchase of wood and quarried stones for repairing the House.[8]

To this, Josiah added the following puzzling—and unlikely—demand:

> "However, no check is to be kept on them for the silver that is delivered to them, for they deal honestly."[9]

Since the text does not tell us why Josiah was waiving financial control, we might suspect that the author of the text, the Deuteronomist, may have wished to signal that financial control in Judah was passing from a compliant Josiah to the chief priest, Hilkiah.

Very soon something remarkable happened:

> Then the high priest Hilkiah said to the scribe Shaphan, "I have found a scroll of the Teaching in the House of the Lord." Hilkiah gave the scroll to Shaphan, who read it. The scribe

> Shaphan then went to the king and reported to the king: "Your servants have melted down the silver that was deposited in the House, and they have delivered it to the overseers of the work who are in charge at the House of the Lord." The scribe Shaphan also told the king, "The high priest Hilkiah has given me a scroll": and Shaphan read it to the king.[10]

Apparently Josiah didn't listen closely enough to perceive that the text, in recounting what had happened to the children of Israel "after they came out of Egypt" betrayed the fact that it had been written long after the time of the legendary Moses:

> This is the law which Moses set before the children of Israel and these are the witness, ordinances and statutes which Moses told the children of Israel after they came out of Egypt, on the other side Jordan in the valley beside Beth-peor in the land of Sihon, king of the Amorites which dwelt at Hesbon, whom Moses and the children of Israel smote after they were come out of Egypt, and conquered his land and the land of Og, king of Bashan, two kings of the Amorites on the other side Jordan toward the sun rising: from Aroar upon the bank of the river Arnon, unto mount Sion which is called Hermon and all the fields on the other side Jordan eastward: even unto the sea in the field under the springs of Pisga...[11]

That Shaphan did not hand the scroll to Josiah for him to read himself suggests that perhaps the king had not been taught how to read. Why else would Shaphan undertake to read it to him? Why hadn't the chief priest, Hilkiah, delivered the scroll to Josiah himself? Was it to give Josiah a proper sense of humility? Was Hilkiah indicating that he considered Josiah to be on the same level as Shaphan? And why had Hilkiah waited—which is suggested by the abruptness of the text—until the silver had been melted down before revealing that a scroll had been discovered?

It may be that the author thought such details were relatively trivial and simply moved on to matters that, in his eyes, were important. However:

> When the king heard the words of the scroll of the Teaching, he rent his clothes.[12]

Josiah was deeply disturbed:

> And the king gave orders to the priest Hilkiah, and to Ahikam son of Shaphan, Achbor son of Michaiah, the scribe Shaphan, and Asaiah the king's minister: "Go, inquire of the Lord on my behalf and on behalf of the people, and on behalf of all Judah, concerning the words of this scroll that has been found. For great indeed must be the wrath of the Lord that has been kindled against us, because our fathers did not obey the words of this scroll to do all that has been prescribed for us.[13]

> And Moses called all Israel, and said unto them, hear, O Israel, the statutes and judgments which I speak in your ears this day, that ye may learn them, and keep, and do them. The Lord our God made a Covenant with us in Horeb… Thou shalt have no other gods before me… thou shalt not make thee any graven image, or any likeness of any thing that is in the heaven above, or that is in the earth beneath, or that is in the waters beneath the earth… (5:1-29) Ye shall walk in all the ways which the Lord your God hath commanded you that ye may live, and that it may be well with you, and that ye may prolong your days in the land which you shall possess.[14]

Had Moses forgotten that the Lord had ordered him to make the image of a golden snake, Neshutan?

There were places everywhere—even, until recently, in the Temple itself, Josiah knew—where the old Canaanite gods were still worshipped and where there were images in great profusion and this, Josiah may have decided, was the reason his father's days had been cut short. He may also have been persuaded that this had been the reason the northern kingdom had been defeated, a hundred years before.

Set in a presumably historical framework, the Deuteronomistic law code claimed to have been dictated by Yahweh to Moses. It forbade giving bad cuts of meat to the priests. It established at least a subsistence wage for the Levite priests. It dealt with a variety of issues involving land and property. It imposed all sort of demands upon the Israelites. It required that not only they, but everyone else—even foreigners—in Judah, worship no god other than Yahweh. It established rules for marriage, divorce, executions, burials. It also warned of severe punishment for failing to observe the provisions of the law code.[15]

Some of it was contradictory. Although a custom seems to have existed that exempted those who were afraid from military service, the Deuteronomistic law code ordered those in combat to be afraid of nothing—even when they were underarmed or vastly outnumbered.[16] This command ignores one of the peculiarities of military service which is that because fear is contagious, it is unwise to have any but the fearless present on the battlefield.

Among the casualties of Josiah's reform were all of the various holidays associated with the various cults that had been suppressed.

Josiah issued an order for all the citizens of Judah to come together in Jerusalem to hear the law read to them. He ordered a Passover celebration in keeping with the requirement in the newly discovered code. Whether or not this was the first Passover celebration ever is not known. Unless there had been an oral tradition of an exodus from Egypt—an exodus which now seems never to have happened—it is unlikely that there had ever been an annual Passover celebration like the one the Jahwist first described in her original version of *Exodus*. And there doesn't seem to be an author before Josiah's time describing the celebration of Passover. Why? Previous authors may have known that the story of the waters parting in *Exodus* had no literal historical basis. This may be the moment at which an allegorical script became, as Harold Bloom put it, "Scripture"—the reading of which would be "numbed by taboo and inhibition."[17] We should, however, at least consider the possibility that the celebration of Passover was the Deuteronomist's own invention for the simple reason that the cultic holidays that had been cancelled needed to be replaced.

Since the author of the *Book of Deuteronomy* appears to be the first to mention the Ark of the Covenant[18] it is possible that the Ark was first constructed during the reign of King Josiah. That the Ark is mentioned in *Numbers, Joshua, Judges, Samuel*, and *Kings* suggests that the thoughtful reader look to see whether references to it were inserted later.

If the Jahwist's Moses were an allegorical representation of King Saul, no Ark would have existed before the beginning of Saul's reign in 1025 BCE. In the Jahwist's *Exodus*, the Jahwist mentions an Ark but we may reasonably assume that if Saul had an Ark it would have been one of a fairly simple design.

The construction of the elaborate gilded Ark of the Covenant described in *Exodus* 25 probably dates to just before discovery of the Deuteronomistic scroll in 621 BCE. While the *Bible* is silent as to whether the scroll was in the Ark when discovered, it would have made an impressive display and would have given instant authority to Hilkiah's scroll.

Young Josiah seems to have believed that the scroll was genuinely old, but was it? Opinions as to when the scroll that was read to Josiah had been written vary from as far back as the time of the legendary Moses in the fifteenth century BCE to the Persian period when the kingdom of Judah was no more.

Philip R. Davies, Professor in the Department of Biblical Studies at the University of Sheffield, England, expresses the opinion that Deuteronomy was written a hundred years or more later than the time of King Josiah. In *Scribes and Schools: the Canonization of the Hebrew Scriptures*, Davies places the writing of Deuteronomy in the Persian period, which is to say, between the time Babylon fell to Cyrus around 539 BCE and the conquest of Persia by Alexander the Great around

332 BCE.

To Davies, the "story of the finding of the law scroll under Josiah… is a complete fiction, and the idea of a monarch seeking to impose religious orthodoxy over the whole society is highly unusual. Monarchs were occasionally concerned about particular cults, but meddling with popular religion makes no sense… The Mosaic lawbook par excellence… is a colonial program that moves power toward the Levites…"[19]

If Josiah were a particularly weak king, a sort of constitutional monarch—with the Yahweh-only priests holding the real power—and a vassal of Babylon, he would have had no more power than a later provincial colonial governor. If this had been the case, then Davies' method for dating Deuteronomy—on the basis of the relative strength of the monarch—might place Deuteronomy, not during the Persian period, but during King Josiah's reign.

In *Introduction to the Literature of the Old Testament*, S. R. Driver puts matters this way:

> Even (if) it were clear that the first four books of the Pentateuch were written by Moses, it would be difficult to sustain the Mosaic authorship of Deuteronomy. For, to say nothing of the remarkable difference of style, Deuteronomy conflicts with the legislation of Exodus-Numbers in a manner that would not be credible were the legislator in both one and the same.[20]

Driver dismisses the notion that the high priest Hilkiah was involved in the writing of Deuteronomy. Arguing that the document

> could hardly have been lost during the early years of Josiah (who appears to have been throughout devoted to the service of Jehovah); but this might easily have happened during the heathen reaction under Manasseh. Hence it is probable that its composition is not later than the reign of Manasseh.[21]

So says S. R. Driver, who goes on to add:

> The influence of Deuteronomy upon subsequent writers is clear and indisputable. It is remarkable, now, that the early prophets, Amos, Hosea, and the undisputed portions of Isaiah, show no certain traces of this influence; Jeremiah exhibits marks of it on nearly every page.[22]

Or, perhaps, it was the other way around?

In *Who Wrote The Bible?* Richard Eliott Friedman sees the work of the Deuteronomist as a collaborative effort involving the prophet Jeremiah and the scribe, Baruch ben Neriyah whose careers bridged the reign of King Josiah and the early years of the exile in Egypt in the early sixth century BCE. [23]

Now it is possible that a law code had been discovered during the temple renovations. Some sort of document could have been placed there by Aaronid priests during the reign of King Hezekiah. Since the scrolls would have been safe during Hezekiah's reign since he was presumably favorably disposed toward the priests, it is more likely that a law code drawn up in Hezekiah's time would been hidden away in the early years of King Manasseh's reign for safekeeping when King Manasseh installed facilities in the temple for the worship of gods other than Yahweh.

If the code Hilkiah's workmen found reflected the interests of the Priestly Source, which is to say, one or more Aaronid priests, it would either have had to be rewritten or replaced with a law code acceptable to the priests under Hilkiah—Mushites, not Aaronids.

Whether Josiah was pious from his youth and started his suppression of the worship of gods other than Yahweh at age 16, over ten years before the discovery of the scroll in the temple—as suggested by *II Chronicles* 34:3-7—or whether he only began such activities at age 28, after the discovery of the laws on the scroll in the temple—as suggested by *II Kings* 23:4-24—we simply do not know. The two accounts differ and cannot be satisfactorily reconciled. Thus it is for the individual reader to weigh the matter and decide which account is correct—or whether neither account has merit.

We may infer, by reading the two accounts, that Josiah purged all Israel of their shrines, altars, the sacred posts, the idols, and the molten images. At his command, the priests demolished the altars of the Baal and the incense stands were cut down. At Josiah's orders, the sacred posts—known as "the asherah or asherim"—were burned on the priests' altars, the idols and images were smashed and ground into dust and strewn onto the graves of those who had sacrificed to them.

The account in *II Kings* implies that Josiah's "reform" entailed a major bloodbath. That seems to be the certain implication of "Josiah also did away with the necromancers and mediums." In Samaria and Bethel Josiah "slew on the altars all of the priests of the shrines who were there… and then he returned to Jerusalem.[24]

II Kings 23:7 provides a titillating detail that the prudish Chronicler later would fail to mention,

> He tore down the cubicles of the male prostitutes in the House of the Lord.[25]

The *Bible* says very little about the nature of prostitution in the temple. It does not say whether male prostitutes were used by women whose husbands had been unsuccessful in fathering a son, leaving us to wonder whether it was to such a prostitute that Samuel's mother, Hannah, had access in the story told in *I Samuel* 1:17-18.

II Chronicles 34:4 describes how the ashes of the sacred posts, idols, and images were strewn "onto the graves of those who had sacrificed to them." *II Kings* 23:6 describes how Josiah burned the Asherah which was in the Temple of Yahweh and scattered "its dust over the burial ground of the common people."[26] A reasonable inference from this is that the worship of the former Canaanite gods was popular not only with a sizeable segment of the working population as well as a majority of the ruling elite and possibly always had been.

For more than a decade, Josiah continued to try to stamp out all the traces of idolatry in his kingdom. In Samaria, in what had been Israel, Josiah abolished all the cult places after having all of their priests slain and burned on their altars. Next, he caused the shrines of the various foreign gods in Jerusalem to be destroyed as well as the various rural shrines to be defiled; and he took care, because of provisions in the recently discovered book, to support the Levites, whose workload had been greatly reduced.

Then, in 609 BCE, Josiah, 39, quite probably a Babylonian vassal and friendly to the Babylonian cause as was Jeremiah, became embroiled in a hopeless and unnecessary war with Egypt's Pharaoh Necho. Necho and his army were on their way to Carchemish when Josiah decided to intercept them at Meggido, a major trading hub. Necho sent ambassadors to Josiah advising him that they were on their way to make war against the Assyrians and had no quarrel with him.

But Josiah persisted. After all, he and the Israelite people had made a Covenant with Yahweh and they had kept their side of the bargain and now it was time for Yahweh to keep His. But while it must have been unimaginable—to Josiah—that any harm could come to as faithful a supporter of Yahweh as he, one of the Egyptian archers, unaware of the Covenant, took aim and mortally wounded him.

The dying Josiah called for the chariot of his second-in-command to take him back to Jerusalem. There Josiah died. Jeremiah composed a lament for the occasion and Josiah was buried—peacefully, as Huldah had prophesied—among the previous kings of Judah.[27]

The four kings after Josiah—Jehoahaz, Jehoiakim, Jehoiachim and Zedekiah—all would be said to have done that which "was displeasing in the sight of the Lord." Having failed to keep the terms of the Deuteronomist's Covenant—not to mention the contract with Nebuchadnezar—punishments of the severest sort, for one and all, were not far off.

Josiah's oldest son, Eliakim, 25, was passed over in favor of Jehoahaz, 23. Three months later Pharaoh Necho attacked Judah, exacted a tax of one hundred talents of silver and one talent of gold, deposed Jehoahaz and sent him off to Egypt where he later died.

Next to rule was Jehoahaz's older brother, Eliakim who ruled for eleven years under the name, Jehoiakim. In historian John Bright's words, Jehoiakim was "a petty tyrant unfit to rule."[28] While Jehoiakim may have pleased some of his subjects with his refusal to continue Josiah's suppression of non-Yahwistic religions, he demonstrated, very quickly and very visibly, his lack of concern for their welfare by squandering a significant portion of Judah's dwindling funds on a new, more magnificent palace:

> With spacious upper chambers, provided with windows, paneled in cedar: Painted with vermilion...[29]

This provoked Jeremiah, "whose contempt for Jehoiakim," in John Bright's words, was "unbounded, to his scathing best."[30]

Caught between the two superpowers of the day, Egypt and Babylon, Jehoiakim vacillated as to what to do. He remained a vassal of Egypt until 603 BCE when he switched his allegiance, temporarily, to Nebuchadnezar and Babylon. Two years later, having become convinced that Egypt would be the victor in its struggle with Babylon, he switched his allegiance back to Egypt. Three years later, in December 598 BCE, Nebuchadnezar was on the march again.

Just what became of Jehoiakim is uncertain. *II Kings* 24:6 merely mentions that Jehoiakim "slept with his fathers,"[31] while *II Chronicles* 36:6 says that he was deported to Babylon.

In any event, Josiah's youngest son, Jehoiachin, 18, became king and ruled for about a year. After a three months' siege, Jehoiachin surrendered to Nebuchadnezar.[32] He and other members of the royal family were deported to Babylon.

Matthaniah ruled under his throne-name, Zedekiah. The relationship between Zedekiah and Jeremiah seem to have been adversarial throughout. According to the Chronicler, who was probably writing sometime in the Persian period, Zedekiah not only did "what was displeasing to the Lord his God," but also "did not humble himself before the prophet Jeremiah who spoke for the Lord."[33] From this it would seem that the monarchy had become subordinated to the priesthood.

In the eleventh year of Zedekiah's reign, the Babylonians discovered that he had been having secret discussions with the Egyptians—something Jeremiah had specifically warned him against—and lost all patience with him and the citizens of Judah. To Nebuchadnezar, Zedekiah seemed not only ungrateful for his having put him on the throne of Judah, he was also a traitor. When Nebuchadnezar's forces captured Zedekiah en route to Jericho, they brought him and his family to Riblah. There Nebuchadnezar forced Zedekiah to watch as all of his sons were killed. Then Zedekiah's eyes were torn out. He was put in chains and taken back to Babylon where he was put on display in a cage.

After looting Solomon's Temple, Nebuchadnezar's men destroyed the walls of the city and burned the Temple and the mansions of "all the notables." And then:

> The chief of the guards also took Seraiah the chief priest and Zephaniah, the deputy priest, and the three guardians of the threshold. And from the city he took a eunuch who was in command of the soldiers; seven royal privy councilors, who were present in the city; the scribe of the army commander, who was in charge of mustering the people of the land; and sixty of the common people who were inside the city, took them and brought them to the king of Babylon at Riblah. The king of Babylon had them struck down and put to death at Riblah, in the region of Hamath."[34]

Many of elite in Jerusalem were taken captive and transported to Babylon. During their exile there, their priests continued to perform the various rituals that the Deuteronomist had previously prescribed. This seems to have been helpful in keeping the people together as a nation without a country, the implied promise being that if the people would re-enter their contract with their God, Jahweh, and keep the contract faithfully—Jahweh would arrange for them to be allowed to return to Jerusalem and that the nation of Israel (including Judah) would be restored.

Not all of the Judahite elite went to Babylon. Some fled to Egypt, taking Jeremiah along with them. Tradition has it that Jeremiah was stoned to death at Taphanes.

The work of the Deuteronomist was not over. Some scholars, referring to the Deuteronomist, see two authors— Dtr1 and Dtr2. The writing attributed to Dtr1 was written before the end of the monarchy in 586 BCE and that attributed to Dtr2 was written afterwards. Because Jeremiah and Baruch ben Seriyah were both active during the monarchy and, in Egypt, after its demise and because the work of Dtr1 and Dtr2 and the *Book of Jeremiah* are all characterized by the same styles for their prose as well as their poetry and use many of the same phrases and metaphors in their work—as Richard Elliott Friedman has pointed out—it is all, very likely, the work of the same team.[35]

Among the exiles who went to Babylon was a twenty-two year old priest who would there design a theocracy and give the exiles a new form of hope.

ENDNOTES

1. *II Kings* 21:20
2. As indicated by the formula "did what was displeasing to the Lord," which appears more often than not in the biographies of the kings in *I and II Kings* and *I and II Chronicles* as well as in *Jeremiah* 52:2, the kings in question permitted the worship of gods other than Yahweh, something which, we may be sure, was displeasing to the priesthood in Jerusalem.
3. *II Kings* 21:23
4. *II Kings* 21:24
5. *II Kings* 18:21
6. *II Kings* 22:2
7. *II Kings* 22:4

8. *II Kings* 22:6
9. *II Kings* 22:7
10. *II Kings* 22:8-10
11. *Deuteronomy* 4:44-49
12. *II Kings* 22:11
13. *II Kings* 22:12-13
14. *Deuteronomy* 5:1-29
15. *Deuteronomy* 17:5-6 and 17:12
16. *Deuteronomy* 6:14
17. Bloom, Harold, *The Book of J*, Grove Weidenfeld, New York, 1990, p 35
18. *Exodus* 25:10-22
19. Davies, Philip R., *Scribes and Schools: The Canonization of the Hebrew Scriptures*, Oxford, 1998, pp 98-99
20. Driver, Samuel Rolles, *An Introduction to the Literature of the Old Testament*, Charles R. Scribner's Sons, New York, 1928, p 82
21. Driver, op cit, p 87
22. Driver, op cit, p 88
23. Friedman, Richard Elliott, *Who Wrote The Bible?*, HarperSanFrancisco, 1997, pp 146-147
24. *II Kings* 23:20
25. *II Kings* 23:7
26. *II Kings* 23:6
27. *II Kings* 22:20 The prophetess Huldah promises Josiah a peaceful burial, not a peaceful death. It is an interesting example of how carefully one must interpret prophecy—an art yielding the best results when practiced long after the events prophesied have occurred.
28. Bright, John, *A History of Israel*, Third Edition, Westminster Press, Philadelphia, 1980, p 325
29. *Jeremiah* 22:14b
30. Bright, op cit, p 326
31. Bright, op cit, p 327. Bright speculates that Jehoiakim was assassinated by his own people in the hope—false, as it turned out, that they would thereby gain milder treatment from the Babylonians.
32. Bright, op cit, p 327
33. *II Chronicles* 36:12
34. *II Kings* 25:18-21
35. Friedman, op cit, pp 146-149

CHAPTER 8

EZEKIEL, THE SECOND PRIESTLY SOURCE

Solomon's temple in Jerusalem was still standing in 597 BCE when Ezekiel, a priest of the temple in Jerusalem, possibly a young man of around twenty-five[1] was deported to Babylon along with King Jehoiachin and a substantial portion of the Judahite aristocracy. There the exiles seem to have functioned—and to have regarded themselves—as a government-in-exile, maintained by Nebuchadnezar at government expense.

As the son of Buzi, a priest, Ezekiel would already have had an insider's view of some extraordinary events in Judah's history. If we are right about his age, he would have been fourteen and living in Jerusalem when King Josiah was buried after being killed by Egyptian soldiers at Megiddo, eighteen when King Jehoiakim burned Jeremiah's book of prophecies,[2] and twenty-one when the vacillating Jehoiakim rebelled against Nebuchadnezar.[3]

Although little is known about Ezekiel, the man, he seems to have lived in comfortable circumstances in a house in the Israelite community at Tel-Abib on a canal in Babylon. In *An Introduction to the Literature of the Old Testament*, S. R. Driver explains that Ezekiel—

> was a priest and as such belonged to the aristocracy of Jerusalem, who formed the bulk of the first captivity under Jehoiachin. The exiles at Tel-abib must have formed a considerable community. Though their circumstances could hardly have

> been affluent, they do not appear to have been in actual want. Ezekiel lived in his own house where the elders of the Israelites are represented as coming to sit and listen to his words; and the houses of others are alluded to.[4]

Ezekiel, like Jeremiah, was strongly pro-Babylonian and, for that reason, may have enjoyed Nebuchadnezar's trust and respect. This would help explain how he was able to give a detailed description of Nebuchadnezar's plans for conquering Tyre, capital of Phoenicia. Ezekiel cast the matter in the form of a prophecy:

> For thus saith the Lord God: Behold, I will bring upon Tyre Nebuchadnezar king of Babylon, a king of kings, from the north, with horses, and with chariots, and with horsemen, and companies, and much people...[5]
>
> And he shall set engines of war against thy walls, and with his axes he shall break down his towers...[6]

Whether Ezekiel was trusted by the Babylonians to the extent that they were willing to share their military plans with him or whether he picked up the information in the streets of Babylon is uncertain. Perhaps the idea appeared to him in a vision or, unlikely as it may be, Yahweh actually revealed the matter to Ezekiel. We will never know for sure.

Ezekiel also seems to have been privy to what was happening in Jerusalem—matters which he regarded with alarm. He may have gotten his information in dispatches from Jerusalem relayed to him by Nebuchadnezar or from friends, relatives, and others who had remained behind. More likely he got it from both but that, too, is a matter for conjecture.

In July 593 BCE, five years after his arrival in Babylon, Ezekiel, possibly around 307, announced that he had had a call to prophesy—a calling he would follow for the next twenty-two years. It was a very vivid call:

> I looked, and lo, a stormy wind came sweeping out of the north—a huge cloud and flashing fire, surrounded by a radiance; and in the center of it, the center of the fire, a gleam as of amber. In the center of it were also the figures of four creatures. And this was their appearance:
>
> They had the figures of human beings. However, each had four faces and each of them had four wings; the legs of each were (fused into) a single rigid leg, and the feet of each were like a single calf's hoof; and their sparkle was like the luster of burnished bronze. They had human hands below their wings. The four of them had their faces and their wings on their four sides. Each one's wings touched those of the other. They did not turn when they moved; each could move in the direction of any of its faces...[7]

So vivid are Ezekiel's visions—whose reflections he seems to have seen in the canal by his house—that they beg the question of whether we should take Ezekiel's words as being literally true. Should they be regarded as an allegory or had Ezekiel had a psychedelic experience? Had he really seen something or had he thought he had and was trying to describe it as precisely as possible. In any event, Ezekiel claimed that the Lord had called him to 'prophesy' to the remnants of Judah wherever they might be.

After describing the creatures and a chariot with four wheels and various loud sounds, he found himself in the Presence of the Lord who then and there called him to prophesy:

> When I beheld it, I flung myself down on my face. And I heard the voice of someone speaking.[8]
>
> And He said to me "O mortal, I am sending you to the people of Israel, that nation of rebels, who have rebelled against Me... that they may know that there was a prophet among them...[9]

Ezekiel relates how the Lord warned him about the difficulty of dealing with the Israelites—who were, the Lord said, a "nation of rebels, who have rebelled against Me—they, as well as their fathers, have defied Me to this very day," the Lord asked Ezekiel to:

> "... eat what is offered you; eat this scroll, and go speak to the House of Israel." So I opened my mouth, and He gave me this scroll to eat, as He said to me, "Mortal feed your stomach and fill your belly with this scroll that I give me." I ate it, and it tasted as sweet as honey to me.[10]

Devoting a full nine chapters to the Lord's complaints about the Israelites and dealing with issues such as idolatry, using vivid sexual imagery—fitting, considering Ezekiel's characterization of Jerusalem as a wanton woman—combining masturbation, cannibalism and coprophagy, Ezekiel predicted that nearly all of the Israelites would suffer—one third from pestilence, one third by the sword, and one third by being dispersed among the various nations of the earth—whereupon the Lord, according to Ezekiel, explained that there were false prophets among the Israelites and told him to:

> say to those who prophesy out of their own imagination: Hear the word of the Lord! Thus saith the Lord God: Woe to the degenerate prophets, who follow their own fancy, without having had a vision! Your prophets, O Israel, have been like jackals among ruins. You did not enter the breaches and repair the walls for the House of Israel, that they might stand up in battle in the day of the Lord. They prophesied falsehood and lying divination; they said, "Declares the Lord" when the Lord did not send them, and then they waited for their word to be fulfilled. It was false visions you prophesied and lying divination you uttered, saying, "Declares the Lord," when I had not spoken...[11]

Ezekiel does not say which prophets had prophesied falsely—he does not say whether they were prophets working in the distant past or whether one might be one of his contemporaries—such as Habakkuk and/or Haggai—nor does Ezekiel say what their prophecies were. It is unfortunate for us that Ezekiel does not explain how false prophecies can be distinguished from true ones.

> The home of Ezekiel's prophetic life was thus on the banks of the Chebar. There he watched from a distance the toils closing round Jerusalem; and there he declared, in every variety of symbolism and imagery, the approaching fall of the city, the ruin of ancient Israel. Israel's chief crime is its idolatry. This has vitiated its history from the beginning and it is rife in it even now. It would seem that in this judgment Ezekiel is not wholly just to the past, and that he has transferred to it unconsciously the associations of the present. But be that as it may, the corruption of Jerusalem is incurable now; and therefore, as he repeatedly insists, Jerusalem must perish. But even the exiles fall far short of what they should be; exile has not yet wrought upon them the moral change which it was to effect. Hence his conviction that further judgments were imminent for them in the future: and his anxiety to win at least the souls of individuals who might form the nucleus of the purified Israel of the future. His advances were received with coldness: he was even, as it seems, obliged to refrain from speaking openly among the exiles and to confine himself to addressing those who visited him specially in his own house, until the fall of Jerusalem in 586 sealed the truth of his predictions, and assured for him a credit which otherwise he would never have attained. The antagonism between Ezekiel and the exiles is manifest; he addresses them repeatedly as a 'rebellious house.' How they felt towards him, and how he viewed them, appears further from such passages as *Ezekiel* 12:21 ff, 14:1 ff, 20:1 ff. Nevertheless, like Jeremiah, he fixed his hopes for the future upon them: Zedekiah and the Jews in Jerusalem he gave up entirely: the exiles, when purged, would form the foundation of a better Israel in the future.[12]

That Ezekiel disliked King Zedekiah—who may have been serving only as a regent for King Jehoiachin rather than as a king in his own right[13]—is evident. How he was able to predict the blinding and exile of Zedekiah—unless the prediction were written after the fact, which is not at all impossible—remains a mystery.

> And the prince that is among them shall bear upon his shoulder in the twilight, and shall go forth: they shall dig through the wall to carry out thereby: he shall cover his face, that he not see the ground with his eyes. My net also will I spread upon him, and he shall be taken in my snare: and I will bring him to Babylon to the land of the Chaldeans: yet shall he not see it, though he shall die there...[14]

THE BOOK OF EZEKIEL

It is widely accepted that the *Book of Ezekiel*—with the possible exception of *Ezekiel* 1:3 which is written in the third person in contrast to all the rest which is written in the first person—is the work of a single author, the prophet, Ezekiel. It consists of four main groups. The first, chapters 1-24, begun in 593 BCE is made up "of visions, discourses, and symbolic acts belonging to the time before the destruction of Jerusalem;"[15] the second, chapters 25-32, begun in 586 BCE consists oracles against foreign countries;[16] the third, chapters 33-39, consists "discourses concerning the future;"[17] and the fourth, chapters 40-48, contains what Kautzsch refers to as "the great vision of the reconstitution of the divine commonwealth, especially of the temple and the cults, in the Messianic Age."[18]

From the outset, the *Book of Ezekiel* is full of the kind of details associated with the Priestly Source, P. Ezekiel is precise about the dates of many of his visions and oracles. He opens the *Book of Ezekiel* with:

> "In the thirtieth year, on the fifth day of the fourth month, when I was..."

His visions, too, as in *Ezekiel* 1:5c-9 are extraordinarily detailed. And the measurements of virtually every aspect of the buildings and the size of the parcels of land on which they were to stand in the new, ideal Jerusalem he describes in *Ezekiel* 41:1-4 Ezekiel gives in numbing detail. Referring to his celestial guide he says:

> He then led me into the great hall. He measured the jambs, 6 cubits on either side; such was the depth of each jamb. The entrance was 10 cubits wide, and the flanking walls of the entrance were each 5 cubits wide. Next he measured the depth [of the hall], 40 cubits, and the width, 20 cubits. And then he entered the inner room. He measured each jamb of the entrance, 2 cubits [deep]; the entrance itself, 6 cubits across; and the width of [the flanking wall on either side of] the entrance, 7 cubits. Then he measured…

This is P, *par excellence.*

Although scholars of the Bible generally refer to a single Priestly Source, using the letter "P," the material attributed to P may well have been the work of at least three writers, the first of whom was active during the reign of King Hezekiah, possibly the prophet Isaiah—which is to say before the time of King Josiah—the second, Ezekiel, during the early years of the exile and the third, Ezra, after the time of Ezekiel, before, during, and after the time of the second return to Jerusalem.

As is also the case with the *Book of Deuteronomy*, the *Book of Leviticus* represents as historical fact stories that had only two hundred years before were almost certainly intended as allegories—and understood as such. Deuteronomy and Leviticus both represent Moses as a historical character who had supposedly dictated the laws that the Aaronid priests would, after the return from Babylon, enforce, with great cruelty. It is with Ezekiel that the Levites lose their privileges to the sons of Zadok, the Aaronid priests. It is possible that Ezekiel wrote some of the text identified as belonging the Priestly Source—the *Book of Leviticus*, for example.

In *An Outline of the History of the Literature of the Old Testament*, Emil Kautzsch estimated that the Priestly Source was writing sometime between 500 and 400 BC. Kautzsch points out, however, that the program:

> for the theocracy of the future—we may briefly say, for the priestly commonwealth—was sketched by Ezekiel. The first attempt to carry out this (program) was contained in the original Law of Holiness… But we have no knowledge as to the Law of Holiness obtaining official recognition in the worship at Jerusalem after the Return. Something quite different can be shown to have happened: even after the Exile the further development of the Priests' Law was most zealously pursued in the priestly circles which had remained behind in Babylon. We say 'In the priestly circles.' For it will appear that differences were not wanting which point to divergent theories and therefore to diverse hands and circles participating in the work. The priestly history and law-book in the Pentateuch was the product of various priestly schools in the period between 400 and 500 BC, first at Babylon, then at Jerusalem. Apart from the 'Law of Holiness,' which was worked up into it, the following strata can be clearly distinguished: the Priests' Code proper (about 500 BC); the 'Law-book of Moses' published 444; in all probability drawn up by Ezra himself; and the final redaction, occasioned probably by the blending of the Priests' Law with the older historical work (JED).[19]

While Kautzsch places the date of the blending of the Priests' Law with the JED historical work at around 400 BCE, the currently prevailing view is that it may have been completed shortly before the return from the exile.

In addition to writing the original *Book of Leviticus*, the Priestly Source, inserted material into other books in the *Hebrew Bible*. In the *Book of Numbers*, for example, the Priestly Source assigned a virtual monopoly on the priesthood to the Aaronid priests:

> You shall make Aaron and his sons responsible for observing their priestly duties; and any outsider who encroaches shall be put to death.[20]

The Priestly Source is commonly credited with having written everything from *Genesis* 1:1 to *Genesis* 2:4a, that is, through the first half of the fourth verse despite its lacking the legalistic approach, genealogical lists and the dull precision which are characteristic of P. In the Priestly Source's account, God is referred to as Elohim while in the Jahwist's account, God is referred to as Yahweh. The use of the two different names for God led Jean Astruc, a physician at Louis XV's court in 1753, to suggest that in composing Genesis, Moses might have relied upon the work of four different authors—authors whom Astruc identified simply as A, B, C, and D.[21]

In *The Book of J*, Harold Bloom suggests that the author of the Priestly Source (corresponding to Astruc's "A") deleted the beginning of J's original account of creation—probably a story of how, in an epic battle, Yahweh conquered the great sea goddess, Rahab, along the lines quoted below:

> Yahweh with one word created the Sun, the Moon, and the Stars. He stretched out the skies like a tent cloth to shroud the Deep and placed his secret court above the skies, founding it upon the Higher Waters. In creating, Yahweh rode above the Deep, which rose against him. Tehom, queen of the Deep, sought to drown out Yahweh's Creation, but he rode against her in his chariot of fire, and bombarded her with hail and with lightning. Yahweh destroyed her vassal Leviathan with one great blow to the monster's skull, while he ended Rahab by thrusting a sword into her heart. The waters fled backward, awed by the voice of Yahweh, and Tehom tearfully surrendered. Yahweh shouted his triumph, and dried up the floods. He set the Moon to divide the seasons, the Sun to divide day

> and night. Observing Yahweh's victory, the Morning Stars sang together, and all the sons of God shouted for joy. Thus the work of Creation was completed.[22]

In *Psalm* 89—which is attributed to Ethan of Ezrah—Yahweh is described as having conquered the Canaanite goddess, Rahab:

> Thou hast broken Rahab in pieces, as one who is slain…[23]

At the time that the Jahwist wrote *Genesis*, the story of Rahab was familiar to the people in the region. In Ugaritic—which is to say, Canaanite, literature—Baal, the storm god, defeats Yam, the god of the sea. In Mesopotamian literature, Marduk defeats Tiamat, the goddess of the deep waters. And there are also parallels in second millennium Hittite literature.

The account which most scholars today attribute to the Priestly Source contains no reference to Rahab or Yam or Tiamat. It begins thusly :

> When God began to create heaven and earth, and the earth then was water and waste and darkness over the deep and God's breath hovering over the waters, God said, 'Let there be light.' And there was light. And God saw the light, that it was good, and God divided the light from the darkness. And God called the light Day, and the darkness He called Night. And it was evening and it was morning, first day…[24]

That the authors and editors of the *Bible* were reluctant to delete anything, suggests another possibility—perhaps *Genesis* 1:1-2:4a was the work, not of the author of the Priestly Source, but of the author of the Elohistic document—who may have been the Jahwist—thus forming yet another of J's doublets!

The Jahwist's Yahweh was a playful God—even to the point of playing hide-and-seek with Adam and Eve in the Garden of Eden—

> And they heard the sound of the Lord God walking about in the garden in the evening breeze, and the human and his woman hid from the Lord God in the midst of the trees of the

> garden. And the Lord God called to the human and said to him, "Where are you?[25]

The Priestly Source's God was much more somber and had an eye for detail. Genealogical lists abound in the writing of the Priestly Source, Buildings are described in detail and so, too, is the Ark of the Covenant. Although Ezekiel liked vivid verbal imagery, he detested fetishes—idols. Over and over he ranted against them. Thus it's probably unlikely that it was constructed during Ezekiel's time.

The very precise dimensions of the Ark, consistent with the Priestly Source's author's penchant for detail, point to a Priestly Source after Ezekiel's time for the origin—or reconstruction—of the Ark, perhaps as late as the fifth century BCE as a prop to be used for the "return" to Jerusalem of people who had never been there.

ENDNOTES

1. Kautzsch, Emil, *An Outline of the History of the Literature of the Old Testament*, Williams & Norgate, London 1898, p. 87, states that Ezekiel's age at the time he was called is nowhere indicated. But his evidently very exact knowledge of the temple allows us to conjecture that he did not leave Jerusalem as a mere youth, but had probably officiated there as priest. It is possible that the words with which Ezekiel opens his book, "Now it came to pass in the thirtieth year..." may refer to his own age at the time since they do not seem to be related to the year of Nebuchadnezar's reign, or to the year of Jehoiachin's reign, or to anything else.
2. *Jeremiah* 22:14b
3. Bright, *A History of Israel*, Third Edition, Westminster Press, Philadelphia, 1980, p. 325
4. Driver, S. R., *An Introduction to the Literature of the Old Testament*, Charles Scribner's Sons, New York 1928, p. 278
5. *Ezekiel* 26:3
6. *Ezekiel* 26:9
7. *Ezekiel* 1:4-9
8. *Ezekiel* 1:28c-d
9. *Ezekiel* 2:3
10. *Ezekiel* 3:1-3
11. *Ezekiel* 13:1-7

12. Driver, op. cit., pp 278-279
13. *Ezekiel* 12:12
14. Kautzsch, op cit., p. 106-107
15. Kautzsch, op cit., p 87
16. Kautzsch, op cit., p 87
17. Kautzsch, op cit., p 88
18. Kautzsch, op cit., p 88
19. It is possible that Ezra—in addition to being the rightly famous Redactor—was a Third Priestly Source, deliberately writing in an archaic, pre-exilic Hebrew. The currently prevailing view, however, is that because the writer never makes the mistake of using any Late Biblical Hebrew word, the Priestly account may have been written prior to the exile.
20. Freedman, David Noel, Editor-in-Chief, *Anchor Bible Dictionary*, Bantam Doubleday, New York 1992, Volume 2, p. 714
21. *Numbers* 3:10
22. Bloom, Harold, *The Book of J*, Vintage Books, New York, 1990, pp 30-31
23. *Psalms* 89:10a
24. *Genesis* 1:1-5
25. *Genesis* 3:8-9

CHAPTER 9

THE LOST ARK OF THE COVENANT

The story of the mysterious Ark of the Covenant is one of the most intriguing of all *Bible* stories. Although some doubt that the Ark ever existed, there is good reason to believe that it did—at least for a brief period between the seventh and fifth centuries BCE.

The story of the Ark begins slightly more than midway through the *Book of Exodus* although none of it was in the Jahwist's original *Book of Exodus*.[1] Most of the story of the Ark was the work of the authors of the Priestly Source and Deuteronomy, writing some seven to nine hundred years after the legendary escape of the Israelites from captivity in Egypt.[2]

Moses is up on the mountain with over two million[3] starving, thirsty, desperate, hungry former slaves waiting for him, none too patiently, down below. Despite being under obvious and immediate pressure, Moses is calmly taking down the Lord's instructions when the Lord orders Moses to take up a collection on His behalf from the refugees:

> And the Lord spake unto Moses saying "Speak to the Israelites that they take Me a donation from every man, as his heart may urge him you shall take My donation. And this is the donation that you shall take from them, gold and silver and bronze, and indigo and purple[4] ...

At first it might seem that these would be unlikely things for the Israelites to have, but fortunately the Israelites, when they were about to leave Egypt, had the presence of mind (apparently at Moses' instigation) to ask the Egyptians for "ornaments of silver and ornaments of gold and cloaks" things which they could trade for food in the course of their journey to the Promised Land. Fortunately, too, the Egyptians either gave or loaned[5] these things to the fleeing slaves, presumably to speed them on their way[6] and thus bring to an end all of the catastrophes which had occurred as a result of Pharaoh's holding the slaves back.

The *Book of Exodus* describes how the Lord ordered Moses to have a golden box built which to serve not only as a container for the two stone tablets on which the ten commandments have been inscribed, but as a place where He could stay and be available to the priests for help guiding the fleeing Israelites on their forty-year, seven hundred mile hike around and through the Sinai desert.

> And they shall make an ark of acacia wood, two and a half cubits its length and a cubit and a half its width, and a cubit and half its height. And you shall overlay it with pure gold, inside and outside you shall overlay it, and you shall make upon it a golden molding all around. And you shall cast for it four golden rings and set them on its four feet, and two rings on its one side and two rings on the other side. And you shall make poles of acacia wood and overlay them with gold, and you shall bring the poles through the rings on the side of the Ark to carry the Ark with them. In the rings of the Ark the poles must be, they shall not come out. And you shall set in the Ark the tablets of the Covenant that I shall give you. And you shall make a cover of pure gold, two and a half cubits its length, and a cubit and a half its width. And you shall make two cherubim of gold, hammered work you shall make them, at the two edges of the cover. And make one cherub at one edge and one cherub at the other edge, from the cover you shall make the cherubim at both its edges. And the cherubim shall spread

> wings above, shielding the cover with their wings, and their faces toward each other, toward the cover of the faces of the cherubim shall be[7]...

The purpose of the Ark was to house the Law which the Lord had given Moses and the terms of the Covenant—the contract between the Lord and the Israelites—as well as, together with the Tabernacle, to serve as a place for Yahweh to stay when the Israelites were in camp; it would be carried in front of the Israelites when they were on the march; it would cause the river Jordan to dry up to let the Israelites cross;[8] and it would be carried into battle as an assurance to the Israelites that they were indeed under Yahweh's special and undivided protection.

Although the *Book of Joshua* describes how the Israelites were victorious with the Ark in their vanguard at Jericho,[9] the time came, however, years later, when the Israelites, despite the presence of the Ark, were defeated near Aphek. The Philistines took the golden Ark and installed it in their temple at Ashdod along their god, Dagon. On the first night Dagon fell to the floor. Righted by the Philistines the next morning, that night Dagon fell again and broke into pieces.

Spooked, the Philistines of Ashdod had the Ark carried to Gath, another Philistine city. When it became just as unwelcome there it was taken next to Ekron where the Philistines there did not want it either. And so it came to rest at Beth-shemesh. Convinced that possession the Ark was more trouble than it was worth, the Philistines of Beth-shemesh put the Ark into a wooden cart, harnessed two cows to the cart, and sent the cows, cart, and Ark on its way. Coming to rest at Kiriath-jearim, it stayed, cared for by Eleazar, son of Abinadab, for twenty years until King Saul had it moved to his capital, Gibeah.

Some time after Saul's death, according to the biblical account, David had the Ark moved to his new capital, Jerusalem. Later, around 921 BCE Solomon is said to have had a temple built to house it. After that it largely drops from sight until the time of King Josiah when its presence is mentioned again. It is possible that when it may have served as a very impressive icon from the time of the Temple renovation around 621 BCE—until King Josiah's death at Meggido in 609 BCE.

WHO WROTE THE STORY OF THE ARK OF THE COVENANT?

If, as S. David Sperling has suggested, the story of Moses is an allegory for King Saul—there having been no captivity in Egypt, no escape from Egypt, and no Moses—then there would have been no Ark prior to King Saul. Earlier, in Chapter 4, it was suggested that the Jahwist's Genesis and Exodus were written as a prequel to Solomon's Court Historian's biography of David to establish the right of the House of David to rule over the Israelites forever. Since neither Solomon's Court Historian nor the Jahwist were concerned with the existence of a Covenant between Jahweh and the Israelites, then the story of the Ark of the Covenant would have had to have been written by a later author.

Two authors—or groups of authors—are principally responsible for the story of the Ark—the Deuteronomist who was a contemporary of King Josiah and one or two of the three authors of the Priestly Source, writing some time after the time of King Josiah. Here and there in the story bits seem to have been added by the Redactor who edited what had previously been written.

The great detail with which the construction of the Ark is described above suggests that this portion of the account had been written by the author of the Priestly Source who was obsessed with detail.[10]

In 1997 *Bible* scholar Richard Elliott Friedman made a very strong case for placing the Priestly Source's writing during the time of King Hezekiah—clearly *before* the time of King Josiah's Deuteronomist (D). Here is how Friedman expressed it in *Who Wrote The Bible?*:

> P was produced after 722 and before 609 B.C. How much more specific can we get? Can we say in which king's reign

> it was? I think we can. The evidence points to Josiah's great-grandfather, King Hezekiah.
>
> P emphasizes centralization of religion: once center, one altar, one Tabernacle, one place of sacrifice. Who was the king who began centralization? King Hezekiah. Both the books of Kings and Chronicles attest that there was no effective centralization before him."[11]

But it seems unlikely that the Priestly Source's author of King Hezekiah's time would have described the Lord as wanting to have the Ark decorated with the sacred images of the Cherubim since King Hezekiah vigorously opposed the use of images. This he is said to have demonstrated when he destroyed the image of the serpent that Moses was said to have made, by divine command, to protect the Israelites from the bite of poisonous serpents.[12]

As early as 1885, Julius Wellhausen had argued that while the "Jehovist (JE) sanctions a multiplicity of altars," and while "Deuteronomy (D) demands local unity of worship... the Priestly Code (RQ) presupposes that unity and transfers it, by means of the Tabernacle, to primitive times"[13] clearly putting P, in Wellhausen's view *after* D.

In 1898, the German *Bible* scholar Emil Kautzsch suggested that the writing of the Priestly account may have involved two post-Deuteronomistic writers—Ezekiel and Ezra. After crediting Ezekiel with having sketched out the plan for the theocracy of the future during his exile in Babylon, Kautzsch goes on to observe:

> even after the Exile the further development of the Priests' Law was most zealously pursued in the priestly circles which had remained behind in Babylon. We say 'In the priestly circles.' For it will appear that differences are not wanting which point to divergent theories and therefore to diverse hands and circles participating in the work. The priestly history and law-book in the Pentateuch was the product of various priestly schools in the period between 500 and 400 BCE, first at Babylon, then

> at Jerusalem. Apart from the 'Law of Holiness,' which was worked up into it, the following strata can be clearly distinguished: the Priests' Code proper (about 500); the 'Law-book of Moses' (published 444), in all probability drawn up by Ezra himself; and the Priests' Law with the older historical work (JED), about 400 B.C.[14]

Although Friedman's analysis runs counter to most of the then prevailing scholarship, such as that described above, his arguments are strong. For example, referring to the spy story in Deuteronomy, Friedman points out that:

> The author of this part of Deuteronomy (Dtr^1) had to have known P, because he quotes the P spy story word for word.[15]

Friedman points out that Jeremiah—whom we may take to be the original Deuteronomist—was hostile to P who thus had to have preceded Dtr^1. And he points out that it was during King Hezekiah's time that the divisions of the Aaronid priests and the Levites were established and worship centralized in Jerusalem.

Nevertheless, there is certainly the possibility that the author who worked on writing the Priestly Source during the time of King Hezekiah—quite possibly the prophet Isaiah or one of Isaiah's contemporaries—was one of three authors, the other two being Ezekiel and Ezra, living and working after the time of the original Deuteronomist.

That King Josiah is said to have ordered that the Ark be returned to the Temple, circa 621 BCE, indicates that the Ark existed at the time—possibly having been constructed to house the Deuteronomistic document which had been discovered during the renovation of the Temple. This would date the Ark's origin to sometime between 639 BCE when Josiah became king and 621 BCE when the Deuteronomistic scroll was discovered.

But the Deuteronomistic records do not describe what the Ark looked like. If the first of the three authors of the Priestly Source had described the physical characteristics of an Ark not yet built, then the high priest of King Josiah's time, Hilkiah, may have used it as the basis for an Ark built in the late seventh century BCE. That King Josiah—probably at Hilkiah's own urging—ordered Hilkiah not to keep track of the workmen's disposition of the gold and silver, may indicate that some of it was to be used on something for which an accurate accounting was not desired—such as the Ark.

Nothing in Egyptian records indicates that they came into possession of the Ark of the Covenant when King Josiah died at Meggido in 609 BCE at the hands of the Pharaoh Neccho. In Chapter 2:4-5 of the apocryphal *Second Book of Maccabees*, the writing of which occurred circa 150 BCE in the form of the Five Books of Jason of Cyrene on the Maccabaean Wars, prior to the writing of the First Book of Maccabees around 90 BCE,[16] there is what appears to be an allusion to Jeremiah's having hid the Ark in a cave on Mount Neccho:[17]

> It was also contained in the same writing, that the prophet, being warned of God, commanded the tabernacle and the ark to go with him, as he went forth into the mountain, where Moses climbed up, and saw the heritage of God. And when Jeremy (sic) came thither, he found an hollow cave, wherein he laid the tabernacle, and the ark, and the altar of incense, and so stopped the door.[18]

Some of the account of the Ark may have been written after the time of King Josiah by the prophet Ezekiel who described having had visions, for example, of how Yahweh traveled about on cherubim—cherubim such as were described to have been constructed for the cover of the Ark. In this event, the Ark that the Priestly Source described may have been a second Ark—based upon recollections of what Jeremiah's Ark had looked like. Or it may have been based upon a new design. But, just when would this have happened?

There is good reason to believe that the final additions to the Priestly Source were written, after the Edict of Cyrus in 538 BCE, by Ezra and his scribes. Indeed, the circumstances of the exiles' "return," laden with gifts from those who had enslaved them are very, very similar. The story of the captivity of Hebrew slaves in Egypt is now seen as being more likely to have been allegorical and not historical. This suggests that a second Ark—represented as having been constructed during the legendary exodus—may have been constructed in Ezra's time as a powerful icon for use in the Second Temple.

So, just when did the Priestly Ark finally disappear, if it had existed at all? Since there is no sign of it on Titus' triumphal arch in Rome which shows, in great detail, the treasures taken from Jerusalem, it would certainly seem to have disappeared before the time of Titus, some time before II Maccabees was composed.

ENDNOTES

1. For a word-by-word, verse-by-verse, chapter-by-chapter identification of the various authors of the *Book of Exodus*, see Friedman, Richard Elliott, *The Bible With Sources Revealed*, HarperSanFrancisco, San Francisco, 2003, pp 119-189 inclusive
2. *I Kings* 6:1 states that "In the four hundred and eightieth year after the Israelites left the land of Egypt, in the month of Ziv—that is, the second month—in the fourth year of his reign over Israel, Solomon began to build the House of the Lord." Assuming that David's forty-year reign began in 1005 BCE and that Solomon succeeded him *I Kings* 6:1 in 925 BCE, then the building of the Temple would have begun in 921 BCE. Thus implies that the exodus began around 1401 BCE. This conflicts, however, with the statement in *Exodus* 12:37 that during the exodus "the Israelites journeyed from Rameses to Succoth" since Rameses was a city named for Rameses II whose reign extended from 1279 to 1212 BCE, more than a hundred years later than *I Kings* 6:1 implies. Even Rameses I's reign, from 1293 to 1291, was long after the date of the biblical exodus.
3. Alter, Robert, *The Five Books of Moses, A Translation with Commentary*, W. W. Norton & Company, New York, 2004, p382fn
4. *Exodus* 25:1-6
5. *Exodus* 12:35-36
6. *Exodus* 12:33
7. *Exodus* 25:10
8. *Joshua* 3-4
9. *Joshua* 6:1-10

10. Friedman, Richard Elliott, *Who Wrote The Bible?*, HarperSanFrancisco, San Francisco, 1987, p 215

11. Friedman, Richard Elliott, *Who Wrote The Bible?*, p 210

12. *Numbers* 21:8-9

13. Kautzsch, op cit, 106-107

14. Kautzsch, Emil, *An Outline of the History of the Literature of the Old Testament*, Williams & Norgate, London, 1898, 106-107

15. Friedman, Richard Elliott, *Who Wrote The Bible?*, p 208

16. *II Kings* 22:7

17. Kautzsch, op cit, pp 204-205

18. *II Maccabees* 2:4-5

CHAPTER 10

BRINGING IT ALL TOGETHER: THE REDACTOR

For a long time after Jean Astruc had first hypothesized, in 1753, that Moses had used various source documents to write the five books that bear his name,[1] it has been generally assumed that someone else, commonly referred to as the Redactor or "R," had taken four original documents known as J, E, D, and P, had spliced them together, added material of his own and had, thereby, created the *Five Books of Moses*.[2]

The first example of the Redactor's editing efforts occurs with his insertion of what is often referred to as the Priestly account of Creation, consisting of *Genesis* 1:1-2:4a,[3] beginning with the familiar:

> In the beginning God created the heaven and the earth. And the earth was without form, and void; and darkness was upon the face of the deep: and the Spirit of God moved upon the face of the waters. And God said, Let there be light: and there was light. And God saw the light, that it was good: and God divided the light from the darkness. And God called the light Day, and the darkness he called Night: and the evening and the morning were the first day.[4]

It is possible, however, that *Genesis* 1:11-24a should be attributed to the Elohist, rather than to the author of the Priestly Source. The reader is also urged to consider the possibility that in addition to writing J, the Yahwist wrote the parallel narrative commonly attributed to the Elohist. Thus *Genesis*, as we now have it, would open with the Elohist's view of creation followed by the Yahwist's account—a single author's attempt to appeal to, and to be seen as being fair to, two quite different constituencies.

The first example of material written by the Redactor, in terms of the order of its appearance in the *Bible*, consists of *Genesis* 2:10-14:[5]

> Now a river runs out of Eden to water the garden and from there splits off into four streams. The name of the first is Pishon, the one that winds through the whole land of Havilah, where there is gold. And the gold of that land is goodly, bdellium is there, and lapis lazuli. And the name of the second river is Gihon, the one that winds through all the land of Cush. And the name of the third river is Tigris, the one that goes to the east of Ashur. And the fourth river is Euphrates.[6]

Sometime prior to the "return" of the second wave of "exiles" from Babylon in 458 BCE—the one hundred and twenty-eighth year of the exile and eighty years after the Edict of Cyrus—major modifications to "the law"—as the first five books were called— were made.[7]

The apparent purpose of these changes was, presumably, to assist in the restoration of Judaea to the control of fourteen of the former elite families who were still living in Babylon voluntarily, eighty years after Cyrus had encouraged them to return to Judah. As noted above,[8] additional material was written and added, material was deleted thus creating a Hebrew *Bible* very much like the one we know today.

The author-editor who performed this relatively complex work is known to *Bible* scholars as "the Redactor." It is quite likely, as noted above, that the *Bible* had been, all along, a continually growing series of scrolls, with redactions made as old material was discarded and new material added, rather than as a single, relatively late redaction of four or more parallel documents. Whatever the case, however, we will refer to the author-editor who produced the *Bible* as it existed in the mid-fifth century BC as "the Redactor."

While we do not know the Redactor's name, it was most likely, Ezra, one of the exiles at Babylon, assisted by the scribe, Baruch ben Seraiah.[9] While we similarly do not know who Ezra's father was, it is likely that he was related to his scribe—in providing himself with a genealogy[10] designed to trace his ancestry back to Moses' brother, Aaron, he said that he was the son of Seraiah, the son of Azariah, the son or descendant of Hilkiah—presumably the same Hilkiah who had claimed to have found the Deuteronomistic law during the renovation of the temple in 621 BC.

If Ezra had been the son of Hilkiah, three or four generations would have had to have been omitted from Ezrah's genealogy. He may have omitted some black sheep in the family; he may have been the 'son' of Seraiah in the same sense that numerous Davidic kings were 'sons' of David—or he may not have been related to the chief priest, Hilkiah, at all.

Elsewhere,[11] we are told that Ezra was the son of Shallum; Shallum was one of those who had "taken strange wives and some of them had wives by whom they had children."

Ezra provided the elite families who would be returning with him to Judaea with ancestors who (had they been alive) could trace their ancestry back to the time of Moses as well. Those ancestries were to prove useful when, in 458 BC, either in response to a request from Ezra or on his own initiative, Darius sent Ezra, whom he regarded as a prominent scholar, well versed in the laws of Moses. And why should Ezra not be regarded as well versed in the laws of Moses? He had written some of Moses' laws especially for the occasion.

Presumably there had been some, perhaps even extensive, communication between Babylon and Jerusalem during the entire period of the Exile. In any case, Ezra seems to have anticipated—and prepared for—the problems he and his fellow "returnees" would encounter upon their arrival in Jerusalem.

When he went to Jerusalem to serve as Darius' governor in Judaea.

Ezra invited around 1,500 men from fourteen families, i.e., the families of Phineas, Ithamar, Schechaniah, Pharosh, Pahath-Moab, Adin, Elam, Shephatiah, Joab, Shelomith, Bebai, Azgad, Adonikam, and Bigvai. They gathered at "the river that runneth to Ahava and there abode we in tents for three days." [12]

After three days, however, it became apparent that not much was getting done. Ezra soon discovered why, "and I viewed the people, and the priests, and found there none of the sons of Levi," who, having been demoted to menial tasks were the ones who presumably would be doing most of the day-to-day work. Ezra quickly sent for "Eliezer, for Ariel, for Shemaiah, and for Elnathan, and for Jarib, and for Elnathan, and for Nathan, and for Zechariah, and for Mesullam, chief men: also for Joiarib, and for Elnathan, men of understanding."[13]

Soon after they had received the gold, silver and other loot that Nebuchadnezar had taken from Jerusalem a hundred and thirty years earlier, they set off, without a military escort, for Jerusalem. Just how long the trip took, the Book of Ezra does not say. Although the Chronicler, author of the Book of Ezra, writing long after Ezra's time presumably had Ezra's memoirs at hand, he either did not know how long the trip took or felt that it was unimportant.

When this band of exiles showed up in Jerusalem, however, it was most unwelcome. When the exiled elite made it known that it wanted its families' former property back they undoubtedly met with resistance from those who now occupied those properties. Furthermore, the people who had stayed behind, and their descendants, were simpler people, interested in getting along with each other. They had intermarried, they now shared the various religious beliefs of the region, they were more interested in growing crops, pressing olives and making oil, making wine… Letting a bunch of effete aristocrats boss them around to rebuild the city walls, to rebuild the temple, to tell them whom they could marry and whom they couldn't, to tell them which god or gods they could worship and which they couldn't, to force them to give a larger percentage of their produce to the temple priests just wasn't their idea of a better life.

Although the exiles had probably had more or less continuous news of what was going on in Jerusalem, Ezra feigned shock at his discovery that those who had stayed behind had intermarried. After throwing a three-day fit, Ezra ordered those who had intermarried to "put away" their wives and children. Those who confessed and agreed to "expel" their foreign wives and made the prescribed sacrificial offerings were apparently spared but the property and, presumably the lives, of those who did not cooperate were taken, condemned, along with the wives and children. The interrogations, acceptance of sacrifices, confiscations, condemnations and bloodbath—if that's what it was—took ten days, from the twentieth of the month until the thirtieth, partly because there were "so many" and partly because of heavy rain.

At that point, Ezra seems to disappear from history. Under the circumstances it seems likely that someone whose family had suffered at his hands murdered him in revenge.

Thirteen years after sending Ezra, Darius sent a new governor, his cupbearer, Nehemiah. Nehemiah, too, seems to have run things with an iron hand for the rebuilding efforts were pursued vigorously; he also had a copy of the redacted *Bible* which returned property to former owners after a fifty-year period, the 'Jubilee'.

When reading from *Genesis* to *II Chronicles* in the Hebrew *Bible*—or Malachi in the Old Testament—the Redactor's work first shows up in *Genesis* 20:18 in the form of a single verse added at the end of the chapter. The first chapter and the first three and a half verses of the second chapter describing Creation is the work of the Priestly author.

Then, early in the second chapter, another author's very different version of Creation appears, giving the reader a choice of Creations which may be what the Redactor wished to provide. Some of the difference between the two versions has to do with the different approaches to the matter of how sacrifices are to be offered. Because there were those who were familiar with either one or both of the two versions, leaving one or both out would call the revised *Bible* into disrepute. Leaving old, but contradictory material in was, perhaps, the better course; it permitted alternative readings of the *Bible*. A few changes here and there seems to have been sufficient for Ezra's purposes.

Just how Ezrah's redaction was accomplished is uncertain. It has been argued that the Elohist author may have added his writing to the Jahwist's and never existed independently. If this is the case, then the Redactor would have merged JE with Deuteronomist's history and law code and the writings of the Priestly Source, though not necessarily in that sequence and made minor modifications to the work of the Court Historian. This approach, however, raises the question of whether the Deuteronomist had already added his material to what was already in front of him (which would seem to be the more logical way to proceed) or whether he produced a complete but separate account which was later used by the Redactor; the same could be said of the Priestly source.

The prevailing view is that the Redactor took pieces of the Priestly Source's writings, the Jahwist's account, the Elohist's comments (for that is what they were), and the Deuteronomist's history and law code and wove them together in as harmonious a fashion as possible. That the Redactor did not eliminate the material favored by the Aaronids or, on the other hand, that favored by the Levites and, instead, left intact the large amounts of material that point to a polytheistic past, was almost certainly the best possible choice. Far too many people at the time the Redactor was doing his work knew about the details of the various materials with which he was working and to modify those documents would have destroyed his credibility.

Furthermore, including the several major points of view made the resultant work useful for all of the different parties those who favored a non-monarchical form of government and those who opposed it, those who favored the interests of the Levites and those who favored the interests of the Aaronids, those who favored the priests and those who favored the king or, in later times, governor or appointed ruler.

The Redactor's work made it possible for the Jewish people to consider themselves a nation despite their lack of a land with borders, despite their having to live in other countries for whatever reasons. Although the Redactor's objective was, perhaps, more than anything else, the re-enfranchisement of the political and priestly elites of his day, in a very real sense, the Redactor's final, magnificent achievement is the survival of Judaism despite enormous odds.

ENDNOTES

1. Astruc, Jean, *Conjectures sur la Genese*, Noesis, Paris, 1999 (originally published anonymously in Brussels, 1753)
2. Kautzsch, Emil, *An Outline of the Literature of the Old Testament*, Williams and Norgate, London, 1898, p 227. Explaining what he meant by "R," Kautzsch says, "R signifies additions, due to the redactor who blended J and E into one work, JEr, or to the one who united JE and Deuteronomy JEDr; or finally to the one who joined JED and P: it also signifies verses or sections originally belonging to J, E or P, but subsequently transplanted by a redactor from another context into their present position."
3. Kautzsch, op cit, p 228
4. *Genesis* 1:1, King James Version
5. *Genesis* 2:10-14, Robert Alter's translation
6. Kautzsch, op cit, p 197
7. Kautzsch, op cit, p 228
8. Kautzsch, op cit, pp 227-228
9. Friedman, Richard Elliott, *Who Wrote The Bible?*, HarperSan Francisco, San Francisco, 1997, pp 217-245
10. *Ezra* 7:1-5
11. *Ezra* 10:42-44
12. *Ezra* 8:15
13. *Ezra* 8:15

CHAPTER 11

THE CHRONICLER

Sometime between 333 BCE and 250 BCE an anonymous writer known as "the Chronicler," compiled the *Book of Chronicles*, the *Book of Ezra*, and the *Book of Nehemiah*. As to the writer's identity, Emil Kautzsch says, in *An Outline of The History of the Literature of the Old Testament*, that "it is certain that the author was a Levite, and, indeed, a temple-singer or musician."[1]

Like the *Book of Samuel* and the *Book of Kings*, the *Book of Chronicles* was originally one book. In the *Book of Chronicles* the Chronicler presented a history of the House of David. To this the Chronicler added his version of the re-establishment of a Jewish government in Judaea circa 458 BCE and the cruel "reforms" which Ezra and Nehemiah had based on their priestly law-book.

Of the Chronicler's source material, used in compiling the *Book of Chronicles*, the most important was the Deuteronomist's *Book of the Kings of Judah and Israel.*

In compiling the *Book of Ezra*, the Chronicler relied, in part, on the memoirs (and recollections of the memoirs) of the Babylonian-born priest and scribe, Ezra, who was said to have returned from Babylon to Jerusalem around 458 BC, some seventy-eight years after the Edict of Cyrus.

In compiling the *Book of Nehemiah*, the Chronicler relied, in part, on the memoirs (and recollections of the memoirs) of Nehemiah, the cupbearer to Artaxerxes, whom Artaxerxes was said to have sent to Jerusalem in 445 BC, thirteen years after Ezra's arrival there, as governor.

The regulations which Ezra had imposed on those Israelites whose families had never left Judah—as well as upon those families who had returned to Jerusalem before his arrival—were harsh:

> And they made proclamation throughout Judah and Jerusalem unto all the children of the captivity, that they should gather themselves together unto Jerusalem: And that whosoever would not come within three days, according to the counsel of the princes and the elders, all his substance should be forfeited, and himself separated from the congregation of those that had been carried away... Now therefore make confession unto the Lord God of your fathers, and do his pleasure: and separate yourselves from the people of the land, and from the strange wives... And they made an end with all the men that had taken strange wives by the first day of the first month.[2]

Those families who had stayed behind had good reason to bitterly resent those who now returned. While the elite had been away in Babylon, those who had stayed behind had gone about their lives, had married local women, had worshipped together harmoniously. In short, those who had stayed behind had probably led much better lives than before.

Ezra's return—and the return of Ezra's fellow "exiles" led to what was, for those who had stayed behind and their descendants, an unwanted orgy of ethnic cleansing. They were ordered to "put away" their "strange" wives and the children whom those wives had borne. Not only that, Ezra ordered they fully comply within three days or face the confiscation of all their property. That they also had to give up the friendships they had with those of other faiths must have been heartbreaking. The sacrifices thus collected—and the property confiscated—must have added greatly to the Temple revenue.

The Chronicler added extensive genealogical tables, statistical data, and other material whose two most apparent objectives were to legitimize the property claims and religious practices of the second wave of elite families returning from Babylon, some seventy-eight years after the Edict of Cyrus.

The Chronicler portrayed every setback that the Israelites had suffered as the result of their ignoring or defying the priests' representations of the wishes of Jahweh; similarly, the Chronicler portrayed every benefit the Israelites received as the result of obeying those same wishes. As Emil Kautzsch noted:

> every transgression brings on speedy punishment, and every calamity is a punishment for transgression... conversely, when there is indubitable prosperity, a blameless piety is implied. Hence the Chronicler says nothing about David's life as a freebooter or as Philistine vassal, nothing about his adultery and behavior towards Uriah, nothing about the wretched proceedings in David's family, nothing about the manner of Solomon's accession, described in I Kings 1.[3]

As Kautzsch went on to note, the Chronicler devoted:

> seven chapters to his account of the collection of building materials (amongst which the gold and silver were worth $450,000,000) and the other preparations made by David. Indeed, the model of the temple and of all its vessels was given to Solomon by David, along with written instructions from the hand of Yahweh.[4]

It is regrettable that the original copy of those instructions—in Jahweh's own hand—has failed to survive.

According to Kautzsch, the Chronicler makes it appear that:

> the number of their warriors correspond to the mechanical view which makes the prosperity and power of the kings stand in precise relation to the degree of their piety. The most pious

> kings dispose of the largest armies. Thus David has more than one and a half-million warriors,[5]

Such an absurd figure is fifteen times recent Israeli archaeologists' estimate of 90,000 as being the total population of Judah and Israel at the time of David and Solomon.

The Chronicler also included entirely new material such as genealogies and details of religious rituals and practices. Its point of view is that the difficulties the kings of Judah and Israel had were the result of not following exactly the commands of Yahweh. In S. R. Driver's words,

> they show a tendency to refer events to their moral causes—to represent, for instance, a great calamity or deliverance as the punishment of wickedness or the reward of virtue. This feature is especially noticeable in the case of discourses attributed to prophets. The prophets in Chronicles are far more frequently than in the earlier historical books brought into relation with the kings, to whom they predict good or ill success, in accordance with their deserts, with much uniformity of expression, and in a tone very different from that of the prophets who appear in the Books of Samuel or Kings.[6]

Although material was taken from the first nine books[7] of the Hebrew *Bible*, from *Genesis* to *Kings*, and rewritten, the new material which was added was, apparently, based upon "general tradition" or written documents, some of which had been written, perhaps, by the exiles after they had returned from Babylon around 536 BC with a view to helping them reestablish their position in the old status quo of Jerusalem.

The Chronicler claims to have used various books such as "the words of Samuel the seer" and "the words of Nathan the prophet," and "the words of Gad the seer" in compiling his account of King David. The point of view of the Chronicler, however, has more in common with Jeremiah and his Deuteronomistic history than with Solomon's Court

Historian or Rehoboam's Jahwist. As noted above, the Chronicler is also given to great exaggeration, portraying Israel's early days as far grander than they actually could have been.

As Donald Harmon Akenson notes in *Surpassing Wonder: The Invention of the Bible and The Talmuds*,

> Both the Book of Ezra-Nehemiah and of Chronicles rewrite the estimate of the editor-writer of Genesis-Kings, a man who, at minimum, was in contact with many eyewitnesses to the Babylonian deportations and they replace the earlier estimates with ones that are less realistic historically and make a different story altogether. According to Ezra (1:1-65) some 4,363 priests and Levites, accompanied by 128 religious singers and 139 temple porters, led a return from Babylon after Cyrus' decree. The number of returnees was said to total 42,360 persons, plus 7,333 servants (presumably of foreign origin). This was a great band indeed, and one could plausibly claim that they were effectively the sum total of the Chosen People. Crucially, in Chronicles (the companion volume to Ezra-Nehemiah), the eyewitness-based report of the Book of Kings is rubbed off the page.
>
> Whereas the editor-writer of Kings made it clear that the lower-caste majority of the population of the former Kingdom of Judah remained in the homeland and was not exiled (see also Jeremiah 39:10), the author of Chronicles (II Chronicles 36:20-21) introduces the new—and certainly historically inaccurate—myth that everyone in Jerusalem was either killed or carried away to Babylon and that the whole land experienced a Sabbath of desolation for seventy years (that is, from 587 to the rebuilding period, 520-15).
>
> Where the material in the *Book of Kings*, balefully accurate though it probably was, was faulty from an ideological point of view, was that it explained all too well the failure, for a

> period of nearly three generations, of the Judahite religion to win over the people of Jerusalem and of the surrounding countryside: the number of returnees was too small, their character was insufficiently authoritative, and the local majority, who had been left behind, had developed religious institutions which resisted successfully the No-Way-But-Yahweh sloganeering of the Judahite returnees.
>
> The Books of Ezra-Nehemiah and of Chronicles replace the testament of the Book of Kings with numbers that explain success, not failure. A vigorous and numerically deep band of Judahists is presented as returning to redeem an empty land.[8]

As to the organization of the books of Chronicles-Ezra-Nehemiah, Driver notes that:

> Moreover, the Book of Ezra-Nehemiah begins exactly at the point at which the Book of Chronicles (which originally was a single scroll) ends, and carries on the narrative upon the same plan to the time when the theocratic institutions under which the compiler lived were finally established through the labors of Ezra and Nehemiah.[9]

The texts of these books—*Chronicles, Ezra*, and *Nehemiah*—vary; the versions found in the Septuagint are different from those found in the Masoretic.

> The entire work, of which I and II Chronicles together form the first part, comprises, but with generally less detail than that found in the originals upon which it was based: the period from Adam to the second visit of Nehemiah to Jerusalem, 432 BC. Although the narrative embraces a wide period, the aim with which it is written is a limited one; it is that, viz, of giving a history of Judah, with special reference to the institutions connected with the Temple, under the monarchy, and after the restoration. The author (who seems to be the same throughout) begins, indeed, after the manner of the later Semitic his-

torians, with Adam; but the genealogies in I Chronicles 1 have merely the object of exhibiting, relatively to other nations, the position taken by the tribe of Judah, to which I Chronicles 2 is wholly devoted, as I Chronicles 3 is devoted to the descendants of King David. In I Chronicles 4-8, dealing with the other tribes, it is the priestly tribe of Levi (I Chronicles 6) that is treated at the greatest length. Incidentally in these chapters, more decidedly in 9 1-84, the interest of the writer betrays itself: his notices have constantly a bearing, direct or indirect, upon the organization and ecclesiastical institutions of the post-exilic community. The introduction (I Chronicles 1-9:84) ended, the history proper begins. The reign of Saul is passed over rapidly by the compiler: I Chronicles 9:35-44, his genealogy is repeated from 8 29-38; I 10 (excerpted from I Samuel 31) proceeds to David's election as king over all Israel at Hebron (2 Samuel 5 1-10), omitting as irrelevant to his purpose the incidents of David's youth, his persecution by Saul, the reign of Ishbosheth. The Chronicler omits similarly events in David's reign of a personal or private nature (e.g. the greater part of 2 Samuel 9-20). The account of Solomon's reign is excerpted from I Kings with tolerable frankness. After the division of the kingdom no notice is taken of the history of the northern kingdom, except where absolutely necessary (as II Chronicles 22:7-9); on the other hand, the history of Judah is presented in a series of excerpts from 1-2 Kings, supplemented by additions contributed by the compiler. Though secular events are not excluded from the record, it is plain the writer dwells with the greatest satisfaction upon the ecclesiastical aspects of the history. The same interest is not less apparent in Ezra-Nehemiah; and hence the entire work (Chronicles Ezra-Nehemiah) has been not inaptly termed by Reuss the 'Ecclesiastical Chronicle of Jerusalem.'[10]

The Chronicler was clearly favorably disposed toward David and favorably disposed to David's successor, Solomon:

> And Solomon the son of David was strengthened in His kingdom and the Lord his God was with him, and magnified him exceedingly.[11]

Of Solomon's son, Rehoboam, the Chronicler reports that:

> And it came to pass, when Rehoboam had established the kingdom, and had strengthened himself, he forsook the law of the Lord, and all Israel with him...[12]

After Rehoboam dismissed the request of the northern tribes for a reduction in taxes and demands for forced labor, the northern tribes seceded and formed a new kingdom, Israel, and drove the Levite priests out:

> ...for Jeroboam and his sons had cast them off from executing the priest's office unto the Lord: and he ordained him (other) priests for the high places, and for the devils, and for the calves which he had made.[13]

From which we may reasonably infer that, in response to widespread popular demand, Jeroboam had restored the traditional polytheistic religion of the northern kingdom. According to the Chronicler, the consequences were disastrous.

> And it came to pass that in the fifth year of king Rehoboam, Shishak king of Egypt came up against Jerusalem, because they had transgressed against the Lord, With twelve hundred chariots, and threescore thousand horsemen: and the people were without number that came with him out of Egypt: the Lubims, the Sukkiims, and the Ethiopians. And he took the fenced cities which pertained to Judah, and came to Jerusalem.[14]

In such fashion, the Chronicler attempted to explain all of Judah's defeats as having been retribution for having ignored the law of the Lord—which is to say, the law attributed to the Lord who had given it to Moses. Just what Rehoboam thought he was doing, if anything, as the Lord's agent is not known.

Conversely, some kings, like Asa (913-873 BCE) whose reigns were not marred by adversity, were said to have done:

> that which was good and right in the eyes of the Lord his God: for he took away the altars of the strange gods and the high places and he brake down the images and he cut down the groves...[15]

Of others, like Ahaz (736-728 BCE), the Chronicler says that he:

> did not that which was right in the sight of the Lord, like David his father: For he walked in the ways of the kings of Israel, and made also molten images for Baalim... Wherefore the Lord his God delivered him into the hand of the king of 'Syria: and they smote him, and carried away a great multitude of them captives, and brought them to Damascus. And he was also delivered into the hand of the king of Israel, who smote him with a great slaughter.[16]

The Chronicler's agenda in his rewriting of the Israelite's history is obvious. As to the date of the rewriting, Driver notes that:

> The only positive clue which the book contains as to the date when the Chronicles, Ezra-Nehemiah books were composed is the genealogy in *I Chronicles* 3 17-24, which (if verse 21 be rightly interpreted) is carried down to the sixth generation after Zerubbabel. This would imply a date not earlier than ca. 350 BC.
>
> More conclusive evidence is afforded by the *Books of Ezra* and *Nehemiah*, which certainly belong to the same age, and are commonly assumed to be the work of the same compiler. As will appear below, these books contain many indications of being the compilation of an author living long subsequently to the age of Ezra and Nehemiah themselves, in fact, not be-

> fore the close of the Persian rule. A date shortly after 333 BC is thus the earliest to which the composition of the *Chronicles* can be plausibly assigned; and it is that which is adopted by most modern critics. From the character of his narrative it is a probable inference that the author was a Levite, perhaps even a member of the Temple choir.
>
> The basis of the *Chronicles* consists of a series of excerpts from the earlier historical books, *Genesis-II Kings*, with which are combined materials derived by the compiler from other sources. These excerpts are not made throughout on the same scale. In the preliminary chapters (I 1-9) they are often condensed, and consist chiefly of genealogical notices: in *I Chronicles* 10 - *II Chronicles* 36 (which is parallel to *I Samuel* 31 - *II Kings* 25) passages are generally transferred in extenso with but slight variations of expression, due, probably, in a few cases (as they exist in our present text) to textual corruption, but more commonly originating with the compiler. Not infrequently, however, the excerpted narratives are expanded, sometimes remarkably, by the insertion either of single verses or clauses, or of longer passages, as the case may be. Minute particulars can naturally only be learnt from a word-for-word collation of the text of *Chronicles* with the original passages of *Samuel* and *Kings*, which the reader is strongly recommended to make for himself, but the following synopsis has been arranged so as to exhibit both the passages excerpted from the earlier narratives, and the more important additions introduced by the compiler.[17]

S. R. Driver provides a useful side-by-side reference guide permitting an easy comparison of the two accounts.[18] Driver states that:

> in many cases they have a didactic aim: in particular, they show a tendency to refer events to their moral causes—to represent, for instance, a great calamity or deliverance as the punishment

> of wickedness or the reward of virtue. This feature is especially noticeable in the case of discourses attributed to prophets. The prophets in the Chronicles are far more frequently than in the earlier historical books brought into relation with the kings, to whom they predict good or ill success, in accordance with their desserts, with much uniformity of expression, and in a tone very different from that of the prophets who appear in the Books of Samuel or Kings.[19]

Using Driver's guide, noted above, a better understanding of what probably occurred can be had by comparing *I* and *II Kings* with *I* and *II Chronicles* and noting each of their many differences. The Chronicler's story of Saul's death makes it appear that the Philistines stripped Saul's body and displayed his armor (and head) in temples throughout Philistia, while Solomon's Court Historian states that it was an Amelekite who removed Saul's diadem and armband.

To see an example of the Chronicler's sanitizing of the earlier accounts, note his total omission of David's alleged seduction of Bathsheba in *II Samuel* in chapters 10 and 11. By 333 BC, however, whatever doubts the citizens of Jerusalem may have had in 965 BC about the identity of Solomon's biological father, had long since become moot and were probably, in the Chronicler's view, best forgotten.

ENDNOTES

1. Kautzsch, Emil, *An Outline of the History of the Literature of the Old Testament*, Williams and Norgate, London 1898, p 124
2. *Ezra* 10:7-8, 11, 17
3. Kautzsch, op cit., p. 124
4. Kautzsch, op cit., p 125
5. Kautzsch, op cit., p 125
6. Driver, S. R., *An Introduction to the Literature of the Old Testament*, Williams & Norgate, London, 1898, p. 526

7. Nine books, that is, counting *I* and *II Samuel* as one book and *I* and *II Kings* as another single book. "Book," however, is not really the right word. Each of the works referred to had been written on a single scroll. When, later, vowels were added to the Hebrew text more space was required. The *Book of Samuel* then required two scrolls, as did the *Book of Kings*.
8. Akenson, Donald Harmon, *Surpassing Wonder: The Invention of the Bible and the Talmuds*, Harcourt Brace & Company, New York, 1998, p. 72
9. Driver, op cit., p 516
10. Driver, op cit., p 517
11. *II Chronicles* 1:1
12. *II Chronicles* 12:1
13. *II Chronicles* 11:14b-15
14. *II Chronicles* 12:2-4
15. *II Chronicles* 14:2-3
16. *II Chronicles* 28:1-5
17. Driver, op cit., p 519
18. Driver, op cit., p 519-525
19. Driver, op cit., p 526

CHAPTER 12

THE WISDOM OF ALEXANDRIA

King Azemilcus was away at sea when word reached the island city of Tyre, in January 333 BC, that the young Macedonian king, Alexander had conquered the cities of Byblus and Sidon on the eastern coast of the Mediterranean and was now advancing towards Tyre. Tyre sent envoys—including King Azemilcus' son—to assure Alexander that while they were, in general, agreeable to his requests, they could not, without violating their long-standing policy of neutrality, honor his request to be allowed, along with some of his men, to make a sacrifice at the Temple of Heracles inside the city walls. Tyre was more afraid of incurring the wrath of Darius, king of the Persians, whom they knew and feared, than of Alexander—whom they did not know. Since Tyre was heavily fortified and was on an island just off the coast, a few miles from Gaza, they hoped that the young Macedonian would soon pass them by.

For Alexander, neutrality was not enough. It would be too risky, to pursue Darius eastward from the coast without the active support of Tyre. With his own small fleet, greatly augmented by 120 ships from Cyprus, he attacked Tyre by sea. He attacked by land, as well, building a causeway from the coast to the island city. At first the Tyrians felt secure—their walls, which were a hundred and fifty feet high and very thick, had protected them from a similar attack by Nebuchadnezar two hundred years before.

Attempting to intimidate Alexander and his men, the Tyrians hauled some of Alexander's emissaries—whom they'd held hostage—up to the top of the battlements, cut their throats in full view of the Macedonian army, and hurled their bodies into the sea. If there were one single miscalculation that the Tyrians made that would prove fatal, this was it.

Fighting with far more than their normal ferocity, Alexander and his men took the city after placing two one-hundred-and-fifty foot towers on the causeway from which they bombarded the city's walls with huge stones and breaching the walls. After slaughtering all eight-thousand Tyrian warriors, who fought bravely to the last, Alexander took twenty thousand women and children and sold them into slavery. Only those who had taken refuge in the Temple of Heracles were spared; they were given a pardon.

The conquest of Tyre had taken eight months and had cost Alexander four hundred men. Alexander continued on south, conquering Gaza, the last town on the edge of the desert as one travels south from Phoenicia to Egypt in late September and early October. He entered Egypt and on November 14th, 332 BC, was proclaimed Pharaoh at Memphis. He spent part of the winter at the oasis at Siwa, where he was proclaimed a god, but took the time to plan the building of Alexandria on the Nile Delta as a replacement for Tyre.

Alexander departed in the late spring of 331 BCE. He spent the next nine years conquering Persia and most of the countries and provinces as far east as India. Then, upon his death in 323 BCE, his empire was split into three pieces. In 305 BCE, one of Alexander's generals, Ptolemy I, seized control of Egypt—the largest and richest of the three pieces—and proclaimed himself Pharaoh.

Meanwhile Alexandria became, in the words of Lionel Casson, "a brand-new city with a population consisting mostly of soldiers and sailors, the Ptolemies' armed forces, bureaucrats and clerks of the administration, and the mixed bag of traders, businessmen, craftsmen, swindlers, and whatnot, who see opportunity in, as it were, a fresh playing field. Intellectuals had to be blandished into coming to a place that to all outward appearances was a cultural wasteland. The Ptolemies offered such irresistible inducements that in the course of the third century BCE, the period of the city's cultural zenith, they were able to gather there a stellar community from Athens. Ptolemy I got not only Euclid but also Strato, the foremost physicist of the age."

In addition to being a general and now, Pharaoh, Ptolemy I was a historian who had written an authoritative account of Alexander's campaigns and was a patron of the arts. Around 283 BCE, on the advice of his son's tutor, Demetrius, Ptolemy I began to gather a collection of books on kingship and ruling in the style of Plato's philosopher-kings. He went on to gather books about all the world's people that he might better understand subjects and trade partners. Demetrius was put in charge of the library which was built to house Ptolemy I's collection but not as Librarian as that task went to Zenodotus of Ephesus who held the post until 245 BCE. Instead, Demetrius was assigned, during the reign of Ptolemy II (285-246 BCE) to supervise the translation of other cultures' works into Greek. The first book to be translated, according to legend, was the Hebrew *Bible*—a task said to have been accomplished by the hiring, housing, and care of 72 rabbis who completed the work in 72 days. In one version of the story, each of the 72 rabbis produced a translation the entire *Bible* in 72 days which was identical in every word to the translations produced by the other 71 rabbis!

In any event, it is to Alexander—and to the Ptolemies who succeeded him in Egypt—that we owe credit for the Hebrew *Bible*, as it existed in the third century BC, being translated into Greek—the translation being known as the Septuagint. Ptolemy II was a rare book or, rather, a rare scroll collector and, according to classics historian Lionel Casson, in *Libraries in the Ancient World*, was so "intent on getting his hands on Athens' official versions of the plays of Aeschylus, Sophocles, and Euripides that he was willing not only to lay out an enormous amount of money but to resort to swindling in the bargain. He asked to borrow the precious scrolls to have copies made of them. The city fathers must have had suspicions, for they insisted that he post a bond of fifteen talents—a huge sum, the equivalent of millions of dollars to ensure their return. He had copies made all right, a deluxe set on papyrus paper of the finest quality—and sent these back instead of the originals. There was nothing the Athenians could do except keep the bond.

In addition to the translation of the Hebrew *Bible* as it then existed, new literature was added to the *Bible* around the same time—the *Song of Songs, Ecclesiastes*, and the *Book of Job*. While all three works show the influence of various works in the Great Library's collection of Greek literature, philosophy, and science, they are not only among the greatest literary works to be found in the *Bible* but point to changes in the way in which Jews in exile saw their relationships among themselves, their relationships with others, and, not least, their concept of God—and their relationship with that concept.

THE SONG OF SONGS WHICH IS SOLOMON'S

Abishag the Shunamite, the beautiful young virgin that David's servants found to help make David's last days pleasant, makes her first appearance at the opening of the *First Book of Kings*.

> Now King David was old and stricken in years: and they covered him with clothes but he gat no heat. Wherefore his servants said unto him, Let there be sought for my lord the king a young virgin and let her stand before the king, and let her cherish him and let her lie in thy bosom, that my lord the king may get heat. So they sought for a fair damsel throughout all the coasts of Israel, and found Abishag, a Shunamite, and brought her to the king. And the damsel was very fair, and cherished the king, and ministered to him, but the king knew her not. (*I Kings* 1:1-4)

Abishag was with King David when Bathsheba whom David had married after her husband Uriah's death—interrupted, with news that Adonijah, David's eldest surviving son, was proclaiming himself king. As prearranged, Nathan the prophet confirmed what Bathsheba had said and David, virtually under house arrest, abdicated in favor of Bathsheba's son, Solomon. When, shortly thereafter, David died, Bathsheba accused Adonijah of having sought Abishag's hand in marriage—a request that would have been, if genuine, tantamount to challenging Solomon's right to David's throne—as a means of justifying Solomon's ordering Adonijah's death it is quite understandable.

Although the *First Book of Kings* gives us all of the details of the palace coup that put Solomon on the throne, it does not tell us what became of Abishag. At this point Abishag, still a virgin, became, by default, the property of Solomon and, at that point, she seems to disappear from history. She disappears from history, that is, until we come to the *Song of Songs*. The *Song of Songs* tells the story, probably fictional, of how Solomon, desiring to have her as his wife, wooed her passionately. But all Abishag wanted, so the *Song of Songs* says, was to return to her shepherd-lover in Shunem.

As S. R. Driver notes:

> The poetry of the Song is exquisite. The movement is graceful and light; the imagery is beautiful, and singularly picturesque; the author revels among the delights of the country; one scene after another is brought before us—doves hiding in the clefts of the rocks or resting beside the water-brooks, gazelles leaping over the mountains or feeding among the lilies, goats reclining on the sloping hills of Gilead: trees with their varied foliage, flowers with bright hues or richly-scented perfume are ever supplying the poet with a fresh picture or comparison: we seem to walk, with the shepherd-lover himself, among vineyards and fig-trees in the balmy air of spring, or to see the fragrant, choicely furnished garden which the

> charms of his betrothed call up before his imagination. The number of animals and plants, as well as works of human art and labour—many not mentioned elsewhere—named in the Song, is remarkable.

Although the original story of David, Solomon, Bathsheba, and Abishag as told in the *First Book of Kings* is attributed to the Court Historian and thus dates to around 920 BC, the *Song of Songs* was attributed to Solomon himself, writing, presumably, in Jerusalem.

There has been considerable controversy over the authorship and meaning of the *Song of Songs*. That Solomon was its author has been generally rejected—it hardly makes sense that Solomon would record his rejection by David's concubine. Some Christian *Bible* scholars, particularly those writing during the prudish Victorian era, while accepting the notion that Solomon was its author (thereby justifying its inclusion in the canon) try to explain away its clearly erotic nature by arguing that it is not what it seems, that it is, instead, an allegory of "the love of Christ for His Church."

Theirs is a heroic effort, not only because it begs the questions of why an allegory would have been necessary or why this form of allegory would have been chosen, but also because it credits Solomon with the foreknowledge of events which would not come about for another thousand years. It would seem reasonable that prophecies must necessarily be fulfilled within the prophet's lifetime. A prophecy which is neither fulfilled in the prophet's lifetime nor in the lifetimes of those with whom the prophecy is shared, is neither intelligible nor useful. Further, a prophecy which goes unfulfilled indicates a false prophet, the punishment for which is death.

Setting aside all such silliness, it is far more likely that the *Song of Songs* was written by an employee of the great library in Alexandria around 250 BC, during the reign of Ptolemy III, which is to say, at about the same time and in the same place that the *Book of Ecclesiastes* was written, possibly by the same hand.

If, instead, we accept it for what it so clearly seems to be, a Greek drama (complete with Greek chorus in the form of the women of Solomon's harem), intended for performance, we can appreciate it as a truly beautiful piece of literature.

There does seem to be evidence that various portions of the Song have been rearranged, that some portions have been lost or were censored, that originally the Song took the form of a Greek drama intended for performance, and that the subject of the Song is the further adventures of Abishag, now referred to as a "Shulamite."

Various attempts have been made to restore the Song to its original form. The idea that there were three principal characters was first proposed by J. S. Jacobi and later developed in some detail by H. Ewald. The principal characters are Solomon, Abishag the Shunamite maiden, and her shepherd lover; playing minor roles are the ladies of the Court who advise Abishag that she is passing up a real opportunity, three citizens who describe the pomp of Solomon's approach to the palace, and the shepherds of Shunem who welcome Abishag and her lover back to Shunem.

In *An Introduction to the Literature of the Old Testament*, S. R. Driver discusses the authorship and meaning of the *Song of Songs* at length and sets forth outlines of two different reconstructions of the *Song of Songs*, one by Friedrich Delitzsch, the other by H. Ewald. Ewald's assignment of the verses to three principal characters is quite convincing as is shown by the following reconstruction based upon Driver's synopsis of Ewald's outline of the Song. The numbers in parentheses at the end of each speech, in this text, refer to the Chapter and Verse in the *Song of Songs*; the verses themselves coming from the Authorised King James Version of the *Bible*. It is worth noting, in passing, that Palestrina composed music for the Latin of the *Song of Songs* as found in the Vulgate.

THE SONG OF SONGS WHICH IS SOLOMON'S

ACT I

Scene I (*Abishag the Shunamite and Ladies of the Court*)

Abishag (*longing for the caresses of her absent shepherd-lover, complaining that she is detained in the royal palace against her will, and inquiring eagerly where he may be found*):
Let him kiss me with the kisses of his mouth: for thy love is better than wine. Because of the savour of thy good ointments thy name is as ointment poured forth, therefore do the virgins love thee. Draw me, we will run after thee: the king hath brought me into his chambers: we will be glad and rejoice in thee, we will remember thy love more than wine; the upright love thee. I am black but comely, O ye daughters of Jerusalem, as the tents of Kedar, as the curtains of Solomon. Look not upon me, because I am black, because the sun hath looked upon me: my mother's children were angry with me: they made me the keepers of the vineyards: but mine own vineyard have I not kept. Tell me O thou whom my soul loveth, where thou feedest, where thou makest thy flock to rest at noon; for why should I be as one that turneth aside by the flocks of thy companions? (1:2-7)

The Ladies of the Court (in reply—ironically): If thou know not, O thou fairest among women, go thy way forth by the footsteps of the flock, and feed thy kids beside the shepherds' tents. (1:8)

Scene II (*Solomon enters*)

Solomon (*seeking to win Abishag's love*):
I have compared thee, o my love, to a company of horses in Pharaoh's chariots. Thy cheeks are comely with rows of jewels, thy neck with chains of gold. We will make thee borders of gold with studs of silver. (1:9-11)

Abishag (*aside*): While the king sitteth at his table, my spikenard sendeth forth the smell thereof. (1:12)

Abishag (*parrying the king's compliments with reminiscences of her absent lover*):
A bundle of myrrh is my well-beloved unto me, he shall lie all night betwixt my breasts. My beloved is unto me as a cluster of camphire in the vineyards of Engedi. (1:13-14)

Solomon: Behold thou art fair, my love, behold thou art fair, thou hast doves' eyes. (1:15)

Abishag (*aside, taking no notice of the king's remark and applying the figures suggested by it to her shepherd-lover*):
Behold thou art fair, my beloved, yea, pleasant, also our bed is green. The beams of our house are cedar: and our rafters of fir. I am the rose of Sharon, and the lily of the valleys. (1:16-2:1)

Solomon: As the lily among thorns, so is my love among the daughters. (2:2)

Abishag (*aside, applying similarly to her lover the comparison suggested by Solomon*):
As the apple tree among the trees of the wood, so is my beloved among the sons. I sat down under his shadow with great delight, and his fruit was sweet to my taste. He brought me to the banqueting house, and his banner over me was love. (2:3-4)

Abishag (*sinking down in a fit of half-delirious sickness, she reminds the ladies of the Court that love is an affection which arises spontaneously, and entreats them not to excite it artificially in Solomon's favour*):
Stay me with flagons, comfort me with apples, for I am sick of love. His left hand is under my head, and his right hand doth embrace me. I charge, O ye daughters of Jerusalem, by the roes, and by the hinds of the field, that ye stir not up, nor awake my love, till he please. (2:5-7)

ACT II

Abishag and Ladies of the Court

Scene I (*Abishag's reminiscence of her lover's visit.*)

Abishag (*recounting a scene from her past life, of a visit which her shepherd-lover once paid her in her rural home, inviting her to accompany him through the fields, and she repeats the words of the ditty which she then sang to him; she declares her present unaltered devotion to him and expresses the wish that the separation between them may quickly be at an end*):
The voice of my beloved! Behold, he cometh leaping upon the mountains, skipping on the hills. My beloved is like a roe or a young hart: behold he standeth behind our wall, he looketh forth at the windows, shewing himself through the lattice. My beloved spake, and said unto me, Rise up, my love, my fair one, and come away. For lo, the winter is past, the rain is over and gone. The flowers appear on the earth; the time of the singing of birds is come, and the voice of the turtle is heard in our land. The fig tree putteth forth her green figs, and the vines with the tender grape give it a good smell. Arise, my love, my fair one, and come away. O my dove, that art in the clefts of the rock, in the secret places of the stairs, let me see thy countenance, let me hear thy voice; for sweet is thy voice, and thy countenance is comely. Take to the foxes, the little foxes, that spoil the vines; for our vines have tender grapes. (2:8-15)

Abishag (*she declares her present unaltered devotion to him and expresses the wish that the separation between them may quickly be at an end*):
My beloved is mine, and I am his: he feedeth among the lilies. Until the day break, and the shadows flee away, turn my beloved, and be thou like a roe or a young hart upon the mountains of Bether. (2:16-17)

Scene II (*Abishag's first dream.*)

Abishag (*narrating a dream which she had recently had whilst in the royal palace; she had seemed to go in search of her absent lover through the city, and to her joy she had found him*):
By night on my bed I sought him whom my soul loveth: I sought him whom my soul loveth: I sought him but I found him not. I will rise now, and go about the city in the streets, and in the broad ways I will seek him whom my soul loveth: I sought him, but I found him not. The watchmen that go about the city found me: to whom I said, Saw ye him whom my soul loveth? It was but a little that I passed from them, but I found him whom my soul loveth: I held him, and would not let him go, until I had brought him into my mother's house, and into the chamber of her that conceived me. I charge you, O ye daughters of Jerusalem, by the roes, and by the hinds of the field, that ye stir not up, nor awake my love, till he please. (3:1-5)

(*The dream reflects the waking feelings and emotions. In the economy of the poem it swerves to explain to the chorus the state of the heroine's feelings; she then urges, appropriately that the ladies of the Court not seek to stir up an unwilling love; even in her dreams she is devoted to another.*)

ACT III

Scene I (*Citizens of Jerusalem assembled in front of one of the gates. In the distance a royal pageant is seen approaching.*)

First Citizen: Who is this that cometh out of the wilderness like pillars of smoke, perfumed with myrrh and frankincense, with all powders of the merchant? (3:6)

Second Citizen: Behold his bed, which is Solomon's: three-score valiant men are about it, of the valiant of Israel. They all hold swords, being expert in war: every man hath his sword upon his thigh because of fear in the night. (3:7-8)

Third Citizen: King Solomon made himself a chariot of the wood of Lebanon. He made the pillars thereof of silver, the bottom thereof of gold, the covering of it of purple, the midst thereof being paved with love, for the daughters of Jerusalem. Go forth, O ye daughters of Zion, and behold king Solomon with the crown wherewith his mother crowned him in the day of his espousals, and in the day of the gladness of his heart. (3:9-11)

(*The intention of the spectacle is to dazzle the rustic girl with a sense of the honour awaiting her if she will consent to become the king's bride. In the palanquin is Solomon himself, wearing the crown of state which his mother gave him on his wedding day.*)

Scene II (*In the Palace. Solomon, Abishag, and the Ladies of the Court.*)

Solomon (*seeking to win Abishag's love*):
Behold, thou art fair, my love, behold, thou art fair; thou has doves' eyes within thy locks; thy hair is as a flock of goats that appear from Mount Gilead. Thy teeth are like a flock of sheep that are even shorn, which came up from the washing: whereof every one bear twins, and none is barren among them. Thy lips are like a thread of scarlet, and thy speech is comely; thy temples are like a piece of a pomegranate within thy locks. Thy neck is like the tower of David builded for an armoury, whereon hang a thousand bucklers, all shields of mighty men. Thy two breasts are like two young roes that are twins, which feed among the lilies. Until the day break, and the shadows flee away, I will get me to the mountain of myrrh and to the hill of frankincense. Thou art fair, my love, there is no spot in thee. (4:1-7)

Scene III (*Abishag and the Ladies of the Court. Abishag and her lover in ideal interview.*)

Abishag (*hearing, in her imagination, her lover's impassioned invitation*): Come with me from Lebanon, my spouse, with me from Lebanon, look from the top of Amana, from the top of Shenir and Hermon, from the lions dens, from the mountains of the leopards. Thou hast ravished my heart, my sister, my spouse; how much better is thy love than wine! and the smell of thine ointments than all spices! Thy lips, O my spouse, drop as the honeycomb honey and milk are under thy tongue and the smell of thy garments is like the smell of Lebanon. A garden inclosed is my sister, my spouse, a spring shut up, a fountain sealed. Thy plants are an orchard of pomegranates, with pleasant fruits, camphire, with spikenard. Spikenard and saffron, calamus and cinnamon, with all trees of frankincense, myrrh and aloes, with all the chief spices. A fountain of gardens, a well of living waters, and streams from Lebanon. (4:8-15)

Abishag (*giving him her reply*):
Awake, O north wind: and come, thou south, blow upon my garden, that the spices thereof may flow out. Let my beloved come into his garden, and eat his pleasant fruits. (4:16)

Abishag (*seeming to hear again his grateful response*):
I am come into my garden, my sister, my spouse. I have gathered my myrrh with my spice. I have eaten my honeycomb with my honey. I have drunk my wine with my milk: eat, O friends, drink, yea, drink abundantly, O beloved. (5:1)

Scene IV (*Abishag's second dream.*)

Abishag (*relating a dream of the past night, in which she had imagined herself to hear her shepherd-lover at the door, but upon rising to open to him, had found him vanished, and sought him in vain through the city*):
I sleep but my heart waketh, it is the voice of my beloved that knocketh, saying, Open to me, my sister, my love, my dove, my undefiled for my head is filled with dew, and my locks with the drops of the night. I have put off my coat: how shall I put it on? I have washed my feet: how shall I defile them? My beloved put in his hand by the hole of the door, and my bowels were moved for him. I rose up to open to my beloved: and my hands dropped with myrrh, and my fingers with sweet smelling myrrh, upon the handles of the lock. I opened to my beloved: but my beloved had withdrawn himself, and was gone: my soul failed

when he spake: I sought him, but I could not find him: I called him but he gave me no answer. The watchmen that went about the city found me, they smote me, they wounded me: the keepers of the walls took away my veil from me. (5:2-7)

Abishag (*the memory of the dream still haunts her, and impels her to make a fresh avowal of her love*):
I charge you, O daughters of Jerusalem, if ye find my beloved, that ye tell him, that I am sick of love. (5:8)

(*The dream of her lover visiting her, and of her failing to secure him, coming at the moment when the king's importunities are threatening to tear her from him for ever, and upon Oettli's view, immediately after her lover's departure, is conceived with great psychological truth.*)

ACT IV

Scene I (*The Ladies of the Court and Abishag*)

The Ladies of the Court (*expressing surprise at Abishag's persistent rejection of the king's advances, and her devotion to one absent*):
What is thy beloved more than another beloved, O thou fairest among women? What is thy beloved more than another beloved, that thou dost so charge us? (5:9)

Abishag (*an enraptured description of her lover*):
My beloved is white and ruddy, the chiefest among ten thousand. His head is as the most fine gold, his locks are bushy, and as black as a raven. His eyes are as the eyes of doves by the rivers of waters, washed with milk, and fitly set. His cheeks are as a bed of spices, as sweet flowers: his lips are like lilies, dropping sweet smelling myrrh. His hands are as gold rings set with the beryl: his belly is as bright ivory overlaid with sapphires. His legs are as pillars of marble, set upon sockets of fine gold: his countenance is as Lebanon, excellent as the cedars. His mouth is most sweet: yea, he is altogether lovely. This is my beloved, and this is my friend, O daughters of Jerusalem. (5:10-16)

Ladies of the Court: Whither is thy beloved gone, O thou fairest among women? Whither is thy beloved turned aside? That we may seek him with thee. (6:1)

Abishag: My beloved is gone down into his garden, to the beds of spices, to feed in the gardens, and to gather lilies. I am my beloved's and my beloved is mine: he feedeth among the lilies. (6:2-3)

Scene II (*Solomon enters.*)

Solomon (*renews his efforts to win Abishag's affection by praising her beauty and describing the honour in store for her*):
Thou art beautiful, my love, as Tirzah, comely as Jerusalem, terrible as an army with banners. Turn away thine eyes from me, for they have overcome me: thy hair is as a flock of goats that appear from Gilead. Thy teeth are as a flock of sheep which go up from the washing, whereof every one beareth twins, and there is not one barren one among them. As a piece of a pomegranate are thy temples within thy locks. There are threescore queens, and fourscore concubines, and virgins without number. My dove, my undefiled is but one: she is the only one of her mother, she is the choice one of her that bare her. The daughters saw her, and blessed her: yea, the queens and the concubines, and they praised her. (6:4-9)

Solomon (*the king's memory passes back to the occasion of his first meeting Abishag in the nut-orchard, and he repeats the words with which the ladies of the Court then accosted her*):
Who is she that looketh forth as the morning, fair as the moon, clear as the sun, and terrible as an army of banners? (6:10)

(*Next Solomon reflects upon her reply, in which she excuses herself for having wandered there alone, and allowed herself to be surprised by the king's retinue; he quotes similarly the request which they then made to her to remain with them; with her reply, and their answer, that they desired to see her dance.*)

Solomon: I went down into the garden of nuts to see the fruits of the valley, and to see whether the vine flourished, and the pomegranates budded. Or ever I was aware, my soul made me like the chariots of Amminadib. Return, return, O Shulamite, return, return, that we may look upon thee. What will be seen in the Shulamite? As it were the company of two armies. (6:11-13)

Scene III

Solomon (*making a final endeavor to gain Abishag's heart by praising her charms in more effusive terms than before*):
How beautiful are thy feet with shoes, O prince's daughter the joints[1] of thy thighs are like jewels, the work of the hands of a cunning workman. Thy navel is like a round goblet, which wanteth not liquor, thy belly is like an heap of wheat set about with lilies. Thy two breasts are like two young roes that are twins. Thy neck is as a tower of ivory, thine eyes like the fishpools in Heshbon, by the gate of Bathrabim, thy nose is as the tower of men of Lebanon, by the gate of Bathrabim, thy nose is as the tower of Lebanon which looketh toward Damascus. Thine head upon thee is like Carmel, and the hair of thine head like purple, the king is held in the galleries. How fair and how pleasant art thou, O love, for delights. This thy nature is like to a palm tree, and thy breasts to clusters of grapes. (7:1-9)

Scene IV

Abishag (*heedless of the king's admiration, Abishag declares her unswerving devotion to her shepherd-lover, and her longing to be with him again in the open fields*):
I am my beloved's and his desire is toward me. Come, my beloved, let us go forth into the field: let us lodge in the villages. Let us get up early to the vineyards, let us see if the vine flourish, whether the tender grape appear, and the pomegranates bud forth: there will I give thee my loves. The mandrakes give a smell, and at our gate are all manner of pleasant fruits, new and old, which I have laid up for thee, O my beloved. O thou that wert as my brother, that sucked the breasts of my mother, when I should find thee without, I would kiss thee, yea, I should not be despised. I would lead thee, and bring thee into my

mother's house, who would instruct me: I would cause thee to drink of spiced wine of the juice of my pomegranate. His left hand should be under my head and his right hand should embrace me. (7:10-8:3)

Abishag (*making her final repulse of the king*):
I charge you, O daughters of Jerusalem, that ye stir not up, nor awake my love, until he please. (8:4)

ACT V (*Shepherds, Abishag, and her lover*)

Scene I

Shepherds of Shunem (*perceiving the Shunamite approaching, leaning on her lover's arm*):
Who is this that cometh up from the wilderness, leaning upon her beloved? (8:5a)

Abishag (*addressing her lover, and pointing to the apple tree, under which she had once aroused him from his sleep, and the spot where he had first seen the light, and declaring passionately the irresistible might of true love*):
I raised thee up under the apple tree; there thy mother brought thee forth: there she brought thee forth that bare thee. Set me as a seal upon thine heart, as a seal upon thine arm: for love is strong as death: jealousy is cruel as the grave: the coals thereof are coals of fire, which hath a most vehement flame. Many waters cannot quench love, neither can the floods drown it; if a man would give all the substance of his house for love, it would be utterly contemned. (8:5b-8:7)

Abishag (*addressing all present, recalling words in which her brothers had planned formerly for her welfare, and declaring how she had fulfilled their best expectations*):
We have a little sister, and she hath no breasts: what shall we do for our sister in the day when she shall be spoken for? If she be a wall, we will build upon her a palace of silver: and if she be a door, we will inclose her with boards of cedar. I am a wall, and my breasts like towers: then

was I in his eyes as one that found favour: he let out the vineyard unto keepers, every one for the fruit thereof two hundred. (8:8-12)

The Lover (*asking his love for a song*):
Thou that dwellest in the gardens, the companions hearken to thy voice: cause me to hear it. (8:13)

Abishag (*singing, and inviting her lover to join her over the hills*):
Make haste, my beloved, and be thou like to a roe or to a young hart upon the mountains of spices. (8:14)

End

ECCLESIASTES

Among the many works acquired by the library were the writings of the Greek philosopher, Epicurus (341 BC-270 BC). Epicurus believed that everything was composed of very small, indivisible particles, that while gods existed, they were not like the gods described in either Greek myth or in any other. He believed that while the gods were immortal, they were unconcerned with human existence.

The author of *Ecclesiastes* seems to have had access to, and to have been influenced by both the ideas and style of the Greek philosopher, Epicurus. Epicurus began his famous letter to his friend, Menoeceus with:

> Let no one be slow to seek wisdom when he is young nor weary in the search of it when he has grown old. For no age is too early or too late for the health of the soul. And to say that the season for studying philosophy has not yet come, or that it is past and gone, is like saying that the season for happiness is not yet or that it is now no more.

As to its authorship and time of writing, Emil Kautzsch points out that:

> the repeated bitter complaints that justice is badly adminis-

> tered, that injustice indeed prevails in the world, would not come very well from a reigning king.

Containing, as it does, an air of resignation more appropriate to a period long after the fall of Jerusalem when all hope of reviving the imagine grandeur of David's day had been long gone, a Solomonic authorship would seem to be out of the question.

So much for when and where it was written, we next must consider why. Kautzsch suggests that *Ecclesiastes* represents:

> the final abandonment of the attempt to solve the riddle of existence" and observes that "The theme of the whole is expressed at the very outset. Everything is vain, troublesome, and at the same time aimless. Vain is the striving after Wisdom, like that after property and pleasure. Man ever stands powerless in the presence of an inevitable and, to him, incomprehensible fate. And thus the only profitable counsel which one may perhaps venture to give (verse 17) is to get the better of the misery of the existence by enjoying life rationally, while, at the same time, not abandoning one's religious faith.

Both Epicurus and the author of *Ecclesiastes* recommend that their readers respect the gods, Epicurus expressing it this way:

> First believe that God is a living being, immortal and blessed, according to the notion of a god indicated by the common sense of mankind and so believing, you shall not affirm of him anything that is foreign to his immortality or that is repugnant to his blessedness.

Similarly, the author of *Ecclesiastes* urges his readers to:

> Fear God, and keep his commandments: for this is the whole duty of man.

In both, a common thread of respect for the state is also recommended. The advice, like that with regard to religion, is in keeping with what is politically expedient. As we would put it today, why make waves?

Both Epicurus and the author of *Ecclesiastes* urge their readers to seek pleasure as the principal object in life—though in moderation. Epicurus says that while he does not mean "the pleasures of the prodigal," and that he believes "pleasure is the end and the aim of life" which bears a striking resemblance to the advice in *Ecclesiastes* to "Go thy way, eat thy bread with joy, and drink thy wine with a merry heart."

Both Epicurus and the anonymous author of *Ecclesiastes* believed that death was, for all living things, the end, after which there was nothing—and therefore, nothing to fear. Epicurus declares that:

> death is the privation of all sentience; therefore a correct understanding that death is nothing to us makes the mortality of life enjoyable not by adding to life a limitless time

This is similar to the observation in *Ecclesiastes* that:

> For the living know that they shall die; but the dead know not anything, neither have they any reward.

The format is that of an older man advising a younger man or of a father advising his son:

> Rejoice, O young man, in the days of thy youth…

Whether the younger man was the author's son or was simply someone he treated as such is not known. It is possible that they both worked for the library as scribes and may have been priests as well.

Ecclesiastes is one of the most famous of all of the books of the Hebrew *Bible*, and justly so. It is great literature and contains some of the most memorable lines of any work of poetry or prose. Who could ever forget the opening lines of *Ecclesiastes*' Chapter 3?

> To every thing there is a season and
> a time to every purpose under the heaven
>
> A time to be born, and a time to die:
> a time to plant, and a time to pluck up that which is planted
>
> A time to kill, and a time to heal;

a time to break down, and a time to build up;
A time to weep, and a time to laugh;
a time to mourn, and a time to dance..."

Perhaps it is to the large number of books being translated and copied by the library staff that the author of *Ecclesiastes* was referring when he said:

> of the making of many books there is no end; and much study is a weariness of the flesh.

Such a statement would have been in keeping with the character of someone employed by the world's then greatest library!

Some *Bible* scholars see a second hand involved in the writing of *Ecclesiastes*. It is possible that at the Council of Jamnia, or at some other council where the composition of the canon was being considered, an admirer of *Ecclesiastes* added a few words here and there which would assure its continued presence in the Tanakh. Attributing its authorship to the wise King Solomon, "the words of the Preacher, the son of David, king in Jerusalem," seems to have been a masterstroke, whoever wrote it, and we are the luckier for it.

THE BOOK OF JOB

The *Book of Job* is also the work of an unknown author, or authors. It may have been in Alexandria around the same time that, or a little after, the *Song of Songs* and *Ecclesiastes* were written—which is to say, around 250 BC.

The author of the *Book of Job*, like the authors of the *Song of Songs* and *Ecclesiastes*, seems, in places, to have been influenced by the philosophy of Epicurus either directly by the writings of Epicurus which were in the library at Alexandria—or indirectly, by the *Book of Ecclesiastes*.

The *Book of Job* seems to be attempt to answer the question of why a presumably omnipotent God would allow bad things happen to good people and good things, to bad people.

It may be a veiled argument against monotheism since it puts its finger, so to speak, on the heart of the problem—those who assert the existence of only one god—to whom is ascribed the responsibility for every thing that exists and every thing that happens, there is then no one else to whom to attribute the blame for injustice. In polytheistic religions, on the other hand, misfortune and injustice are often explained away as resulting from conflicts among the gods themselves.

The *Book of Job* opens with a description of how various divine beings happened to run into each other. The Lord, spotting Satan among them, asked "Where have you been?" to which Satan replied "Roaming all over the earth."

Next, the Lord, as if He and Satan were merely talking shop, inquired "Have you noticed my servant, Job? There is no one like him on earth, an upright and blameless man who fears God and shuns evil!" to which Satan replied "Why it is You who have fenced him round, him and his household and all that he has. You have blessed his efforts so that his possessions spread out in the land. But lay Your hand upon all that he has and he will surely blaspheme You to Your face." Whereupon the Lord accepts the offer of the wager and gives the power to afflict Job, his household, and possessions to test Job's resolve.

One day, soon thereafter, a messenger approaches Job with some bad news. "The oxen were plowing and the asses were grazing alongside them when Sabeans attacked them and carried them off, and put the boys to the sword. I alone have escaped to tell you." A second messenger came with some more bad news, a big wind had come up and Job's house had fallen in, killing all of Job's children—only the messenger had survived.

Instead of cursing the Lord, Job prepared himself to mourn his children, tearing his robe, cutting off his hair and, falling to the ground, began to worship the Lord. And, the *Book of Job* notes, "For all that,

Job did not sin nor did he cast reproach on God."

As Job's torments continue, Job does not curse the Lord. Neither, however, does he praise him; he simply falls silent.

In the distant past, it was believed that the story was based upon an actual man and actual events. Such a belief, however, raises a variety of essentially unanswerable questions. Why were God and Satan on such seemingly friendly terms? Why would an omnipotent God bet on the outcome of Satan's tormenting of Job—tormenting approved of by God—only to achieve a draw?

More recently Job has been viewed as a fictional character in a morality tale.

It is also possible that the *Book of Job* is an allegory about the situation in which the Jewish people found themselves in the third century BC.

ENDNOTES

1. The word "joints" appears to be the translator's euphemism for an expression which very likely was intended to indicate female genitalia. The author's eye is clearly moving upwards from Abishag's feet to her navel, locating the place where the two curves of her thighs join as being somewhere in between.

   Verses 7.2 and 7.3 might more faithfully reflect the original author's meaning if rendered as "How beautiful is the sound of your sandals as you dance the Mahanaim, O daughter of nobility, the joining of the curves of your two thighs is like jewelry, the work of an artist's hands. Your navel is a bowl of roundness—May mixed wine not be lacking. Your belly is a mound of wheat, fenced about with lilies."

   The Mahanaim was probably a popular, highly sexual dance in the third century BCE which had originated in a town in the Trans-Jordan by that name, just as the Charleston was a dance—originally of West African origin—popular first among black dockworkers in Charleston, South Carolina in the early twentieth century and later with the smart set during the Roaring Twenties.

CHAPTER 13

THE STRUGGLE FOR JUDAEA

To understand what happened between the time that the Hebrew Bible was approaching its completion and the period just before the birth of Christ, the following short history of the struggle for Judaea following its conquest by Alexander in 332 BCE, has been provided. This short history has been taken, verbatim, from Julius Wellhausen's Prolegomena to the History of Israel, *Edinburgh, 1885, pp. 513-526.*

Palestine fell into Alexander's possession in 332; after his death it had an ample share of the troubles arising out of the partition of his inheritance. In 320 it was ruled by Ptolemy I, who on a Sabbath-day took Jerusalem; but in 315 he had to give way before Antigonus. Even before the battle of Ipsus, however, he recovered possession once more, and for a century thereafter Southern Syria continued to belong to the Egyptian crown, although the Seleucidae more than once sought to wrench it away.

In the priestly dynasty during the period of the Ptolemies, Onias I ben Jaddua was succeeded by his son Simon I, after whom again came first his brothers Eleazar and Manasseh, and next his son Onias II; the last-named was in his turn followed by his son Simon II, whose praises are sung by the son of Sirach (xlix. 14-16). At the side of the high priest stood the Gerusia of the town of Jerusalem, as a council of state, including the higher ranks of the priesthood. The new sovereign power was at once stronger and more just than the Persian—at least under the earlier Ptolemies; the power of the national government increased; to it was entrusted the business of raising the tribute.

As a consequence of the revolutionary changes which had taken place in the conditions of the whole East, the Jewish dispersion (diaspora) began vigorously to spread. It dated its beginning indeed from an earlier period—from the time when the Jews had lost their land and kingdom, but yet, thanks to their religion, could not part with their nationality. They did not by any means all return from Babylon; perhaps the majority permanently settled abroad. The successors of Alexander (diadochi) fully appreciated this international element, and used it as a link between their barbarian and Hellenic populations. Everywhere they encouraged the settlement of Jews—in Asia Minor, in Syria, and especially in Egypt. Alongside of the Palestinian there arose a Hellenistic Judaism which had its metropolis in Alexandria. Here, under Ptolemy I and II, the Torah had already been translated into Greek, and around this sprung up a Jewish-Greek literature which soon became very extensive. At the court and in the army of the Ptolemies many Jews rose to prominent positions; everywhere they received the preference over, and everywhere they in consequence (suffered) the hatred of, the indigenous population.

After the death of Ptolemy IV (205) Antiochus III attained the object towards which he and his predecessors had long been vainly striving; after a war protracted with varying success through several years, he succeeded at last in incorporating Palestine with the kingdom of the Seleucidae. The Jews took his side, less perhaps they had become disgusted with the really sadly degenerate Egyptian rule, than because they had foreseen the issue of the contest, and preferred to attach themselves voluntarily to the winning side. In grateful acknowledgment, Antiochus confirmed and enlarged certain privileges of the "holy camp," i.e., of Jerusalem (Josephus, Antiquities, xii 3, 3). It soon, however, became manifest that the Jews had made but a poor bargain in this exchange. Three years after his defeat at Magnesia, Antiochus III died (187), leaving to his son Seleucus IV an immense burden of debt, which he had incurred by his unprosperous Roman war. Seleucus, in his straits, could not afford to be over-scrupulous in appropriating money where it was to be found: he did not need to be twice told that the wealth of the temple at Jerusalem was out of all proportion to the expenses of the sacrificial service. The sacred treasure accordingly made the narrowest possible escape from being plundered; Heliodorus, who had been charged by the king to seize it, was deterred at the last moment by a heavenly vision. But the Jews derived no permanent advantage from this.

It was a priest of rank, Simon by name, who had called the attention of the king to the temple treasure; his motive had been spite against the high priest Onias III, the son and successor of Simon II. The circumstance is one indication of a melancholy process of disintegration that was at that time going on within the hierocracy. The high-priesthood, although there were exceptional cases, such as that of Simon II, was regarded less as a sacred office than as a profitable princedom; within the ranks of the priestly nobility arose envious and jealous factions; personal advancement was sought by means of the favour of the over-lord, who had something to say in the making of appointments. A collateral branch of the ruling family, that of the children of Tobias, had by means of the ill-gotten wealth of Joseph ben Tobias attained to a position of ascendancy, and competed in point of power with the high-priest himself. It appears that the above-mentioned Simon, and his still more scandalous brother Menelaus, also belonged to the Tobiadae, and relying upon the support of their powerful party (Josephus, Antiquities xii 5, 1), cherished the purpose of securing the high-priesthood by the aid of the Syrian king.

The failure of the mission of Heliodorus was attributed by Simon to a piece of trickery on the part of Onias the high priest, who accordingly found himself called upon to make his own justification at court and to expose the intrigues of his adversary. Meanwhile Seleucus IV died of poison (175), and Antiochus IV Ephiphanes did not confirm Onias in his dignity, but detained him in Antioch, while he made over the office to his brother Jason, who had offered a higher rent. Possibly the Tobidae also had something to do with this arrangement; at all events, Menelaus was at the outset the right hand of the new high priest. To secure still further the favour of the king, Jason held himself out to be an enlightened friend of the Greeks, and begged for leave to found in Jerusalem a gymnasium and an ephebeum, and to be allowed to sell to the inhabitants there the rights of citizenship in Antioch—a request which was readily granted.

The malady which had long been incubating now reached its acute phase. Just in proportion as Hellenism showed itself friendly did it present elements of danger to Judaism. From the periphery it slowly advanced towards the centre, from the diaspora to Jerusalem, from mere matters of external fashion to matters of the most profound conviction. Especially did the upper and cultivated classes of society begin to feel ashamed, in presence of the refined Greeks, of their Jewish singularity, and to do all in their power to tone it down and conceal it. In this the priestly nobility made itself conspicuous as the most secular section of the community, and it was the high priest who took the initiative in measures which aimed at a complete Hellenising of the Jews. He outdid every one else in paganism. Once he sent a considerable present for offerings to the Syrian Hercules on the occasion of his festival; but his messenger, ashamed to apply the money to such a purpose, set it apart for the construction of royal ships of war.

The friendship shown by Jason for the Greek king and for all that was Hellenic did not prevent Antiochus IV from setting pecuniary considerations before all others. Menelaus, intrusted with the mission of conveying to Antioch the annual Jewish tribute, availed himself of the opportunity to promote his own personal interests by offering a higher sum for the high-priesthood, and having otherwise ingratiated himself with the king, gained his object (171). But though nominated, he did not find it quite easy to obtain possession of the post. The Tobiadae took his side, but the body of the people stuck to Jason, who was compelled to give way only when Syrian troops had been brought upon the scene. Menelaus had immediately, however, to encounter another difficulty, for he could not at once pay the amount of tribute which he had promised. He helped himself so far indeed by robbing the temple, but this landed him in new embarrassments. Onias III, who was living out of employment at Antioch, threatened to make compromising revelations to the king; he was, however, opportunely assassinated. The rage of the people against the priestly temple-plunderer now broke out in a rising against a certain Lysimachus, who at the instance of the absent Menelaus had made further inroads upon the sacred treasury. The Jews' defence before the king (at Tyre) on account of this uproar resolved itself into a grievous complaint against the conduct of Menelaus. His case was a bad one, but money again helped him out of his straits, and the extremely penalty of the law fell upon his accusers.

The feelings of the Jews with reference to this wolfish shepherd may easily be imagined. Nothing but fear of Antiochus held them in check. Then a report gained currency that the king had perished in an expedition against Egypt (170); and Jason, who meanwhile had found refuge in Ammanitis, availed himself of the prevailing current of feeling to resume his authority with the help of one thousand men. He was not able, however, to hold the position long, partly because he showed an unwise vindictiveness against his enemies, partly (and chiefly) because the rumor of the death of Antiochus turned out to be false. The king was already, in fact, close at hand on his return from Egypt, full of anger at an insurrection which he regarded as having been directed against himself. He inflicted severe and bloody chastisement upon Jerusalem, carried off the treasures of the temple, and restored Menelaus, placing Syrian officials at his side. Jason fled from place to place, and ultimately died in misery at Lacedaemon.

The deepest despondency prevailed in Judaea; but its cup of sorrow was not yet full. Antiochus, probably soon after his last Egyptian expedition (168), sent Apollonius with an army against Jerusalem. He fell upon the unsuspecting city, disarmed the inhabitants and demolished the walls, but on the other hand fortified Acra, and garrisoned it strongly, so as to make it a standing menace to the whole country. Having thus made his preparations, he proceeded to carry out his main instructions. All that was religiously distinctive of Judaism was to be removed; such was the will of the king. The Mosaic cult was abolished, Sabbath observance and the rite of circumcision prohibited, all copies of the Torah confiscated and burnt. In the desecrated and partially destroyed temple pagan ceremonies were performed, and upon the great altar of burnt offering a small altar to Jupiter Capitolinus was erected, on which the first offering was made on 25th Kislev 168. In the country towns also heathen altars were erected and the Jews compelled, on pain of death, publicly to adore the false gods and to eat swine's flesh that had been sacrificed to idols.

The princes and grandees of the Jews had represented to Antiochus that the people were ripe for Hellenisation; and inasmuch as, apart from this, to reduce to uniformity the extremely motley constituents of his kingdom was a scheme that lay near his heart, he was very willing to believe them, that the very opposite was the case must of course have become quite evident very soon; but the resistance of the Jews taking the form of rebellious risings against his creatures, he fell upon the hopeless plan of coercion—hopeless, for he could attain his end only by making all Judaea one vast graveyard. There existed indeed a pagan party; the Syrian garrison of Acra was partly composed of Jews who sold themselves to be the executioners of their countrymen. Fear also influenced many to deny their convictions; but the majority adhered firmly to the religion of their fathers. Jerusalem, the centre of the process of Hellenisation, was abandoned by its inhabitants, who made their escape to Egypt, or his themselves in the country, in deserts and caves. The scribes in especial held fast by the law; and they were joined by the party of the Asidaeans (i.e., pious ones).

THE HASMONAEANS

At first there was no thought of meeting violence with violence; as the Book of Daniel shows, people consoled themselves with thoughts of the immediate intervention of God which would occur in due time. Quite casually, without either plan or concert, a warlike opposition arose. There was a certain priest Mattathias, of the family of the Hasmonaeans, a man far advanced in life, whose home was in Modein, a little country town to the west of Jerusalem. Hither also the Syrian soldiers came to put the population to a positive proof of their change of faith; they insisted upon Mattathias leading the way. But he was steadfast in his refusal; and when another Jew addressed himself before his eyes to the work of making the heathen offering he killed him and the Syrian officer as well, and destroyed the altar. Thereupon he fled to the hill country, accompanied by his sons (Johannes Gaddi, Simon Thassi, Judas Maccabaeus, Eleazar Auaran, Jonathan Apphus) and other followers. But he resolved to defend himself to the last and not to act as some other fugitives had done, who about the same time had allowed themselves to be surrounded and butchered on a Sabbath-day without lifting a finger. Thus he became the head of a band which defended the ancestral religion with the sword. They traversed the country, demolished the altars of the false gods, circumcised the children, and persecuted the heathen and heathenishly disposed. The sect of the Asidaeans also intrusted itself to their warlike protection (*I Maccabees* ii 42).

Mattathias soon died and left his leadership to Judas Maccabaeus by whom the struggle was carried on in the first instance after the old fashion; soon, however, it assumed larger dimension, when regular armies were sent out against the insurgents. First Applonius, the governor of Judea, took the field; but he was defeated and fell in battle. Next came Seron, governor of Coelesyria, who also was routed near Bethhoron (166). Upon this Lysias, the regent to whom Antiochus IV, who was busied in the far east, had intrusted the government of Syria and the charge of his son, Antiochus Philopator, a minor, sent a strong force under the command of three generals. Approaching from the west, it was their design to advance separately upon Jerusalem, but Judas anticipated their plan and compelled them to quit the field (166). The regent now felt himself called on to interpose in person. Invading Judaea from the south, he encountered the Jews at Bethsur, who, however, offered an opposition that was not easily overcome; he was prevented from resorting to the last measures by the intelligence which reached him of the death of the king in Elymais (165).

The withdrawal of Lysias secured the fulfilment of the desires of the defenders of the faith in so far as it now enabled them to restore the Jerusalem worship to its previous condition. They lost no time in setting about the accomplishment of this. They were not successful indeed in wresting Acra from the possession of the Syrians, but they so occupied the garrison as to prevent it from interfering with the work of restoration. On 25th Kislev 165, the very day on which, three years before, "the abomination of desolation" had been inaugurated, the first sacrifice was offered on the new altar, and in commemoration of this the feast of the dedication was thenceforth celebrated.

As it was easy to see that danger still impended, the temple was put into a state of defence. But the favorable moment presented by the change of sovereign was made use of for still bolder attempts. Scattered over the whole of Southern Syria there were a number of Jewish localities on which the heathens now proceeded to wreak their vengeance.

For the purpose of rescuing these oppressed co-religionists, and of bringing them in safety to Judaea, the Maccabees made a series of excursions, extending in some cases as far as to Lebanon and Damascus. Lysias had his hands otherwise fully occupied, and perhaps did not feel much disposed to continue the fight on behalf of the cult of Jupiter Capitolinus. Daily gaining in boldness, the Jews now took in hand also to lay regular siege to Acra. Then at last Lysias yielded to the pressure of Syrian and Jewish deputations and determined to take serious steps (162). With a large force he entered Judaea, again from the south and laid siege to Bethsur. Judas vainly attempted the relief of the fortress; he sustained near Bethzachariah a defeat in which his brother Eleazar perished. Bethsur was unable to hold out, being short of provisions on account of the sabbatical year. The Syrians advanced next to Jerusalem and besieged the temple; it also was insufficiently provisioned, and would soon have been compelled to surrender, had not Lysias been again called away at the critical moment by other exigencies. A certain Philip was endeavouring to oust him from the regency; as it was necessary for him to have his hands free in dealing with this new enemy, he closed a treaty with the temple garrison and the people at large, in accordance with which at once the political subjection and the religious freedom of the Jews were to be maintained. Thus the situation as it had existed before Antiochus IV was restored only no attempt was made to replace Menelaus as high priest and ethnarch; this post was to be filled by Alcimus.

The concessions thus made by Lysias were inevitable; and even King Demetrius I, son of Seleucus IV, who towards the end of 162 ascended the throne and caused both Lysias and his ward to be put to death, had no thought of interfering with their religious freedom. But the Maccabees desired something more than the status quo ante; after having done their duty they were disinclined to retire in favour of Alcimus whose sole claim lay in his descent from the old heathenishly-disposed high-priestly family. Alcimus was compelled to invoke the assistance of the king, who caused him to be installed by Bacchides. He was at once recognized by the scribes and Asidaeans, for whom, with religious liberty, everything they wished had been secured; the claims to supremacy made by the Hasmonaeans were of no consequence to them. Doubtless the masses also would ultimately have quietly accepted Alcimus, who of course refrained from interference with either law or worship, had he not abused the momentary power he derived from the presence of Bacchides to take a foolish revenge. But the consequence of his action was that, as soon as Bacchides had turned his back, Alcimus was compelled to follow him. For the purpose of restoring him a Syrian army once more invaded Judaea under Nicanor (160), but at Kapharsalama and afterwards at Bethhoron was defeated by Judas, and almost annihilated in the subsequent flight, Nicanor himself being among the slain (13th Adar = Nicanor's day). Judas was now at the acme of his prosperity; about this time he concluded his (profitless) treaty with the Romans. But disaster was impending. In the month of Nisan, barely a month after the defeat of Nicanor, a new Syrian army under Bacchides entered Judaea from the north; near Elasa, southward from Jerusalem, a decisive battle was fought which was lost by Judas, and in which he himself fell.

The religious war properly so called had already been brought once for all to an end by the convention of Lysias. If the struggle continued to be carried on, it was not for the faith but for the supremacy—less in the interests of the community than in those of the Hasmonaeans. After the death of Judas the secular character which the conflict had assumed ever since 162 continually became more conspicuous. Jonathan Apphus fought for his house and in so doing used thoroughly worldly means. The high-priesthood, i.e., the ethnarchy, was the goal of his ambition. So long as Alcimus lived, it was far from his reach. Confined to the rocky fastnesses beside the Dead Sea, he had nothing for it but, surrounded by his faithful followers, to wait for better times. But on the death of Alcimus (159) the Syrians refrained from appointing a successor, to obviate the necessity of always having to protect him with military force. During the interregnum of seven years which followed, Jonathan again came more and more to the front, so that at last Bacchides concluded an armistice with him on the basis of the status quo (*I Maccabees* ix 73). From his residence at Michmash Jonathan now exercised a de facto authority over the entire nation.

When accordingly Alexander Balas, a reputed son of Antiochus IV, rose against Demetrius, both rivals exerted themselves to secure the alliance of Jonathan, who did not fail to benefit by their competition. First of all, Demetrius recognized him as prince of Judah; in consequence of this he removed to Jerusalem, and expelled the heathen and heathenishly disposed, who continued to maintain a footing only in Acra and Bethsur. Next Alexander Balas conferred on him the title of "high priest of the nation and friend of the king;" in gratitude for which Jonathan went over to his side (152). He remained loyal, although Demetrius now made larger offers; he was justified by the event, for Demetrius I had the worst of it and was slain (150). The victorious Balas heaped honors upon Jonathan, who maintained his fidelity, and fought successfully in his interests when in 147 Demetrius II, the son of Demetrius I, challenged a conflict. The high priest was unable indeed to prevent the downfall of Alexander in 145; but Demetrius II, won by presents, far from showing any hostility, confirmed him in his position in consideration of a tribute of 300 talents.

Jonathan was grateful to the king, as he showed by going with 3,000 men to his aid against the insurgent Antiochenes. But when the latter drew back from his promise to withdraw the garrison from Acra, he went over to the side of Trypho, who had set up a son of Alexander Balas (Antiochus) as a rival. In the war which he now waged as Seleucidstrategus against Demetrius he succeeded in subduing almost the whole of Palestine. Meanwhile his brother Simon remained behind in Judaea, mastered the fortress of Bethsur, and resumed with great energy the siege of Acra. All this was done in the names of Antiochus and Trypho, but really of course in the interests of the Jews themselves. There were concluded also treaties with the Romans and Lacedaemonians, certainly not to the advantage of the Syrians.

Trypho sought now to get rid of the man whom he himself had made so powerful. He treacherously seized and imprisoned Jonathan in Ptolemais, and made an attack upon the leaderless country. But on the frontier Simon, the last remaining son of Mattathias, met him in force. All Trypho's efforts to break through proved futile; after skirting all Judaea from west to south, without being able to get clear of Simon, he at last withdrew to Peraea without having accomplished anything. On the person of Jonathan, whom he caused to be executed, he vented the spleen he felt on the discovery that the cause for which that prince had fought was able to gain the victory even when deprived of his help. Simon, in point of fact, was Jonathan's equal as a soldier and his superior as a ruler. He secured his frontier by means of fortresses, made himself master of Acra (141) and understood how to enable the people in time of peace to reap the advantages that result from successful war; agriculture, industry, and commerce (from the haven of Joppa) began to flourish vigorously. In grateful recognition of his services the high-priesthood and the ethnarchy were bestowed upon him as hereditary possessions by a solemn assembly of the people, "until a trustworthy prophet should arise."

Nominally the Seleucidae still continued to possess the suzerainty. Simon naturally had detached himself from Trypho and turned to Demetrius II, who confirmed him in his position, remitted all arrears of tribute, and waived his rights for the future (142). The friendship of Demetrius II and of his successor Antiochus Sidetes with Simon, however, lasted only as long as Trypho still remained in the way. But, he once removed, Sidetes altered his policy. He demanded of Simon the surrender of Joppa, Gazara, and other towns, besides the citadel of Jerusalem, as well as payment of all tribute resting due. The refusal of these demands led to war, which in its earlier stages was carried on with success, but the scales were turned after the murder of Simon, when Sidetes in person took the field against John Hyrcanus, Simon's son and successor. Jerusalem capitulated; in the negotiations for peace the surrender of all the external possessions of the Jews was insisted upon; the suzerainty of the Syrians became once more a reality (135). But in 130 the powerful Antiochus Sidetes fell in an expedition against the Parthians, and the complications anew arising in reference to the succession to the Syrian throne placed Hyrcanus in a position to recover what he had lost and to make new acquisitions He subjugated Samaria and Idumaea, compelling the inhabitants of the latter to accept circumcision. Like his predecessors, he too sought to secure the favour of the Romans, but derived no greater benefit from the effort than they had done. After a prosperous reign of thirty years he died in 105. B Josephus he is represented as a pattern of all that a pious prince ought to be; by the rabbis as representing a splendid high-priesthood.

The darkness of the succeeding age lent a brighter color to his image.

The external splendor of the Hasmonaean kingdom did not at once die away—the downfall of the Seleucidae, which was its negative condition, being also a slow affair. Judah Aristobulus, the son of Hyrcanus, who reigned for only one year, was the first to assume the Greek title of royalty; Ituraea was subdued by him, and circumcision forced upon the inhabitants. His brother Jonathan (Jannaeus) Alexander (104-79), in a series of continual wars which were never very prosperous, nevertheless succeeded in adding the whole coast of Philistia (Gaza) as well as a great portion of Peraea to his hereditary dominions. But the external enlargement of the structure was secured at the cost of its internal consistency.

From the time when Jonathan, the son of Mattathias, began to carry on the struggle no longer for the cause of God but for his own interests, the scribes and the Asidaeans, as we have seen, had withdrawn themselves from the party of the Maccabees. There can be no doubt that from their legal standpoint they were perfectly right in contenting themselves, as they did, with the attainment of religious liberty, and in accepting Alcimus. The Hasmonaeans had no hereditary right to the high-priesthood, and their politics, which aimed at the establishment of a national monarchy, were contrary to the whole spirit and essence of the second theocracy. The presupposition of that theocracy was foreign domination; in no other way could its sacred—i.e., clerical—character be maintained. God and the law could not but be forced into the background if a warlike kingdom, retaining indeed the forms of a hierocracy, but really violating its spirit at every point, should ever grow out of a mere pious community. Above all, how could the scribes hope to retain their importance if temple and synagogue were cast into the shade by politics and clash of arms? But under the first great Hasmonaeans the zealots for the law were unable to force their way to the front; the enthusiasm of the people was too strong for them; they had nothing for it but to keep themselves out of the current and refuse to be swept along by it. Even under Hyrcanus, however, they gained more prominence, and under Jannaeus their influence upon popular opinion was paramount, for under the last-named the secularization of the hierocracy no longer presented any attractive aspects; it was wholly repellent. It was looked upon as a revolting anomaly that the king, who was usually in the field with his army, should once and again assume the sacred mantle in order to perform the sacrifice on some high festival, and that his officers, profane persons as they were, should at the same time be holders of the highest spiritual offices. The danger which in all this threatened "the idea of Judaism" could not in these circumstances escape the observation of even the common people; for this idea was God and the law, not any earthly fatherland. The masses accordingly ranged themselves with ever-growing unanimity on the side of the Pharisees (i.e., the party of the scribes) as against the Sadducees (i.e., the Hasmonaean party).

On one occasion, when Alexander Jannaeus had returned to Jerusalem at the feast of tabernacles, and was standing in his priestly vestments before the altar to sacrifice, he was pelted by the assembled crowd of worshippers with citrons from the green branches they carried. By the cruelty with which he punished this insult he excited the populace to the highest pitch, and when he lost his army in the disaster of Gadara, rebellion broke out. The Pharisees summoned the Syrian king Demetrius Eucaerus; Jannaeus was worsted and fled into the desert. But as he wandered in helplessness there, the patriotism of the people and sympathy for the heir of the Maccabees suddenly awoke; nature proved itself stronger than that consistency which in the cause of the Divine honour had not shrunk from treason. The insurgents for the most part went over to the side of the fugitive king; the others he ultimately overpowered after a struggle which lasted through several years, Demetrius having withdrawn his intervention. The vengeance which he took upon the Pharisees was a bloody one; their only escape was by voluntary exile. Thenceforward he had peace so far as they were concerned. His last years were occupied with the re-acquisition of the conquests which he had been compelled to yield to the Arabs during the civil war. He died in the field at the siege of Ragaba in Peraea (79).

Under Queen Salome, his widow, matters were as if they had been specially arranged for the satisfaction of the Pharisees. The high-priesthood passed to Salome's son, Hyrcanus II; she herself was only queen. In the management of external affairs her authority was absolute (Antiquities, xiii, 16, 6); in home policy she permitted the scribes to wield a paramount influence. The common assertion, indeed, that the Synedrium was at that time practically composed of scribes is inconsistent with the known facts of the case; the Synedrium at that time was a political and not a scholastic authority. In its origin it was the municipal council of Jerusalem (so also the councils of provincial towns are called synedria, Mark xiii 9), but its authority extended over the entire Jewish community; alongside of the elders of the city the ruling priests were those who had the greatest number of seats and votes. John Hyrcanus appears to have been the first to introduce some scribes into its composition; it is possible that Salome may have increased their number, but even so this high court was far from being changed into a college of scribes like that at Jamnia. If the domination of the Pharisees at this time is spoken of, the expression cannot be understood as meaning that they already held all the public offices, but only at most that the holders of those offices found it necessary to administer and to judge in their spirit and according to their fundamental principles.

CHAPTER 14

OLD WINE IN NEW BOTTLES

The characters and ideas in the Hebrew *Bible* live on in the literature of the three cultures which are derived, directly or indirectly, from it—Judaism, Christianity, and Islam. While it is clearly impossible to trace all of the vast number of ways that the Hebrew *Bible* has influenced those three cultures, a few references to some of the literature which could not have been created without it may prove interesting or useful—or both.

JUDAISM

After the Hebrew *Bible* was translated from Hebrew into Greek in Alexandria in the third century BCE, it acquired a number of additions—such as *Ecclesiastes, The Song of Songs, The Book of Ruth, The Book of Daniel,* and *The Book of Jonah.* There were others, such as the *Book of Jubilees,* which are believed to have been rejected at the Council of Jamnia around 90 CE—after the destruction of the Second Temple in 70 CE but before the disastrous Bar Kochba Revolt of 132-135 CE.

Over the centuries the Hebrew *Bible* continued to inspire the creation of Judaic literature the Jerusalem and Babylonian *Talmuds*, the *Agadic Tales*, various commentaries and codes. There were also mystic works such as the *Kabbalah* in the 12th century CE and the *Zohar*. And, as an aid to worship, liturgy in the form of the Siddur.[1]

Books about Israel's King David continue to be published to this day—ranging from scholarly works such as Baruch Halpern's *David's Secret Demons*, historical fiction such as Stefan Heym's thoroughly entertaining *The King David Report* which gives a fictional account of how Solomon's Court Historian wrote or rewrote an account of David in such a fashion as to validate Solomon's rise to David's throne.

Noteworthy, too, in the literature of the twentieth century, however, are the short stories based on biblical themes, written by Bruno Schultz, a Polish Jew, in the 1930s. The two principal characters of his two surviving masterpieces, *The Sanatorium Under the Sign of the Hourglass* and *The Street of Crocodiles*, are Jacob and his son, Joseph. His novel, *Moses*, is believed to have been lost during the German occupation during World War II. Schultz himself was shot in his hometown, Drogobych in Eastern Poland, by a Gestapo officer in 1942.

CHRISTIANITY

The Hebrew *Bible* can be said to be the cornerstone of Christianity since it was the *Bible* Jesus knew and to which he referred. Whether Jesus knew that there had been no captivity in Egypt, that there had been no Exodus, no Moses, and that most of "the law" had simply been made up is not known. It will be interesting to see just how the archaeological findings and biblical scholarship of the past ninety years will reshape Christianity itself.

Alexandria, the city where the Hebrew *Bible* was translated into Greek, may have played a role in the life of Jesus. According to the *Gospel of Matthew* (2:13), an angel of the Lord appeared unto Joseph in a dream, "saying, Arise, and take the young child and his mother, and flee into Egypt, and be thou there until I bring thee word: for Herod will seek the young child to destroy him." The gospels are silent as to just where in Egypt Joseph took Mary and Jesus, but inasmuch as Egypt (circa 2 BC) had been under Roman rule since around 30 BC, Alexandria would have been a good place for them to settle if, as would seem likely, a good education were a consideration. Although Plutarch (circa 45-120 CE), states that the Great Library was destroyed accidentally by a fire set by Julius Caesar's troops (circa 45 BC), it is more likely that the Library itself was still in existence during Jesus' childhood and that only the warehouses where books awaiting cataloguing were lost to fire. Anecdotal information, reported in classicist Lionel Casson's *Libraries of the Ancient World*, suggests that the Great Library survived until at least the seventh century CE.

An enormous number of works were generated as Christianity gained in popularity. Many of these, such as the *Gospel of Thomas* and the *Gnostic Gospels*, were condemned, at the time, as being heretical and were suppressed. New interest in these has been generated by such respected writers as Elaine Pagels.

The *Malleus Maleficarum* (the 'Witches' Hammer'), the Church's medieval manual on the interrogation, torture, and execution of people suspected of witchcraft is certainly in keeping with the priestly tradition of suppressing all other religions; Jeremiah and Ezra would certainly have understood.

The story of how the Christian New Testament came to be written is told, with great thoroughness and in more detail than anywhere else, in Burton Mack's *Who Wrote the New Testament?*, a book that can be recommended without reservation.

The *Book of Mormon* is said to have been translated into English by Joseph Smith in upstate New York between 1823 and 1830. That Smith chose the style of the King James Version raised questions about its authenticity, as did rumors of its having been based upon a somewhat earlier novel by Samuel Spaulding. The *Book of Mormon* was published in 1830, was subsequently revised, and has remained in print ever since. Those who are interested in the history of the Church of Latter Day Saints are fortunate to be able to obtain a digital copy of the first edition of the *Book of Mormon* from Octavo, Oakland, California.

It goes without saying, however, that the influence of the Hebrew *Bible* on the literature of predominantly Christian countries is enormous. Obvious examples include Oscar Wilde's *The Selfish Giant* and D. H. Lawrence's *The Man Who Died*.

One of Wal-Mart's all-time best sellers, *Left Behind: A Novel of the Earth's Last Days* by Tim Lahaye and Jerry B. Jenkins, deals with the apocalyptic 'end-times' prophesied in the hallucinogenic *Book of Revelation. Left Behind,* itself shaped by Ezekiel's very vivid visions, testifies to the reading tastes of the large and apparently growing number of 'evangelical' Christians.

ISLAM

When Allah, acting through the Angel Gabriel, began dictating the *Qu'ran* to Muhammad around 610 CE, Muhammad had probably already become familiar with the stories of the patriarchs of the Hebrew *Bible* through his contacts with Jewish merchants in the course of his career as a spice merchant.

References to the stories of the patriarchs are found not only in the Qu'ran but also in the poetry of Muslim poets such as Farid Ud-Din Attar (*The Conference of the Birds*), Hafiz (*The Songs of Hafiz*) , Omar Khayaam (*The Rubyaat*), and the thirteenth century Sufi poet, Jelaluddin Balkhi, (1207-1273) better known simply as "Rumi." Rumi's poem, *Moses and the Shepherd*, below, requires no commentary, speaking eloquently enough for itself.

MOSES AND THE SHEPHERD

Moses heard a shepherd on the road praying,
"God,
where are you? I want to help you, to fix your shoes
and comb your hair. I want to wash your clothes

and pick the lice off. I want to bring you milk
to kiss your little hands and feet when it's time
for you to go to bed. I want to sweep your room
and keep it neat. God, my sheep and goats
are yours. All I can say, remembering you,
is ayyyy and ahhhhhhhh."
Moses could stand it no longer.
"Who are you talking to?"

"The one who made us,
and made the earth and made the sky."
"Don't talk about shoes
and socks with God! And what's this with your little hands
and feet? Such blasphemous familiarity sounds like
you're chatting with your uncles.
Only something that grows
needs milk. Only someone with feet needs shoes. Not God!
Even if you meant God's human representatives,
as when God said, 'I was sick, and you did not visit
even then this tone would be foolish and irreverent.
Use appropriate terms. Fatima is a fine name
for a woman, but if you call a man Fatima,
it's an insult. Body-and-birth language
are right for us on this side of the river,
but not right for addressing the origin,
not for Allah."
The shepherd repented and tore his clothes and sighed
and wandered out into the desert.
A sudden revelation came then to Moses. God's voice:

You have separated me
from one of my own. Did you come as a Prophet to unite,
or to sever?

I have given each being a separate and unique way
of seeing and knowing and saying that knowledge.
What seems wrong to you is right for him.
What is poison to one is honey to someone else.
Purity and impurity, sloth and diligence in worship,
these mean nothing to me.
I am apart from all that.
Ways of worshiping are not to be ranked as better
or worse than one another.
Hindus do Hindu things.
The Dravidian Muslims in India do what they do.
It's all praise, and it's all right.
It's not me that's glorified in acts of worship.
It's the worshipers! I don't hear the words
they say. I look inside at the humility.
That broken-open lowliness is the reality,
not the language! Forget phraseology.
I want burning, burning.
Be friends
with your burning. Burn up your thinking
and your forms of expression!
Moses,
those who pay attention to ways of behaving
and speaking are one sort.
Lovers who burn
are another.
Don't impose a property tax
on a burned-out village. Don't scold the Lover.
The "wrong" way he talks is better than a hundred
"right ways of others.
Inside the Kaaba
it doesn't matter which direction you point
your prayer rug!

The ocean diver doesn't need snowshoes!
The love-religion has no code or doctrine.
Only God.
So the ruby has nothing engraved on it!
It doesn't need markings.
God began speaking
deeper mysteries to Moses. Visions and words,
which cannot be recorded here, poured into
and through him. He left himself and came back.
He went to eternity and came back here.
Many times this happened.
It's foolish of me
to try and say this. If I did say it,
it would shatter all writing pens.
Moses ran after the shepherd.
He followed the bewildered footprints,
in one place moving straight like a castle
across a chessboard. In another, sideways,
like a bishop.
Now surging like a wave cresting,
now sliding down like a fish,
with always his feet
making geomancy symbols in the sand,
recording his wandering state.

Moses finally caught up with him.
"I was wrong. God has revealed to me
that there are no rules for worship.
Say whatever
and however your loving tells you to. Your sweet blasphemy
is the truest devotion. Through you a whole world
is freed.
Loosen your tongue and don't worry what comes out.

It's all the light of the spirit."

The shepherd replied,
"Moses, Moses,
I've gone beyond even that.
You applied the whip and my horse shied and jumped
out of itself. The divine nature and my human nature
came together.
Bless your scolding hand and your arm.
I can't say what has happened.
What I'm saying now
is not my real condition. It can't be said."
The shepherd grew quiet.
When you look in a mirror
you see yourself, not the state of the mirror.
The flute player puts breath into a flute,
and who makes the music? Not the flute.
The flute player!
Whenever you speak praise
or thanksgiving to God, it's always like
this dear shepherd's simplicity.
When you eventually see
through the veils to how things really are,
you will keep saying again
and again,
"This is certainly not like
we thought it was!"

—from *The Essential Rumi*, Translations by Coleman Barks with John Moyne, Castle Books, pp 165-168.

It goes without saying that the importance of reading—carefully, thoughtfully, respectfully—the *Qu'ran*, or *Koran*, as it is perhaps more familiarly known, cannot be overestimated. Without an in-depth understanding of the *Qu'ran*, those of us who live in 'Western' countries cannot possibly understand the points of view of the world's one billion Muslims.

What is to be gained by reading the poetry of Attar, Hafiz, Khayaam, and Rumi is another matter altogether. Their poems are greatly revered by Muslims, it is true, but for those Westerners who take the time to 'discover' will find a delicious treat ahead of them... as Moses and the Shepherd has just shown.

The History of The Writing of The Hebrew Bible

ca 3500 BCE	Canaanite highlands settled; eventually there were almost a hundred villages and larger towns scattered throughout the central ridge.
ca 2200 BCE	By now the Canaanite settlements had disappeared and the Canaanite highlands were only sparsely settled.
ca 2000 BCE	A second wave of settlement in the Canaanite highlands. Eventually there were about two hundred and twenty settlements, ranging from villages to towns to fortified regional centers.
ca 1600 BCE	End of the second wave of settlement.
ca 1574 BCE	Seqenenre Tao, ruler of Egypt at Thebes, reads a letter he said had been sent to him by Apepi I, the Hyskos king at Avaris, which addresses him as the "Prince of the Southern City," i.e., Thebes, and demands that Seqenenre Tao remove the hippopotami from the Canal at Thebes—which was 500 miles away—because the noise is keeping him from being able to sleep, day or night. It was this absurd complaint that began the war between Thebes and Avaris which resulted in the expulsion of the Hyskos from Egypt around 1570

BCE and gave Egypt control of the eastern end of the Mediterranean—including Canaan and Midian.

ca 1207 BCE Pharaoh Merenptah memorialized his victories in Canaan including the complete annihilation of Israel, an indigenous Canaanite tribe, on a stele.

ca 1150 BCE Coinciding with the end of the Late Bronze Age and the beginning of Iron Age I, Egyptian control of Canaan ended and a power vacuum ensued. Canaanite habiru and Canaanite peasants withdrew from the control of the Canaanite rulers of the city-states who had served as Egyptian vassals and became the proto-Israelites. For reasons that are not entirely clear, the proto-Israelites distinguished themselves from their neighbors, the Philistines, Ammonites and Moabites, by neither raising pigs nor eating their flesh.

ca 1147 BCE Rameses V becomes pharaoh of Egypt.

ca 1143 BCE Rameses V stricken with smallpox; his brother, Rameses VI, becomes co-regent.

ca 1141 BCE Rameses V dies. Rameses VI withdraws Egyptian troops from Timna where the Midianites/Kenites had long been mining for copper. The Midianites destroyed the temple of Hathor, the Egyptian goddess of love, joy, and pleasure. Although Hathor was patroness of miners, the Midianites overturned and defaced her images and began the worship of a new, invisible God, Yahweh. The Midianites had, apparently, long worshipped images of a serpent god similar to that which Yahweh was later said to have told Moses to fashion. Worshipped (or revered) under the name of Neshutan, the image was said to have been able to cure (if looked upon by the victim) the bite of venomous snakes—a common occurrence among miners.

ca 1055 BCE	Saul, son of Kish, born.
ca 1035 BCE	David, son of Jesse, born; Jonathan, son of Saul, born around this time, too.
ca 1025 BCE	Saul, son of Kish, became Israel's first king. He instituted the worship of a warrior God, Jahweh, as one means of unifying the tribal federation which he ruled for about twenty years; he established a legal code to replace the justice system of the judges (of whom Samuel seems to have been the last); and he caused *The Book of the Wars of Jahweh* to be compiled. Although little is known about *The Book of the Wars of Jahweh*, it probably contained *The Song of Deborah*, generally considered to be the oldest piece of Hebrew poetry; it may also have contained the original of *Psalm 18*, the *Blessing of Jacob*, the *Blessing of Moses*, and the *Song of the Sea*. Saul's insistence upon the exclusive worship of the Midianites' Jahweh may have met with sufficient resistance as to encourage a revolt.
ca 1009 BCE	David, 26, one of Saul's three thousand warriors, saw the opportunity and organized four to six hundred malcontents to serve as mercenaries and hired himself and his men out to Saul's principal enemy, the Philistine king, Achish of Gath.
ca 1007 BCE	Achish gives Ziklag, a small village in the Negev Desert, to David.
ca 1005 BCE	Soon King Achish came to see David's potential as a vassal king. With help from the Amelekites, the Philistines killed Israel's King Saul and two of his sons. After his soldiers stripped Saul and his sons of their armor, Achish sent an Amelekite to David with Saul's headpiece and armband—symbols of Saul's

royal authority—thereby offering King Saul's throne to David—who would become his vassal. Accusing the courier of being involved in King Saul's death, David had him slain immediately. In an effort to distance himself from any blame for Saul's death, David composed an elegy lamenting the deaths of Saul and Jonathan. When the Amelekite warriors returned from Gath, they were slain by David and his men. David took the Amelekites' cattle and other possessions and distributed it among his men and the elders of the various tribes that Saul had ruled. David moved to Hebron appointed himself king of Judah.

David assigned Abiathar, the sole surviving priest from Saul's slaughter of Canaanite priests at Nob (Shiloh?), the task of compiling a comprehensive account of the brave deeds of David and his men together with the stories of the legendary heroes of the various tribes that David sought to rule; this compilation became the now long-lost *Book of Jashar* the second of the books that later became the *Bible*. During the next seven years David systematically eliminated all of Saul's descendants who might be eligible for the throne as well as Abner, the leader of Israel's warriors. David's *Book of Jashar* would also have contained detailed denials of David's complicity in any of the deaths which resulted in him becoming king of Israel in addition to becoming king of Judah. Left with little or no choice in the matter, the leaders of the ten northern tribes elected David as their king.

ca 965 BCE An ailing David was forced to abdicate in favor of his wife Bathsheba's son, Solomon. Solomon commissioned a Court Historian to write a biography of David biased so as to legitimize Solomon's succession to David's throne. The Court Historian based his account on material from the *Book of Jashar*, eyewitness accounts from survivors, and, in the case of the story of David's alleged seduction of Bathsheba and his complicity in the murder of Bathsheba's first husband, Uriah, and David's subsequent marriage to Bathsheba, his own imagination. The Court Historian's account forms much of the present *I Samuel* and *II Samuel*.

ca 931 BCE Upon Solomon's death, his son Rehoboam became king and almost immediately alienated the leaders of the ten northern tribes who have asked for reductions in taxes and forced labor. Rehoboam refused and the ten northern tribes refused to anoint Rehoboam as king of Israel. Instead, the ten northern tribes anointed Jeroboam, a former overseer of forced labor for Solomon who has been living in exile in Egypt at the expense of Pharaoh Sheshonq I, as king. A protege of the Court Historian who was associated with the royal court began the creation of a prequel to the Court Historian's history of David. Because this author, probably a woman of royal rank, refers to God as Jahweh, this author was later referred to, by Bible scholars, as "J."

J's wrote her account in an effort to bring about the reconciliation of the northern kingdom of Israel and the southern kingdom of Judah. J's account consists of ancient legends and myths combined with a series of allegories intended to describe the situation in Canaan prior to the rise of David to the throne. J is the original author of the story of the Israelite captivity in Egypt and the exodus of the Israelites from Egypt under the leadership of Moses; her story of Moses is an allegory about Saul's establishment of Israel as a nation.

At about this time an author, possibly J herself, inserted passages into J's prequel which represent the views of the people of the northern kingdom. Bible scholars generally refer to this author as "E" because of E's use of the word Elohim to indicate God. Whether written by one person or two, the J and E accounts were designed to appease the people of the northern kingdom (who preferred to continue to worship the old Canaanite gods as being more appropriate to an agricultural people than the worship of the warrior god) without alienating the Judahites, Jahweh. J's account extends from *Genesis* 2:4b through the early chapters of *I Samuel*.

The Annals of the Kings of Judah are said to have been kept during the reign of Rehoboam (931-914 BCE) by Semaiah and Iddo the Seer and by Iddo the Seer during the reign of Abijam (914-911 BCE). It is reasonable to assume that the accounts of Rehoboam and Abijam were effectively appended to *The Annals of Solomon*.

Scribes recorded the deeds of King Jeroboam I of Israel (931-909 BCE).

ca 911 BCE Unknown scribes kept an account of the forty-one year reign of King Asa of Judah (911-870 BCE) which were to be found in *The Annals of the Kings of Judah and Israel*. It is purely a matter of conjecture, but the Judahite scribes may well have begun keeping accounts of the kings of Israel beginning sometime during the reign of King Asa.

ca 909 BCE A period of instability and civil war began in the northern kingdom of Israel. Israel was ruled by King Nadab (909-908 BCE), King Baasha of Israel (908-885 BCE), King Elah (885-884 BCE), and King Ahab (873-852 BCE). While details of these three kings were derived from unspecified sources, we may assume that they were taken from *The Annals of the Kings of Israel.*

ca 870 BCE Whether accounts of the reigns of King Jehosophat of Judah (870-846 BCE), Jehovah (851-843 BCE, King Ahaziah (840 BCE) and Queen Athaliah (839-833 BCE) were added to the *Annals of the Kings of Judah and Israel* or not is not known but seems likely.

ca 852 BCE In 852 BCE, King Ahaziah (852-851 BCE) became king of Israel. Instability and civil war continued, apparently fomented by the clerical faction. Following Ahaziah's death, Israel was ruled by King Joram (851-842 BCE), King Jehu, son of Hanani, the seer (842-814 BCE). Murder seems to have been the order of the day. The *Book of Chronicles* does not specify how details of the reigns of these three kings were derived but they may well have been taken from *The Annals of the Kings of Israel.*

ca 836 BCE An account of the thirty-eight reign of King Jehoash of Judah (836-798 BCE) was said to have been kept in the *Book of Kings.*

ca 817 BCE Scribes recorded the deeds of King Jehoahaz of Israel (817-800 BCE)

ca 800 BCE Scribes recorded the deeds of King Joash of Israel (800-769 BCE)

ca 798 BCE Details of the thirteen-year reign of King Amaziah (798-785) of Judah are said to have been kept in the *Book of the Kings of Israel and Judah.*

ca 788 BCE Scribes recorded the deeds of King Jeroboam II (788-747 BCE)

ca 779 BCE Details of the thirty-year reign of King Uzziah of Judah (785-755 BCE), also known as King Azariah, were either written by or edited by the prophet Isaiah. King Uzziah's reign was among the most prosperous of all the kings of Judah.

King Uzziah may have sent Amos—better known as a reform-minded prophet—to meddle in King Jeroboam II's affairs to cover Amos' activities as a spy and revolutionary who exploited the unrest among the poor in the northern kingdom who were well aware of the widening gulf between peasants and the elite despite the great increase in the average per capita income. In Israel, the poor and weak—of whom there were many—found in Amos, a champion for their cause, causing Amaziah, the chief priest at the shrine at Beth-el, to warn King Jeroboam of Amos' meddling. Jeroboam authorized Amaziah to order Amos to return to Judah. After his return, Amos wrote the *Book of Amos* which consists of nine chapters of prophecies—oracles against foreign nations and Israel, oracles of indictment against Israel for her sins and injustices, and visions and words of judgment. Amos' only ally in Israel (other than the poor who, if they had been aware of it, may have found his message appealing) would have been the prophet Hosea.

Like the prophet Amos, the prophet Hosea, too, lived during the reign of Jeroboam II, King of Israel. The *Book of Hosea*, written by Hosea, is a collection of oracles composed and arranged by Hosea and his disciples. Like his contemporary, the great prophet of social justice, Amos, Hosea was a prophet of doom; but he held out a hope to the people that the Day of Yahweh contained not just retribution but also the possibility of renewal.

ca 747 BCE Unknown scribes recorded the deeds of King Zeccaiah of Israel (747 BCE), King Shallum of Israel (747 BCE), and King Menahem of Israel.

ca 739 BCE After reigning for forty years, however, Uzziah attempted to curb the power of the priesthood. Uzziah attempted to demonstrate that incense could be offered to Jahweh directly rather than paying the priesthood to offer it. When he put his incense into the censer, however, it exploded and Uzziah's face was burned—burns which the priests quickly diagnosed as leprosy. Uzziah was banished to a luxurious villa two and a half miles south Jerusalem at Ramat Rahel and his son, Jotham, reigned in his stead as Prince Regent. The prophet Isaiah, who may have been related to the royal family, now took up the cause of clerical reform.

Details of the regency of King Uzziah's son, Jotham (755-745 BCE), Jotham's subsequent two-year reign (745-743 BCE) and the reign of Jotham's successor, King Ahaz of Judah (743-727 BCE), may have been written by the prophet Isaiah and added to the *Book of Kings of Israel and Judah*.

ca 737 BCE Scribes recorded the deeds of King Pekahiah of Israel (737-735 BCE)

ca 735 BCE Scribes recorded the deeds of King Pekah of Israel (735-732 BCE)

ca 732 BCE Scribes recorded the deeds of King Hoshea of Israel (732-724 BCE) ca 727 BCE King Ahaz dies and his son, Hezekiah, becomes king of Judah.

ca 721 BCE Samaria fell and the days of the Kingdom of Israel were over. In addition to writing an account of the reign of King Hezekiah of Judah (727-698 BCE), Isaiah may have begun the writing of the Priestly Code based upon the concept of entering into a Covenant with Jahweh which would preclude the worship of the gods which had been brought into Jerusalem by refugees from the fallen Kingdom of Israel. Hezekiah is given credit by later authors of the *Hebrew Bible* for instituting reforms although what is more likely is that his destruction of the most potent Levite icon, a bronze serpent coiled around a bronze rod—said to have been created by Moses—was intended to strengthen the position of the Aaronid priests in the Temple in Jerusalem in exchange for their support of his monarchy rather than the survivors of any of the royal factions who were among the refugees in Jerusalem.

It may have been around this time that J's allegories began to be represented by the priests as being historical fact.

ca 720 BCE The prophet Micah wrote the *Book of Micah* in which he attacked social injustice and the corruption of those in high places. His book consists of judgments against Judah and Jerusalem (Chapters 1-3) and promises of restoration for Judah coupled with judgments against other nations (Chapters 4-7).

ca 698 BCE The deeds of King Manasseh were recorded. Later Jewish tradition blames Manasseh for the death of the prophet Isaiah by "sawing asunder."

ca 647 BCE King Josiah and the prophet Jeremiah were both born around this time; Josiah in Jerusalem and Jeremiah in the village of Anathoth. Jeremiah's father, Hilkiah, may have been the same Hilkiah who was the high priest of the temple in Jerusalem.

ca 641 BCE King Manasseh died and his son, Amon, 22 became king of Judah (641-640 BCE). Amon's two-year reign was marked by religious tolerance which incited the wrath of the Temple priests. Amon, 24, was murdered and the courtiers who had been blamed for the murder were slaughtered by the militia (known as "the people of the land") who had come under the control of the priesthood.

ca 639 BCE Amon's son, Josiah, 8, becomes king of Judah; he received his early education from the temple priests along with his contemporary, Jeremiah.

ca 631 BCE As a result of his education, the sixteen-year old Josiah became interested in what was represented to have been the religion of Judah's legendary King David.

Having learned about the traditions of his subjects, particularly the prophecies of Hosea, from his father as well as from other priests, Jeremiah began keeping a personal journal which would later serve as the basis for the *Book of Jeremiah*. Jeremiah's early messages to the people were condemnations of them for their false worship of the successors to the old Canaanite gods and social injustice with summons to repentance. Jeremiah proclaimed the coming of a foe from the north, symbolized by a boiling pot facing from the north in one of his visions, that would cause great destruction. This foe has been identified with the Scythians, nomads from southern Russia who supposedly descended into western Asia in the 7th century BCE and attacked Palestine.

ca 627 BCE At twenty Josiah began a systematic destruction of the temples, altars, and priests who worshipped the successors to the ancient Canaanite gods, believing that his actions would cause Jahweh to protect Judah as well as to give him and his descendants control over the now-lost northern kingdom of Israel. There should be little doubt that Josiah's motives were pure. Similarly, there should be little doubt that while Jeremiah had to have been fully aware of the extent of his invention of the story of Moses, he believed that Josiah would be confident enough to successful in war if he and his subjects believed that they would have divine help.

At about this time Jeremiah began the writing of the Deuteronomist law code which further defined the "Covenant" envisioned by the authors of the original Priestly Law Code around the time of King Hezekiah. The Ark of the Covenant, described in minute detail in *Exodus*, 25:10 et seq, may have been constructed around this time and the Deuteronomistic history, that further described the Covenant between the Israelites and Jahweh, was created by inserting appropriate bits and pieces into the existing JE and P texts.

ca 625 BCE The *Book of Zephaniah*, the ninth book of the Twelve Minor Prophets, was written in three chapters and was an attack on the worship of Baal and astral deities. Zephaniah predicted the coming catastrophe of the "Day of the Lord." Zephaniah denounced both foreign nations and Judah, but issued a promise of the restoration of Israel: "Sing aloud, O daughter of Zion, shout, O Israel! Rejoice and exult with all your heart, O daughter of Jerusalem." The reason for exultation? Yahweh was about to deliver his people.

ca 621 BCE Jeremiah's father, the high priest Hilkiah, "discovered" the original of the *Book of Deuteronomy* during the renovation of the temple in 621 BCE. At Hilkiah's request, the scribe Shaphan took the book to Josiah and read it to him. Expressing shock at what Shaphan had read to him, Josiah had the newly-found scroll read to the public and, using the emotion of the moment, entered into a covenant, together with his subjects, with Jahweh. Josiah ordered the priests to install the Ark of the Covenant, apparently "discovered" along with the Deuteronomistic law code (though not admittedly so), permanently in the temple to house the newly found scroll.

In writing *Deuteronomy*, Jeremiah had made it appear that Moses had mandated the celebration of Passover. King Josiah was alarmed that the Judahites (and, previously, the Israelites) had ignored Jahweh's wishes, not realizing that it was a new ritual.

Jeremiah was a prolific writer. In addition to the original *Book of Jeremiah* and the original *Book of Deuteronomy*, he created the Deuteronomistic history (sometimes referred to as "the Court History," adding to—and editing—*Genesis, Exodus, Numbers, Joshua, I and II Samuel*, and editing the *Book of the Kings of Israel and Judah* so as to make it seem that those kings who suppressed the worship of all gods other than Jahweh fared who fare well while those who tolerated the worship of other gods would be punished, however belatedly.

ca 621 BCE Ezekiel, "son of Buzi," was born.

ca 619 BCE The *Book of Nahum* was probably written by the prophet Nahum between 626 and 612 BCE (the destruction of Nineveh, the Assyrian capital) containing three chapters directed against Assyria; it also contains oracles and hymns. It expresses a small-minded regret that Jahweh saved Judah from potential devastation by the Assyrians.

ca 609 BCE Overly confident that he would be protected from any physical harm, as a reward for having done what was good in the eyes of the Lord, King Josiah was killed at Megiddo when he and his army tried to stop Pharaoh Necho who was marching north. It is possible that his identity was betrayed by the elegance of his chariot.

Jeremiah may have composed the original *Book of Kings* which included biographies of Josiah, Jehoahaz, Jehoiachim, Hehoiachin, and Judah's last king, Zedekiah. Jeremiah also worked on a redaction of earlier royal biographies, thus creating the *Book of the Kings of Judah and Israel*—known today as *I and II Kings*—which was later modified and incorporated into the original *Book of Chronicles*.

ca 605 BCE Written down by the scribe, Baruch, Jeremiah's predictions were burned by King Jehoiakim; they were rewritten by Baruch after Jeremiah amplified them.

ca 602 BCE King Jehoiakim (born Elioakim, he was Josiah's first son) rebelled against Nebuchadnezar and Judah was devastated by hostile invasions.

ca 601 BCE The *Book of Habbukuk* was written about this time by an unknown author. Habbukuk may have been a professional prophet connected with the Temple circa 605 BCE-597 BCE.

ca 597 BCE After a long siege, Jerusalem surrendered and the deportation of the entire court to Babylon began. The temple and royal palace were pillaged. The twenty-four year old future prophet Ezekiel was among those deported to Babylon, where he was located at Tel-abib on the Kebar canal near Nippur. ca 586 BCE

In the *Book of Obadiah*, the prophet Obadiah heaped curses upon the Edomites for gloating when the temple in Jerusalem was destroyed in 586 BCE. Some writers have suggested that parts of Obadiah date back to as early as the ninth century BCE but this seems unlikely since archaeological evidence discovered during the past forty years (Cohen, Finkelstein, Mazar, et al) has established that Edom was essentially undeveloped before the seventh century BCE.

The *Book of Lamentations* is believed to date from about this time. The scribe, Baruch, combined Jeremiah's predictions with narratives concerning him, forming the *Book of Jeremiah*. A number of Jews fled, first to Bethlehem and then to Egypt, taking an unwilling Jeremiah with them. Jeremiah, according to one legend, was stoned to death at Tahpanhes by the Jews.

ca 591 BCE Ezekiel, thirty, receives his "call" to prophesy. Over the next twenty-two years Ezekiel will write (a) the *Book of Ezekiel*, (b) a substantial portion of the *Book of Leviticus*, and will add material to what is generally referred to as the Priestly Source.

Ezekiel's early oracles, in the *Book of Ezekiel*, date from around 592 BCE, were pronouncements of violence and destruction; his later statements addressed the hopes of the Israelites exiled in Babylon. The faith of Ezekiel in the ultimate establishment of a new covenant between God and the people of Israel profoundly influenced the postexilic reconstruction and reorganization of Judaism. Ezekiel's periods of active prophesying extended from 592 BCE to 573 BCE. His last statements, following an apparent period of silence, date from around 571 BCE.

ca 561 BCE The nucleus of the *Law of Holiness* and the *Song of Moses* may date to around this time during the reign of the Babylonian king, Evil Merodach (Marduk), 561-560 BCE. With the addition of material attributed to the Second Deuteronomist, the text of Deuteronomy became close to that which we have today. Material from JE (*Judges, Samuel* and *Kings*) was blended with the work of the Deuteronomists. Material added to the *Book of Isaiah* included Chapter 13: 1-18, Chapter 14: 1-23, Chapter 21: 1-10, all of Chapter 34, and Chapters 40 through 45.

ca 550 BCE The (second) Priestly Source, identified by Coote and Ord in *In the Beginning, Creation and the Priestly History* as an Aaronid priest, added to and edited the books of *Genesis, Exodus, Numbers, Joshua* and completed much of the *Book of Leviticus*—a pseudo-Mosaic legal code even more restrictive than the *Book of Deuteronomy*. One of the principal objects of the *Book of Leviticus* was to undo the reforms that protected the Levite priests.

ca 520 BCE The prophet Haggai wrote the *Book of Haggai* around this time. Haggai's book contains four oracles. The first calls for Zerubbabel, the governor of Judaea, and

Joshua, to rebuild the Temple. A drought and poor harvest had, according to Haggai, been caused by the failure of the returnees from Babylon to rebuild the Temple. (It was, rather, the failure of the returnees from Babylon who considered themselves too elite for heavy work, to persuade the common people who had stayed behind to rebuild the temple. We can easily understand how those who had stayed behind, and their descendants, would be none too thrilled, after having Jerusalem essentially to themselves for almost fifty years, to have the returnees attempt to reclaim their parents' and grandparents' former properties. We can also understand how those who had stayed behind and who were quite comfortable with living amongst those who worshipped the old Canaanite gods would resent the 'returnees' attempts to reimpose the religious system that had served King Josiah so poorly).

Haggai's second oracle, addressed to the political and religious leaders and the people, sought to encourage them in their rebuilding efforts. The third oracle was issued against the people for not acting in a holy manner (that is, not setting aside the old, but still perfectly serviceable, Canaanite gods yet once again), and the fourth proclaimed that Zerubbabel would be established as the Davidic ruler. This 'promise,' however, went unfulfilled. It seems apparent that Zerubbabel (or, perhaps, the high priest, Joshua), as Haggai's client, should be seen as the author of the *Book of Haggai*.

ca 520 BCE The *Book of Zecharaiah* gives us glimpses into the post-exilic period. Like Haggai, Zecharaiah wished to see the Temple rebuilt. He, too, urged Zerubbabel and the high priest Joshua, to push harder for its "reconstruction." He attempted to console everyone, especially those who had seen Solomon's temple in their childhood, that the glory of the second temple would, eventually, be greater than that of the first. And he ran the risk of offending the high priest, Joshua, by prophesying that sacrifices would be useless if the people failed to work zealously on the temple's reconstruction.

ca 500 BCE The Priests' Code was composed or completed in Babylon, having been blended with the *Law of Holiness* at about this time.

ca 475 BCE An anonymous writer, possibly Ezrah, writing under the pseudonym, Malachi, wrote the *Book of Malachi*, ostensibly by a prophet who would come to be known as the last of the twelve 'minor' prophets. The *Book of Malachi* is concerned with spiritual degradation, religious perversions, social injustices, and alleged unfaithfulness to the Covenant. Malachi condemned priests for failing to instruct the people on their Covenant responsibilities, attacked 'idolatry,' and heaped scorn on men for deliberately forgetting their marriage vows as their wives aged.

ca 458 BCE The priest and scribe, Ezra, was authorized by Artaxerxes I to take about 1,500 members of prominent Judaean and Benjamite families back to Jerusalem and what remained of Judah. Finally, the Redactor, whom Professor Friedman believes to have been Ezra, edited *Genesis, Judges, I and II Samuel, I Kings* and wrote the *Book of Ezra*. In *Surpassing Wonder, The Invention of the Bible and the Talmuds*, Professor Donald Harmon Akenson, credited the Redactor with being the true author of the *Bible* because the form in which we now have it is essentially that which he created. The Aramaic Documentary Source, Q, mentioned in *Ezra* 4-6, dates to about this time as does the *Book of Ruth*.

ca 444 BCE Artaxerxes sent his cupbearer, Nehemiah, to Jerusalem to serve as governor, an indication that Ezra had, not surprisingly, failed to gain control of the people there. Nehemiah served as governor in Jerusalem for twelve years. Nehemiah published the Priestly Code which Ezra had written earlier, while still in Babylon, and used it as the basis for his authority in ruling Judaea. Nehemiah's memoirs, kept during this period, were later used by the Chronicler as the principal basis for the *Book of Nehemiah*.

ca 440 BCE The *First Book of Psalms* was compiled; it includes *Psalms* 3-41. While some may date back to the Davidic period, not all of those ascribed to David date back to that time.

ca 400 BCE The *Book of Joel* was written by a priest who lived in the vicinity of the Temple in Jerusalem. While dating the writing of the *Book of Joel* is difficult, the destruction of Jerusalem had long since occurred and the exiles and/or their descendants had 'returned.' Scholars point out that *Joel* 3:5 plainly refers to long-familiar prophetic utterances.

ca 350 BCE An unknown author wrote the *Book of Jonah*, ostensibly written about a reluctant prophet purported to have lived during the reign of King Jeroboam II. Opinions as to the meaning of the book vary. One of the more interesting views is that of various nineteenth century bible scholars (notably Kleinert, Cheyne, and C. H. H. Wright), as described by S. R. Driver, that "Jonah symbolizes Israel as a nation, and the narrative is an allegory of Israel's history. Israel as a nation, it implies, had been entrusted with a prophetical commission to be a witness and upholder of Divine truth; but Israel shrank from executing this commission, and often apostatized; it was in consequence 'swallowed up' by the world-power Babylon as Jonah was swallowed by the fish; in exile, however, like Jonah, it sought its Lord, and thus was afterwards disgorged uninjured; after the return from exile, there were many who were disappointed that the judgments uttered by the prophets did not at once take effect and that the cities of the nations still stood secure, just as Jonah was disappointed that the judgment pronounced against Nineveh had been averted."

The *Second and Third Books of Psalms* were compiled.

The *Book of Proverbs* may have been completed at about this time. Few, if any, of the proverbs are believed to have been written by Solomon despite the tradition that he had. Some believe that the *Book of Proverbs* may have been written and/or redacted as late as 250 BCE.

ca 332 BCE — Onias I was the high priest in Jerusalem when Alexander the Great conquered Judaea and put Palestine under a Macedonian governor. The following year Alexander founded Alexandria. During this period all sorts of additions were made to the writings of the earlier prophets.

ca 323 BCE — Alexander the Great died in Babylon and a divisive struggle for control of his empire began. Three years later, Antigonus conquered Palestine. Thus began

	the Hellenistic period in Palestine; it lasted until 37 BCE.
320 BCE	The *Book of Job*, possibly an allegory by an unknown author about the treatment of Judah by Jahweh, may have been written at about this time.
ca 301 BCE	The Chronicler produced the *Book of Chronicles*, a vigorously edited version of the *Book of Kings*. It was designed to show that, among other things, the failure of certain kings, including all of the kings of the northern kingdom of Israel to suppress the worship of the old Canaanite gods had caused Jahweh to withdraw His support of Israel and Judah. The *Book of Ezra* and the *Book of Nehemiah* date to about this time.
ca 250 BCE	*Ecclesiastes* was written by a translator or copyist at the Library in Alexandria Egypt; the work was heavily influenced by the writings of Epicurus, the Greek philosopher who had died around 270 BCE. A few verses which conflict with the bulk of the book appear to have been added to *Ecclesiastes* before it was incorporated into the Jewish canon. The *Song of Songs* was written at about the same time and in the same place and by someone similarly employed. It is possible they were the product of the same hand.
197 BCE	Judaea became a province of the Seleucid Empire (Syria)
187-175 BCE	Seleucus IV. Beginning of Hellenistic infiltration, resisted by the Zadokite High Priest Onias III.
ca 175 BCE	The *Book of Esther*, written by a now unknown author, was a sort of early historical novel, primarily literary in nature. The version of the *Book of Esther* which appears in the *Hebrew Bible* does not so much

	as mention God once, a failing that was corrected by the later, revisionist editors who portrayed Esther as devout in their then new "Old Testament."
	Antiochus IV, Ephiphanes, began to Hellenize Judaea by force; the high priest, Onias III, was forced to yield control to his brother, Jason.
172 BCE	Menelaus assassinated Onias III and expelled Jason.
170 BCE	Jason returned from exile.
	Antiochus IV returned from Egypt and, the following year, took vengeance on the inhabitants of Jerusalem and plundered the temple.
168 BCE	Antiochus IV erected an altar to Zeus on the altar of the burnt offering at Jerusalem.
166 BCE	Rising of the Maccabees under leadership of Mudas Macccabee
ca 165 BCE	The *Book of Daniel*, though said to have been written during the early years of Nebuchadnezar, was, instead, a thinly disguised allegorical commentary on Antiochus Ephiphanes' savagely cruel treatment of the Jews (175-163 BCE).
	Daniel 11:3 appears to be describing Alexander, "Then a warrior king will appear who will have an extensive dominion and do as he pleases... but after his appearance, his kingdom will be broken up and scattered to the four winds of heaven, but not for any of his posterity, nor with dominion like that which he had..."
	Daniel 11:31 appears to be describing, in sufficiently vague terms, the setting up, by Antiochus IV, of the altar to Zeus, "Forces... will desecrate the temple, the fortress; they will abolish the regular offering and set

	up the appalling abomination."
160 BCE	Alcimus, the last Hellenizing High Priest died of a stroke; Syrian military intervention ends.
152-145 BCE	Alexander Balas seizes the Seleucid throne and appointed Jonathan High Priest.
145 BCE	Antiochus VI, son of Alexander, raised to the throne by Tryphon, his father's general. Jonathan named governor of Syria. Simon, his brother, made military governor of Palestine.
143 BCE	Jonathan arrested by Tryphon; Simon becomes High Priest and ethnarch.
142 BCE	Jonathan executed in prison.
ca 140 BCE	Simon's titles are confirmed as hereditary. The Maccabaean, or Hasmonaean, dynasty founded.
	The *Fourth and Fifth Books of Psalms* were added to the *Psalter* and the *Book of Judith* was written.
135 BCE	Simon murdered by his son-in-law; John Hyrcanus becomes High Priest and Ethnarch.
104 BCE	Aristobulus I becomes High Priest and king.
103-76 BCE	Alexander Jannaeus becomes High Priest and king but is opposed by the Pharisees.
76 BCE	Alexandra, widow of Jannaeus, becomes queen and is supported by the Pharisees; Hyrcanus II becomes High Priest.
67 BCE	Hyrcanus II becomes king—as well as High Priest—but is deposed by his brother, Aristobulus who becomes High Priest and King.
63 BCE	Aristobulus is taken prisoner by Pompey after the fall of Jerusalem. Judaea becomes a Roman province; Hyrcanus II reinstated as High Priest without the roy-

	al title.
40 BCE	Antigonus, son of Aristobulus II, takes the throne with Parthian support. Hyrcanus II exiled.
37 BCE	Herod the Great becomes king and rules until 4 BCE.
30 BCE	Hyrcanus II executed.
27 CE	Augustus, Emperor of Rome; rules until 14 CE.
ca 6 BCE	Jesus of Nazareth born.
4 BCE	Archaelaus ethnarch of Judaea and Samaria.
14 CE	Tiberius becomes emperor of Rome; rules until 37 CE.
26 CE	Pontius Pilate appointed prefect of Judaea.
ca 30 CE	Jesus executed for sedition.
66 CE	First Jewish War begins.
70 CE	Jerusalem captured, Jews slaughtered in vast numbers, and Temple destroyed.
ca 73	Masada falls.

Appendix 2

An Outline of The Book of Jashar

Beginning in the eighteenth century three works have been published claiming to be translations of the long-lost *Book of Jashar* or *Book of Jasher*. Although each of the three have interesting stories as to their provenance, all are believed to be forgeries. It is unlikely, but not entirely impossible, however, that a copy may someday be discovered in some desert cave.

The rarest of the three is the 414-page *The Book Jashar, The Lost Book of the Bible*, translated from the Original Hebrew by Rev. Dr. Edward B. M. Browne, published in New York by the United States Publishing Company in 1876. Whoever wrote the book translated by the Reverend Doctor Browne forgot to include David's elegy which would seem to indicate that it is either a forgery or incomplete.

There is a 254-page *Book of Jashar* originally published in the nineteenth century by J. H. Parry and a 63-page *Book of Jashar* published by the Rosicrucians in the twentieth century. Reprints of both of these books are currently available.

Emil Kautzsch attributed parts of *I Samuel* and *II Samuel* to a "David Source" and among those parts is David's elegy. He also identified parts of Joshua and Judges to a source of "Hero Stories." The material attributed to these two sources are, perhaps, all that is left, today, of David's original *Book of Jashar*. The locations of these verses—and fragments of verses—are briefly listed and summarized below. From them can be formed a better picture of what the *Book of Jashar* contained and, from that, we may be able to see how David intended to sway the loyalties of the various tribal elders.

Not surprisingly, there is relatively little that is favorable to Saul that would have appeared in the *Book of Jashar*. What little there is that is favorable about Saul would most likely have been added to the record some thirty or forty years after David's death—so sensitive was the issue—and, even then, as we shall see, hidden away in the form of an allegory where Saul is portrayed as Moses.

One method of determining which parts of the Hebrew *Bible* may have been included in the *Book of Jashar* is to first identify the source of *II Samuel* 1:17-27—and then find all other material attributed to that source and, second, to identify the source of *Joshua* 10:12-14—and then find all other material attributed to that source. Using Emil Kautzsch's identification of sources, the use following fragments is suggested as a possible way to partially reconstruct the *Book of Jashar*.

I Sam 16:14-23	Saul, having been abandoned by God (according to Samuel) begins to have spells. A search for a lyre-player results in David, son of Jesse, being invited to Saul's court to play music to cure the spells.
I Sam 18: 6-11	David gains fame as a warrior. Women sing that Saul has killed thousands but that David has killed tens of thousands. Saul begins to resent David's popularity. Saul hurls his spear at David in an apparent attempt to frighten David away, but David does not abandon Saul.
I Sam 20: 1-3	David and Jonathan meet to discuss how Saul plans to treat David.
I Sam 20: 11	Jonathan suggests that he and David go out into the open field.

I Sam 20: 18-39	David and Jonathan part.
I Sam 21: 1	David flees to Nob for food and a sword; Ahimelech, the high priest of the shrine inquires of David why it is that he is alone; David lies and says that he is on a secret mission for King Saul; Ahimelech supplies the food. When Saul finds out that David has escaped with Ahimelech's help, he orders that Ahimelech and all of the other priests be killed. Only Ahimelech's son, Abiathar, escapes and joins David.
I Sam 23: 1-5	David fights the Philistines.
I Sam 23: 7-13	Saul is told that David has gone to Keilah; David consults the ephod (Abiathar) and is advised that Saul will lay siege to Keilah and that the people of Keilah will turn him over to Saul; David and his six-hundred men leave Keilah immediately.
I Sam 23: 19	Ziphites advise Saul that David is hiding in the strongholds of Horesh; Saul sets out to capture David but turns back when he is advised that the Philistines have invaded Israel.
I Sam 24: ctd-13	David and his men hide out in the wilderness of En-gedi; Saul pursues David and, quite by chance, goes into a cave to relieve himself, unaware that David and his six-hundred men are hiding in the back of the cave; David sneaks up on Saul and cuts a piece of Saul's robe off; after Saul leaves the cave, David calls to him, shows him the piece of robe, whereupon Saul apologizes.
I Sam 25: 1b-44	Death of Samuel. David plays protection racket at Carmel. Nabal dies, his widow, Abigail, marries David who gets Nabal's property.

I Sam 27:	David hires out to Achish—and Achish pleased with David.
I Sam 28:1-2	Samuel dies and is buried at his home.
I Sam 28: 4-16	Saul visits the witch of Endor and asks to talk with Saul.
I Sam 28: 19b-25	Samuel's ghost predicts doom for Saul. Witch invites Saul to eat.
I Sam 29	David and Achish meet up with other Philistines at Aphek; David sent back because of opposition of other Philistine leaders; David leaves at daybreak the following day to return to Ziklag.
I Sam 30	David claims to have found Ziklag burned, and that his wives and those of his men, their children, and their property taken by the Amelekites while he and his men were meeting with Achish in Gath—and that it was for this reason that he then set out to take revenge on the Amelekites. It is more likely, however, that the Amelekite warriors are with Achish at Mount Gilboa, as will be seen below.
I Sam 28:3-25	A very frightened Saul seeks out a witch who can summon the dead. Saul orders her to summon up the ghost of Samuel so that he can ask for Samuel's help and advice. After reminding Saul that Saul had forbidden such practices, he assures her that she will not be punished; she then summons a very annoyed Samuel who refuses to help, reminds Saul that the Lord is no longer with him, and that he and his sons will die on the morrow.
I Sam 31	Battle at Mount Gilboa, Saul and three of his sons, including Jonathan, are slain.

II Sam 1:1-4 — An Amelekite warrior, acting as courier, brings David Saul's royal headpiece and armband. Amelekite claims to have killed Saul, thinking it would please David. David, however, punishes Amelekite for regicide. Though nothing is said about the Amelekites serving Achish as mercenaries, the presence of this Amelekite would seem to suggest that had been the case.

II Sam 1:11-12 — David and his men tear their clothes and mourn Saul and Jonathan.

II Sam 1:17-27 — David sang the following lament for Saul and Jonathan which is said to have appeared in the *Book of Jashar* at Ziklag, circa 1005 BC:

"The splendor, O Israel,
  on your heights lies slain,
How have the warriors fallen!
Tell it not in Gath,
  proclaim not in Ashkelon's streets,
Lest the Philistine daughters rejoice,
  lest the daughters of the uncircumcised gloat.
O hills of Gilboa—no dew
  and no rain upon you, O lofty fields
For there the warriors' shield was besmirched,
  the shield of Saul unfurnished with oil.
From the blood of the slain,
  from the warriors' fat—
Jonathan's bow did not retreat
  and the sword of Saul
  never turned away empty.
Saul and Jonathan, beloved and dear,
  in their life and their death
  they were not parted

They were swifter than eagles,
  and stronger than lions.
O daughters of Israel, weep over Saul,
  who clothed you in scarlet and bangles.
  who studded your garments
  with jewelry of gold.
How have the warriors fallen
  in the midst of the battle.
Jonathan, upon your heights slain!
I grieve for you my brother, Jonathan.
  Very dear you were to me.
More wondrous your love to me
  than the love of women.
How have the warriors fallen,
  and the gear of battle is lost."
(*II Samuel* 1:17-27 RA)

II Sam 2:1-9	David calls for ephod (Abiathar) and asks God whether he should go up to Hebron.
II Sam 2:10b-12	The Lord (Abiathar) advises David to go to Hebron.
II Sam 2:17-end	Battle between Joab's (David's) men and Abner's men; Abner kills Joab's brother.
II Sam 3:1	David's forces getting stronger.
II Sam 3: 6b-29	Abner getting stronger than Ishbosheth; Joab kills Abner.
II Sam 3: 31-39	David orders Joab and his men to mourn Abner; David sings lament.
II Sam 4: 1-3	Ishbosheth informed of Abner's death.
II Sam 4: 5-12	Rechab and Baanah, two of Ishbosheth's commanders, murder Ishbosheth and report Ishbosheth's death to David; David orders his men to

	kill Rechab and Baanah; his men cut their hands and feet off and hang them up.
II Sam 5:1-2	The elders of the tribes of Israel meet and elect David king of Israel.
II Sam 5: 17-25	The Philistines hear that David has become king of Israel and attack; David defeats them and once more there is peace.

Abiathar, presumably David's longtime personal scribe, outlived David and while he was shortly thereafter banished to the small village of Anathoth, a few miles outside Jerusalem, he may have added the following two items to his copy of the B*ook of Jashar*.

II Sam 21: 15-22	David's last battle. Troops fear defeat if David were to be killed.
II Sam 23: 8-39	David's last words.

In addition to the stories praising David there were stories about the legendary heros of the dozen or so tribes whom Saul and, later, David, sought to unite. Kautzsch identifies two sources (though sometimes with reservations) for the remnants of the "Hero Stories," the first of which is an "older stratum of the ancient Hero-Stories," listed below.

Judges 8:4-10a	Gideon crosses the Jordan.
Judges 8:11-21	Gideon captures the two kings of Midian.
Judges 8:24-27a	Gideon collects the Israelites gold to make a golden ephod.
Judges 8:29-32	Gideon's son, Abimelech, is born; Gideon dies.
Judges 9:1-37	Abimelech kills his 70 brothers, he conquers Schechem by fire, he dies.

The second part "from the early part of the Kingly period," are listed below.

Judges 3:15b-26	Ehud, a left-handed Benjamite, kills the Moabite king, Eglon.

Judges 3:27-28	The conquest of Moab.
Judges 4:4-22	Deborah, an Israelite prophetess, kills Sisera, a Canaanite army commander.
Judges 5:1-31a	The Song of Deborah and Barak.
Judges 6:2b-6	Troubles between the Israelites and the Midianites.
Judges 6:11-33	Gideon destroys his father's altar to Baal.
Judges 6:36-40	The miracle of the fleece and the threshing floor.
Judges 7:1-11	The story of a victory by the few over the many.
Judges 7:13-25	The warrior's dream, Gideon's interpretation and victory.
Judges 8:1-3	Gideon and Ephraim.
Judges 8:22-23	Israelites offer to be ruled by Gideon.
Judges 10:8a	Abimelech.
Judges 11:1-11	Jepthah, his "men of low character," and the Amorites.
Judges 11:30-40	Jepthah and the sacrifice of his daughter.
Judges 12:1-6	Jepthah, the Gideonites, and the Ephraimites.
Judges 13:2-3	Zorah, a Danite, to have a son, the first to deliver Israel from the Philistines.
Judges 13:5-25	Zorah has a son, Samson.
Judges 14:4	Samson, the lion, and the riddle of the honey.
Judges 15:1-19	Samson and the Philistines.
Joshua 10:12-14	Joshua commands the sun to stand still during the Israelites battle.

THE AUTHORS OF THE BOOK OF SAMUEL: WHO WROTE WHAT

The way in which the *Book of Samuel*—originally all in one book—was put together, was described in the *Die Heilige Schrift des Alten Testaments*, translated and edited by Emil Kautzsch, a professor of theology and Hebrew at the University of Halle, Germany. In the 1895 edition, Kautzsch attributed the verses of *I* and *II Samuel* and the first two chapters of *I Kings* to the following dozen or so authors listed, chronologically, below.

Kautzsch used the letter **S** to indicate the "Saul-Source, a Judahite or Benjamite history of Saul, dating from the tenth or ninth century" BCE.

The letters **Da** indicate the "David-Source, in all probability a Judahite history of David, contemporary with **S**, perhaps from the same hand". The elegy that David composed at Ziklag in 1005 BCE upon learning of the deaths of Saul and all but one of his sons at Mount Gilboa originally appeared in the long lost *Book of Jashar*; it now appears in *II Samuel*:19-27

Kautzsch used the letters **Je** to indicate the "Jerusalem-Source, an old history of David, written most probably in Jerusalem, in any case in Judah, dating from the time of Solomon or Rehoboam."

Kautzsch used the letters **SS** to indicate a "considerably later history of Samuel and Saul, probably Ephraimite, a combination of diverse traditions, perhaps dating from the second half of the eighth century" BCE.

E was the letter Kautzsch used to indicate those passages he believed to be "Ephraimite narratives… extracts from a historical work which appeared in the northern kingdom, dating probably from the ninth century" BCE. In examining the material Kautzsch attributed to **E**, it seems more likely that the author was the Priestly Source, **P**, working sometime between the reign of King Hezekiah and the exile in Babylon.

Kautzsch used the letters **Dt** to indicate the Deuteronomist working during the reign of King Josiah in the late 7th century BCE.

R was the letter Kautzsch used to indicate the Redactor who is generally believed to have combined pieces of a wide variety of documents into a nearly final version of the books between *Genesis* and the end of *II Kings*.

Two other authors were simply identified as **Ri**, and **(H)**, while passages of unidentified origin were simply indicated with a question mark, "?"

I SAMUEL

1: 1-5a **SS**, 5b **R**, 6-28 SS

2: 1-10 R, 11-26 SS, 27-36 **Dt**

3: 1-21a SS, 21b R

4: 1-18a **E***, 18b R, 19-21a E*, 22 R

5: 1-12 E*

6: 1-14E*, 15 R, 16 E*, 17-18a R, 18b-21 E*

7: 1 E*, 2a R, 2b-16 Dt, 17 R

8: 1-22 SS

9: 1-8 S, 9 R, 10-27 S

10: 1-7 S, 8 R, 9-16 S, 17-24 SS, 25-27 R

11: 1-11 S, 12-15 R

12: 1-25 **Ri** (Dt)

13: 1 R, 2-7 S, 8-15a R, 15b-18 S, 19-22 R, 23 S

14: 1-1-46 S, 47-51 Ri, 52 R

15: 1-35 S

16: 1-13 R, 14-24 **Da**

17: 1-11 SS, 12a (Ri)R, 12b-14 (**H**)SS, 15 (H) R, 16-31 (H)SS, 32-38a SS, 38b (H)SS, 39-40a R, 40b H, 48c SS, 48d (H), 49 SS, 50 (H)SS, 51-54 SS, 55-58 (H)SS

18: 1-5 (H)SS, 6a (H)Da, 6b R, 6c -7 Da, 8a (H)R, 8b-11 Da, 12a SS, 12b (H)SS, 13-15 SS

19: 1-19 (H)SS, 20-21a Da, 21b H?, 22-26a Da, 26b (H)R, 27 Da, 28 SS, 29-30 (H)SS

20: 1a R, 1b-11 Da, 12-17 ?, 18-39 Da, 40-42 R

21: 1 Da, 2-10 SS, 11-16 ?

22: 1-23 SS

23: 1-5 Da, 6 R, 7-13 Da, 14-18 R, 19-28 Da

24: 1-23 Da

25: 1a R, 1b-44 Da

26: 1-25 SS

27: 1-12 Da

28: 1-2 Da, 3 R, 4-16 Da, 17-18 R, 19-25 Da

29: 1-11 Da

30: 1-33 Da

31: 1-15 Da

II SAMUEL

1: 1-4 Da, 5 R, 6-16 SS, 17-27 Da

2: 1-9 Da, 10a R, 10b Da, 11 R, 12 Da, 13-16 ?

3: 1 Da, 2-5 ?, 6-29 Da, 30 R, 31-20 Da

4: 1-3 Da, 4 R, 5-12 Da

5: 1-2 Da, 3 Je, 4-5 R, 6-7a Je, 7b R, 8-15 Je

6: 1-23 **Je**

7: 1-29 (Je)Dt

8: 1-10 (?)R, 11 R, 13-18 (?)R

9: 1-13 Je

10; 1-19 Je

11; 1-27 Je

12: 1-9 Je, 1-12 R, 13-31 Je

13: 1-39 Je

14: 1-33 Je

15: 1-37 Je

16: 1-23 Je

17: 1-29 Je

18: 1-32 Je

19: 1-44 Je

20: 1-26 Je

21: 1-2a ?, 2b R, 3-14 ?, 15-22 Da

22: 1-2a, R, 2b-51 ?

23: 1a R, 2b-7 ?, 8-38 Da

24: 1-25 ?

I KINGS

1: 1-53 Da

2: 1-9 Dt, 10-12 R, 13-26 Da, 27 Dt, 28-46 Da

APPENDIX 4

AN OUTLINE OF THE DEUTERONOMIST'S WORK

The verses cited below are attributed to the Deuteronomist by Emil Kautzsch in *An Outline of the History of the Literature of the Old Testament*. The scroll discovered during the Temple renovation in 621 BCE may have included material beginning with the verses cited below in the original of the *Book of Deuteronomy*:

4:44-49	"This is the teaching that Moses set before the people..."
5:1-29	Establishes Covenant
6:1-25-36	Establishes Law Israelites required to slaughter their enemies
7:1-36	Israelites required to slaughter their enemies
8:1-20	Reviews the Exodus and renews promises to the Israelites
9:1-29	"Reminds" Israelites of the original Covenant
10:1-5	Moses told to create second set of commandments
10:10-32	Moses told to build an Ark
11:1-28	Reminds Israelites of Exodus and Covenant
12:1-31	Israelites ordered to eliminate worship of all other gods
13:1-19	Orders Israelites not to add to, nor to subtract from, the Law

14:1-29	Specifies death rituals and establishes laws for food, taxes, and care of the Levites
15:1-23	Mandates concern for the poor and needy, establishes a tax code
16:1-22	Establishes Passover holiday
17:1-20	Mandates quality of sacrifices, makes religious deviation a capital offense
18:1-32	Establishes rules regarding Levites, foreigners, and prophets
19:1-21	Establishes rules for acquiring and subdividing land
20:1-20	Admonishes Israelites not to fear enemies who outnumber them or are better equipped
21:1-23	Establishes rules regarding murder, slaves, defiant children, executions
22:1-29	Establishes rules concerning divorce and defaming of virgins
23:1-26	Prohibition of help to strangers except Egyptians and Moabites
24:1-22	Rules for marriage, divorce, military service, and hired help
25:1-19	More marriage laws, fair weights and measures, slaughter of Amelekites
26:1-15	Formulae for appropriating land belonging to others
28:1-68	Blessings for the righteous and curses for the wicked
31:9-13	Tells how Moses wrote down this teaching and required it to be read

Using a large number of previously existing records of kings' reigns, stories of old prophets, etc, the Deuteronomist wove them together. Thus the original of the *Book of Kings* probably dates to this time.

In addition to the writing of the original *Book of Deuteronomy*, the Deuteronomist also inserted material into the then-existing books of Joshua and Samuel.

JOSHUA

1:3-9	Inserts a description of the Covenant
1:12-18	Orders the taking of Canaan and makes disobedience a capital offence
2:9b-11	Reminds the Israelites of an incident of Exodus
2:24	States that their enemies are powerless
3:7	Yahweh promises His support as His end of the bargain
4:14	Emphasizes the power of Jahweh
4:21-24	Emphasizes the power of Jahweh
5:1	Recapitulates the borders of the land Yahweh has promised the Israelites
8:1-2	Admonition to be fearless
8:27	"Only the cattle and spoil of that city Israel took for a prey unto themselves
8:31-35	Joshua reads the terms of the Covenant to the Israelites
9:1-2	Israelites enemies unite to fight Joshua
9:27c	"even unto this day, in the place which he should choose"
10:1	"Now it came to pass, when Adonizedec, king of Jerusalem, had heard
10:25	"And Joshua said unto them, Fear not nor be dismayed, be strong . . ."
10:28-43	"And that day Joshua took Makedah and smote it with the edge of his sword

11:10-23	Joshua makes the sun stand still; Joshua captures five kings hiding in a cave
12:1-24	"Now these are the kings of the land, which the children of Israel smote"
13:1-14	"Now Joshua was old and stricken in years"
14:6-15	Joshua recalls old times and places including their stay at Kadesh-Barnea
21:43-45	"And the Lord gave unto Israel all the land which He sware to give"
22:1-6	Joshua praises the Reubenites, Gadites, and the half-tribe of Manasseh"
23:1-16	Joshua's farewell address reminds the Israelites of their Covenant obligations

I SAMUEL

2:27-31a	Jahweh upset at Eli's sons placing themselves above Him
2:32a	Jahweh predicts early deaths for Eli's male descendants
2:33-36	Jahweh promises to raise up a faithful priest (Samuel) to be Eli's successor
7:2b-16	Ark is stranded in Kirjath-jearim for twenty years
14:47-51	Saul wages war against the Philistines and Amelekites

II SAMUEL

7:1-12	David discusses a more appropriate home (a temple) for the Ark
7:14-29	The Lord promises to establish David's descendants as kings forever

I KINGS

2:1-9	David tells Solomon to keep the Covenant with the Lord
3:1-2	Solomon builds a palace for Pharaoh's daughter while the people worship on hilltops
3:4	Solomon goes to a hilltop himself where he has a dream
3:14	The Lord tells Solomon to keep the Covenant as his father, David, had
4:13b	Territorial data
4:19b-34	Territorial data
5:1	Hiram of Tyre introduces himself to Solomon as an admirer of David
5:16-23	Details of Solomon's building of the temple
6:7	Details of Solomon's temple
6:9	Details of Solomon's temple: construction of cedar
6:11-14	Lord renews his Covenant with Solomon
6:18-22	Details of the richness of Solomon's temple
6:28-30	"And he overlaid the cherubims with gold . . ."
6:32	"The two doors were of olive tree and he carved upon them"
6:35	"And he carved thereon cherubims"
6:38	Completion of the temple after seven years of effort.
8:2	Gathering of "men of Israel"
8:3b	"and the priests took up the Ark"
8:9	"There was nothing in the Ark save he two tables of stone"
8:14-43	"And the king turned his face about, and blessed all the congregation"

8:52-64	Public recitation of the Covenant by Solomon
8:65-66	Claims that Solomon celebrated a seven day Passover holiday
9:10-11	Hiram, who had built Solomon's palace and temple, complains
9:19-21	Description of Solomon's wealth and policies
9:25-28	States that Solomon offered burnt offerings
10:11-12	Describes Solomon's navy bringing gold and precious stones from Ophir
10:14-15	"Now the weight of the gold... was six-hundred three-score and six talents
10:20b-27	Of Solomon's throne, "there was not the like made in any kingdom"
11:1-9a	Solomon loved many strange women, together with Pharaoh's daughter
11:11-13	"...the Lord said unto Solomon... thou has not kept my covenant"
11:29-39	The prophet Ahijah prophesies that Jeroboam will rule over ten tribes
11:41-43	"the rest of the acts of Solomon... in the book of the acts of Solomon?"
12:15	The Lord causes Rehoboam to act foolishly and lose the northern kingdom
12:26-31	Jeroboam worries about losing his kingdom to Rehoboam
13:33b-34	"Jeroboam... made... the lowest of the people priests"
14:1-18	Jeroboam sends his wife to see the prophet Abijah at Shiloh
14:19-24	"the rest of the acts of Jeroboam, how he warred, and how

	he reigned"
14:29-31	"the rest of the acts of Rehoboam, and all that he did, are they not written in"
15:1-5b	"in the eighteenth year of king Jeroboam... Abijam reigned over
15:7-15	"Now the rest of the acts of Abijam, and all that he did"
15:23-34	"The rest of all the acts of Asa"
16:5-11	"Now the rest of the acts of Baasha"
16:14-20	"Now all the rest of the acts of Elah, and all that he did"
16:23	"In the thirty and first year of Asa king of Judah began Omri to reign"
16:29	End of Omri's kingdom
21:20b-22	Prophesies doom for house of Ahab
21:24	"Him that dieth of Ahab in the city the dogs shall eat"
22:39-54	"Now the rest of the acts of Ahab"

APPENDIX 5

A BRIEF COMMENTARY ON THE ORIGIN OF THE PSALMS

A new song book, *The Book of Psalms*,[1] may have been among the many innovations Ezra introduced with the hope of unifying the Jewish people after the rebuilding of the temple in Jerusalem the fifth century BCE. Originally a single pair of books, the *Book of Psalms* was repeatedly rearranged, divided, added to, and edited until by the time the Hebrew *Bible*, having assumed its final form, it was translated into Greek in Alexandria circa 250 BCE. Additions continued until the time of the Maccabees.

Some of the songs in the original compilation circa 440 BCE were undoubtedly old. Determining the age of each psalm or, indeed, any of the psalms, is far from a straightforward matter. That seventy three of the one hundred fifty psalms are credited to David does not establish a tenth century BCE date for the origin of those psalms because, as will subsequently be shown, it is unlikely that David wrote any of the psalms attributed to him.

That a dozen psalms are attributed to Asaph and one each to Ethan, and Heman—men reputed to have been leading Temple singers in the days of David—does not establish their antiquity. The *Book of Chronicles* would seem to establish Asaph and Heman[2] as contemporaries and an insertion in *I Kings*, which states, referring to King Solomon:

> For he was wiser than all men; than Ethan the Ezrahite, and Heman, and Chalcol and Darda, the sons of Mahol; and his

fame was in all nations roundabout.[3]

would seem to establish Ezra and Heman as Solomon's contemporaries but, such was not the case despite the Chronicler's reporting their having such roles. They—the psalms as well as their putative authors and composers—date to a time not earlier than the Second Temple period though they may have used other material as a base.

Similarly those attributed to the Korahites, a clan of famous temple singers, do not date to the time of Moses.

Certain psalms not betrayed by clues pointing to a relatively late period, are of a universal nature, useful in any age. These we may believe to be genuinely old or adapted from songs that were. Provenance, however, is not the issue, utility is.

Since the five books of psalms seem to be arranged in a chronological sequence—though some individual psalms may have been moved from one book to another—the discussion of authorship or composition which follows looks at each of the five books and their contents in the sequence in which they now appear.

Ezra may have caused Book I and Book II of the *Book of Psalms* to be produced at the same time, to serve two different constituencies: Book I for the Yahwists, Book II for the Elohists.

BOOK I

With 272 references to Yahweh and only 15 to Elohim, Book I is primarily a Yawistic song book.

The compilation of Book I, consisting of forty-one psalms, Psalms 1 through 41 inclusive, may have begun as early as the time of the Exile. Throughout Book I, as throughout all of the five books of psalms, there are numerous instances of great poetic beauty. While the provenance of the psalms poses a number of problems for scholars, that does not affect the beauty of the psalms themselves.

Although of the forty-one psalms in Book I thirty-seven are attributed to David, it is unlikely that any of them were written by David. Psalm 7, at verse 9, for example, clearly indicates that the congregation is ruled by a theocracy. Psalm 9, verse 18, would seem, because of its mention of Sheol,[4] to indicate a relatively late origin, certainly not Davidic; the same criterion would apply to Psalm 16, verse 10. The knowledge of metallurgy implied by Psalm 12, verse 7, indicates a post-Davidic time.

The only four psalms in Book I not attributed to David are Psalm 1 which expresses the fundamental ethical ideas of the *Psalter*, Psalm 2 which supports the theocracy and Israel's messianic, post-monarchic hopes, and Psalms 10 and 33. Since, together, Psalms 1 and 2 provide a program for the entire *Psalter*,[5] it is likely that they were the last, or among the last psalms, to be added.

In general, the speaker in the psalms is not a single godly man but the godly community of the post-exilic time[6]—a fact which would tend to rule David out as a possible author, not only of the psalms in Book I, but of any of the psalms in the entire *Psalter*.

BOOK II

With 164 references to Elohim and only 30 references to Yahweh, Book II is primarily an Eloistic song book. Consisting of thirty-one psalms, Psalms 42 through 72 inclusive, Book II is believed to have been compiled around the time of Ezra.[7] Eighteen of the thirty-one psalms are attributed to David."

Seven of the psalms, Psalms 42 and 44 through 49 inclusive, are attributed to the Sons of Korah—which is surprising since all of the sons of Korah were supposed to have perished after their rebellion against the legendary Moses and Moses' brother, Aaron. The interest of the Korahites in the burning of incense indicates a much later time than that of Moses and Aaron. Korahites may have existed during the time of King

Uzziah[8] who, in his later years, took an unsuccessful and nearly fatal interest in breaking the sons of Aaron's incense monopoly.

Psalm 50 is attributed to Asaph, a Levite in charge of the singing at the Temple. Although I Chronicles places him as living at the time of King David, his psalms are said to have been used during the reign of King Hezekiah.[9] Psalm 50's reference to the Covenant would seem to place its origin as being no earlier than King Hezekiah and the origin of the Priestly Code. It is only somewhat more likely to have originated during the reign of King Josiah. In either of these two cases, it would seem to have been passed on orally until its inclusion in Book II. The inclusion of Psalms 73 and 83, attributed to Asaph, in Book III would seem to place Asaph himself at sometime in the Persian age.[10]

Of particular note are the references to Tyre, Assyria, and other nations in Psalm 83, verses 6 through 12 which would suggest a date long after the reign of King David and King Solomon.

One of the psalms, Psalm 72, is attributed to King Solomon but Solomonic authorship is unlikely, principally because, it refers, throughout, to the king in the third person. The wish, referring to the king, that:

> "May his name be eternal; while the sun lasts, may his name endure; let men invoke his blessedness upon themselves, let all nations count him happy"

would seem exceptionally vain, even for King Solomon, if it had come from his hand!

Book II concludes, at verse 20 of Psalm 89, with

> "End of the prayers of David son of Jesse,"

implying, it would seem, that any psalms attributed to David in any of the remaining three books would have been misattributed. It is possible that verse 20 of Psalm 89 was added to Book II by the compiler of Book III, thus identifying it as being suited to post-monarchic times.

BOOK III

Book III, consisting of seventeen psalms, Psalms 73 through 89 inclusive, is believed to have been compiled toward the end of the Persian age.[11] According to Emil Kautzsch, Book III was created by:

> "a redactor who wished to supplement a collection of David poems by a gleaning of non-Davidic ones (already, however, ascribed to David's choirmasters).[12]

One of the seventeen psalms, Psalm 86, is attributed to David, probably erroneously since Psalm 72 states that the "psalms of David end here. It could be convincingly argued that the psalms in the Psalter have been rearranged, but that, too, poses a problem since, in that case, the ending verse of Psalm 72 would then be an embarrassing error.

Two psalms, Psalms 73 and 83 are attributed to Asaph; two psalms, Psalms 84 and 87 are attributed to the Sons of Korah. The comments about the sons of Korah above, with reference to Book III, apply here, too.

One psalm, Psalm 88 is attributed to Heman, said to have lived in the time of King David and King Solomon though, for a variety of reasons, that is unlikely. Much more likely would be the time of King Hezekiah or even much later.

One psalm, Psalm 89 is attributed to Ethan of Ezrah said to have lived in the time of King Solomon. If so, Psalm 89 would seem to have been passed down orally—a perfectly reasonable thing for a song. Psalm 89 makes an interesting reference to the Canaanite god, Rahab:

> You crushed Rahab; he was like a corpse

In Book III, references to Elohim outweigh references to Yahweh by 107 to 44.

BOOK IV

Book IV, consisting of seventeen psalms, Psalms 90 through 106 inclusive, is believed to have been compiled around 300 BCE. Two of the psalms are attributed to David, probably erroneously since Psalm 72 concludes, at verse 20, as noted above, by saying "End of the prayers of David son of Jesse."

One psalm, Psalm 90, is attributed to Moses, almost certainly erroneously. First, it refers to the span of human life as:

> "seventy years, or, given the strength, eighty years"[13]

something that Moses, said to have died in good health at the age of one-hundred and twenty,[14] would have found too limiting although, admittedly, we do not know how old Moses was supposed to be when he wrote this psalm. There is also no mention in Exodus of Moses having written any psalms, but that does not prove that Moses did not write Psalm 90. Instead, as has been discussed earlier in this book, if the biblical character Moses were allegorical, and based upon Israel's first king, Saul, then such attribution would have been known, by its author, to be false.

In Book IV Yahweh is the only divine name used.

BOOK V

Book V, consisting of forty-four psalms, Psalms 107 through 150 inclusive, is believed to have been completed around the time of Simon, the founder of the Hasmonean dynasty, circa 142 BCE.[15] At least one of the psalms, Psalm 127, appears to have been written as early as 250 BCE, perhaps in Alexandria.

All but one of the references to a divine name in Book V are to Yahweh. The one exception occurs in Psalm 108. Since the five books are arranged more or less chronologically, the ebb and flow of the use of one divine name or the other would seem to provide some sort of historical insight.

Fifteen of the psalms—Psalm 108-110, 122, 124, 131, 138-145—are attributed to David. We can say that such attribution is probably erroneous since, as noted previously, Psalm 72 states that the "psalms of David end here."

Further, the observation in Psalm 108, that God has:

> "rejected us… you do not march with our armies…"

does not sound like David at all! For one thing, David's principal use of priestly skills involved divination; for another, it is almost unthinkable that David would risk a deterioration of his soldiers' morale with such a negative statement.

Psalm 109 has some of the same spirit as Psalm 108 and Psalm 110 is positively anti-monarchic—something one would not expect from David. Psalm 122 was obviously written long after the time of David, "There the thrones of judgment stood, thrones of the house of David." Psalm 131's

> "O Israel, wait for the Lord now and forever"

is hard to imagine coming from the mouth or hand of David. Psalms 138-145 all seem to indicate having been written long after the time of David.

Emil Kautzsch has noted that Psalm 119, which is anonymous, makes frequent references throughout to the law, something which occurs but infrequently in the psalms.

Psalm 127 is the second psalm in the Psalter attributed to King Solomon but its thought, though less secular than Ecclesiastes, also attributed to Solomon, seems more akin to the spirit of the author of Ecclesiastes. If so, it would seem to have been written circa 250 BCE. Psalm 127 speaks for itself:

A song of ascents. Of Solomon
Unless the Lord builds the house
  its builders labor in vain on it
  unless the Lord watches over the city
  The watchman keeps vigil in vain
In vain do you rise early
  and stay up late,
  you who toil for the bread you eat;
He provides as much for His loved ones while they sleep
Sons are the provision of the Lord
  the fruit of the womb, His reward.
Like arrows in the hand of a warrior
  are sons born to a man in his youth.
Happy is the man who fills his quiver with them;
  they shall not be put to shame
  when they contend with the enemy in the gate.

ENDNOTES

1. *II Chronicles* 29:25 refers to the existence of psalteries in King Hezekiah's time. While this is entirely possible, it is unlikely that any psalteries existing in Hezekiah's time closely resemble any of the current five books of Psalms.
2. *II Chronicles* 5:12; see also *II Chronicles* 29:25
3. *I Kings* 4:31
4. See *Surpassing Wonder, The Invention of the Bible and the Talmuds*, by Donald Harmon Akenson, Harcourt Brace, New York, 1999, pp 167, 186
5. Kautzsch, Emil, *An Outline of the Literature of the Old Testament*, Williams and Norgate, London, 1898, p 146
6. Kautzsch, op cit., p 147
7. Kautzsch, op cit., p 146
8. *II Chronicles* 26:16-21
9. See Kautzsch, op cit., p 146
10. Kautzsch, op cit., p 145

11. Kautzsch, op cit., p 145

12. Kautzsch, op cit., p 144

13. *Psalm* 90, verse 10

14. *Deuteronomy* 34:5-7 reads "So Moses the servant of the Lord died there, in the land of Moab, at the command of the Lord. He buried him in the valley in the land of Moab, near Beth-peor; and no one knows his burial place to this day. Moses was a hundred and twenty years old when he died; his eyes were undimmed and his vigor unabated." Deuteronomy implicitly attributes this statement to Moses' authorship, which, aside from being unlikely in the extreme, is one of the things that caused Hobbes and Spinoza to question the nature of the Mosaic authorship of the Pentateuch! How could Moses have known that the site of his grave would go unknown 'til the time of King Josiah?

15. Kautzsch, op cit., p 145

BIBLIOGRAPHY

Akenson, Donald H., *Surpassing Wonder, the Invention of the Bible and the Talmuds*, Harcourt, 1998

Albright, William, *Archaeology, Historical Analogy and Early Biblical Tradition*, Louisiana State University Press, Baton Rouge 1966

Alter, Robert, *Genesis*, W. W. Norton, New York, 1996

Alter, Robert, *The Art of Biblical Narrative*, Basic Books, 1991

Alter, Robert, *The David Story*, W. W. Norton, New York, 1999

Alter, Robert, *The Five Books of Moses*, W. W. Norton, New York, 2004

American Bible Society, *The Holy Bible*, New York, 1860

Astruc, Jean, *Conjectures sur La Genese*, Noesis, Paris, 1999 (originally published 1753)

Barks, Coleman (translator), *The Essential Rumi*, Castle Books, Edison, New Jersey, 1995

Barr, James, *The Literal, The Allegorical, and Modern Biblical Scholarship*, Journal for the Study of the Old Testament (JSOT) 44, 3-17, 1989

Ben-Tor, Amnon, *The Archaeology of Ancient Israel*, New Haven, 1992

Bloch, Ariel and Chana Bloch, *The Song Of Songs, A New Translation*, University of California Press, Berkeley and Los Angeles, 1995

Bloom, Harold, *The Book of J*, Random House, New York, 1990

Booth, Wayne C., *The Rhetoric of Fiction*, University of Chicago Press, 1970

Bright, John, *A History of Israel, Third Edition*, Westminster John Knox Press, Louisville, 1981

Browne, Edward B. M., translator, *The Book of Jashar*, New York, 1876

Budde, K., under the editorial direction of Paul Haupt, T*he Books of Samuel, Critical Edition of the Hebrew Text*, Johns Hopkins Press, Baltimore 1894

Burton, Captain Sir Richard F., *The Gold Mines of Midian and the Ruined Midianite Cities*, Paul Kegan & Co., London, 1878

Carlson, R, David, *The Chosen King*, Almqvist & Wiksell, Uppsala, 1964

Carroll, R. P., *Psalm LXXVIII: Vestiges of a Tribal Polemic*, Vetus Testamentum (VT) 21/2 (1971) 133-50

Casson, Lionel, *Libraries of the Ancient World*, Yale University Press, New Haven, 2001

Clayton, Peter, *Chronicle of the Pharaohs*, Thames & Hudson, London, 1994

Clements, Ronald E., *Abraham and David*, SCM Press, London, 1967

Clements, Ronald E., *The World of Ancient Israel*, Cambridge University Press, 1991

Bibliography

Coote, Robert, *In Defense of Revolution, the Elohist Narrative*, Fortress Press, Philadelphia, 1991

Coote, Robert, and Ord, Robert, *The Bible's First History*, Fortress Press, Philadelphia, 1989

Coote, Robert, and Ord, Robert, *In the Beginning, the Priestly Narrative*, Fortress Press, Philadelphia

Cross, Frank Moore, *Canaanite Myth and Hebrew Epic*, Harvard University Press, Cambridge, 1973

Day, John, *Pre-Deuteronomic Allusions to the Covenant in Hosea and Psalm LXXVIII*, VT 36, 1

Daniell, David, *William Tyndale, A Biography*, Yale University Press, New Haven, 1994

Davies, Philip R., *Scribes and Schools*, Westminster John Knox Press, Louisville, 1998

Dever, William, *Who Were the Early Israelites and Where Did They Come From?*, 2003

Driver, Samuel Rolles, *Introduction to the Literature of the Old Testament*, Scribners', New York, 1913

Driver, Samuel Rolles, The Polychrome Bible, Part 3, *The Book of Leviticus*, Dodd Mead, and Company, New York 1898

Duff, Archibald, *History of Old Testament Criticism*, Watts & Co., London, 1910

Eco, Umberto, *Misreadings*, Harcourt, Inc., Orlando, Florida, 1993

Ehrman, Bart D., *Jesus, Apocalyptic Prophet Of The New Millennium*, Oxford University Press, New York, 1999

Ehrman, Bart D., *Misquoting Jesus*, HarperSanFrancisco, San Francisco, 2005

Eichorn, *Einleitung ins Alte Testament*, Leipzig, 1780

Emerton, J. A., *The Riddle of Genesis 14*, VT 21/4 (1971) 403-39

Falk, Marcia, *The Song Of Songs, A New Translation and Interpretation*, HarperSanFrancisco, 1990

Finkelstein, Israel, *Archaeological and Historical Aspects of Early Israel*, Yad Ben-Zvi, 1990

Finkelstein, Israel, *The Archaeology of the Israelite Settlement*, Israel Exploration Society, 1986

Finkelstein, Israel, and Silberman, Neil Asher, *David and Solomon*, Free Press, a Simon & Schuster imprint, 2006

Finkelstein, Israel, and Silberman, Neil Asher, *The Bible Unearthed*, Simon & Schuster, 2002

Finkelstein, Israel, *The Emergence of the Monarchy in Israel*, JSOT 44, 43-74, 1989

Fredericks, Daniel C., *Life's Storms and Structural Unity in Qoheleth 11.1-12.8*, JSOT 52, 95-114

Freedman, David, *The Anchor Bible Dictionary*, Doubleday, New York, 1992

Friedman, Richard Elliott, *Who Wrote The Bible?,* Harper, 1987

Friedman, Richard Elliott, *The Hidden Book In The Bible*, Harper, 1998

Friedman, Richard Elliott, *The Bible With Sources Revealed*, HarperSanFrancisco, San Francisco, 2003

Garsiel, Moshe, *I Samuel: A Literary Study*, Rubin Mass Ltd, Jerusalem, 1990

Geisler, Norman L., and Nix, William E., *A General Introduction to the Bible*, Moody Press, Chicago 1968

George, Andrew, *The Epic of Gilgamesh*, Allen Lane, Penguin Press, 1999

Gersh, Harry, *The Sacred Books of the Jews*, Stein & Day, New York, 1968

Gibson, John, *Canaanite Myths and Legends*, T&T Clark Publishers Ltd., Dulles, 1978

Glueck, Nelson, *Rivers In The Desert*, Grove Press, New York, 1960

Golb, Norman, *Who Wrote The Dead Sea Scrolls?*, Scribner, New York, 1995

Gray, Edward M., *Old Testament Criticism*, Harper, New York, 1923

Green, William Henry, *Moses and the Prophets*, Hurst & Co., New York, 1882

Greenberg, Moshe, *Ezekiel 1-20 A New Translation and Commentary*, Doubleday, New York 1983

Greenberg, Moshe, *Ezekiel 21-37 A New Translation and Commentary*, Random House, New York 1995

Gunkel, Hermann, *The Legends of Genesis*, The Open Court, Chicago, 1901

Halpern, Baruch, *David's Secret Demons*, William B. Eerdmans Publishing Co., Grand Rapids, 2001

Hamilton, Edith, *Spokesmen for God*, W. W. Norton & Company, Inc., New York, New York 1949

Haupt, Paul, *The Polychrome Bible, Part 6, The Book of Joshua*, New York, 1899

Heidel, Alexander, *The Gilgamesh Epic and Old Testament Parallels*, University of Chicago, 1946

Heller, Joseph, *God Knows*, Alfred A. Knopf, New York, 1984

Heym, Stefan, *The King David Report*, G. P. Putnam's Sons, New York, 1972

Hobbes, Thomas, *Leviathan*, Penguin Books, London, 1968 (first published, London, 1651)

Hoffman, Yain, *The Doctrine of the Exodus in the Bible*, Tel Aviv University Press, 1983

Hoffman, Yain, *A North Israelite Typological Myth and a Judaean Historical Tradition*, VT 39, 2

Hupfeld, Hermann, *Die Quellen der Genesis und die Art ihrer Zusammensetzung*, Berlin, 1853

Ilgen, Karl David, *Die Urkunden des Jerusalemischen Tempelarchivs in ihrer Urgestalt*, Halle 1798

James, Lawrence, *The Golden Warrior, The Life and Legend of Lawrence of Arabia*, Abacus, London, 1995

Jewish Publication Society, *Tanakh, The Holy Scriptures*, Philadelphia, 1985

Josephus, Flavius, *The Jewish War*, translated by G. A. Williamson, Penguin Books, London, 1981

Kautzsch, Emil, *An Outline of the Literature of the Old Testament*, London, 1898

Kautzsch, Emil, *Die Heilige Schrift des Alten Testaments*, Halle, 1913

Keller, Werner, *The Bible as History in Pictures*, William Morrow & Co., New York, 1964

Kennedy, James, *Peasants in Revolt: Political Allegory in Genesis 2-3*, JSOT 47, 3-14

Kirsch, Jonathan, *King David, The Real Life of the Man Who Ruled Israel*, Ballantine, 2000

Kovacs, Maureen Gallery, *The Epic of Gilgamesh*, Stanford University Press, 1985

Lahaye, Tim and Jenkins, Jerry B., *Left Behind: A Novel of the Earth's Last Days*, Tyndale House, Wheaton, Illinois, 2000

Lawrence, D. H., *David, A Play*, Alfred A. Knopf, New York, 1926

Lawrence, T. E., *Seven Pillars of Wisdom*, Anchor Books, New York, 1991

Levy, Thomas E., editor, *The Archaeology of Society in the Holy Land*, Facts on File, Inc., New York, 1995

Mack, Burton L., *Who Wrote the New Testament?*, HarperSanFrancisco, San Francisco, 1995

Marcus, Amy Dockser, *The View From Nebo*, Little, Brown & Co., Boston, 2000

Mazar, Amihai, *Archaeology of the Land of the Bible*, Doubleday, New York, 1990

McDowell, Josh, *Evidence That Demands A Verdict*, Here's Life Publishers, Inc., San Bernardino, California 1972

McDowell, Josh, *More Evidence That Demands A Verdict*, Here's Life Publishers, San Bernardino, California, 1972

McDowell, Josh, *The Best of Josh McDowell, A Ready Defense*, Thomas Nelson, Nashville, 1993

McKenzie, Stephen, *King David*, Oxford University Press, Oxford, England, 2000

McKenzie, Stephen, *The Trouble With Kings: The Composition of the Book of Kings*, 1991

Meier, Sam, *Job I-II: A Reflection of Genesis I-III*, VT 39, 2

Mendenhall, George E., *The Hebrew Conquest of Palestine*, Biblical Archaeologist (BA), XXV/3, 1962, pp 66-87

Mendenhall, George E., *The Tenth Generation*, Johns Hopkins University Press, Baltimore, 1973

Miles, Jack, *God, A Biography*, Alfred A. Knopf, New York, 1995

Negbi, Ora, *Canaanite Gods in Metal*, Israel Exploration Society, Jerusalem, 1976

Noth, Martin, *The Chronicler's History*, Sheffield, 1987

Noth, Martin, *The History of Israel*, Harper, New York, 1958

O'Connor, Eugene, translator and editor, *The Essential Epicurus*, Prometheus Books, Amherst, NY, 1993

Pagels, Elaine, *The Gnostic Gospels*, Vintage, New York, 1979

Palmer, Edward Henry, *The Desert of the Exodus*, Deighton Bell, Cambridge, 1871

de la Peyrere, Isaac, *Prae Adamitae (Men Before Adam)*, Brussels, 1655

Plaut, Steven, *The Scout*, Gefen Books, Hewlett, New York, 2002

Plaut, W. Gunther, *The Torah: A Modern Commentary*, New York, 1981

Porter, Barbara Nevling, *Images, Power and Politics*, American Philosophical Society, Philadelphia, 1993

Redford, Donald, *A Study of the Biblical Joseph Story*, Leiden, 1970

Redford, Donald, *Egypt, Canaan, and Israel in Ancient Times*, Princeton University Press, 1972

Renault, Mary, *The Nature of Alexander*, Pantheon Books, New York

Robinson, Edward, *Biblical Researches in Palestine, 11th Edition*, Crocker & Brewster, Boston, 1874

Robertson-Smith, W., *Lectures on the Religion of the Semites, Third Edition*, A&C Black, London, 1927

Rosenberg, Joel, *King and Kin, Political Allegory*, Indiana University Press, Bloomington, 1986

Rost, Leonard, *The Succession to the Throne of David*, The Almond Press, Sheffield, England, 1982

Rothenberg, Beno, *Were These King Solomon's Mines? Excavations in the Timna Valley*, Stein and Day, New York, 1972

Runions, J. E., *Exodus Motifs in I Samuel*, Evangelical Quarterly 52, 1980

Scholem, Gershon, *Kabbalah*, Dorset Press, New York, 1987

Scholem, Gershon, *Origins of the Kabbalah*, Princeton University Press, Princeton, New Jersey, 1990

Scholem, Gershon, *Sabbatai Sevi, The Mystical Messiah*, Princeton University Press, Princeton, 1973

Shaw, Ian, *The Oxford History Of Ancient Egypt*, Oxford University Press, Oxford, 2000

Smith, W. Robertson, *The Old Testament in the Jewish Church*, Second Edition, London, 1892

Sperling, S. David, *The Original Torah: The Political Intent of the Bible's Writers*, NYU Press, 1998 de Spinoza, Benedict, *A Theologico-Political Treatise*, Dover Publications, New York, 1951 (1670)

Spong, John Shelby, *Rescuing the Bible from Fundamentalism*, Harper SanFrancisco, SF, 1991

Thompson, Thomas, *The Historicity of the Patriarchal Narratives*, Trinity Press International, 2002

Trumbull, H. Clay, *Kadesh-Barnea, Its Importance and Probable Site*, Hodder-Stoughton, London, 1884

Tuch, F., *Kommentar uber die Genesis*, Halle, 1838

Tyndale, William, *The Old Testament*, Yale University Press, New Haven, 1992

Van der Toorn, Karel, *Dictionary of Deities and Demons*, Leiden, Brill, 1995

Van der Toorn, Karel, *Saul and the Rise of Israelite State Religion*, VT 63, 4, 1993

van Seters, John, *Abraham in History and Tradition*, Yale University Press, New Haven, 1987

van Seters, John, *The Pentateuch: A Social-Science Commentary*, Sheffield, 1999

van Seters, John, *The Terms "Amorite" and "Hittite" in the Old Testament*, VT 22/1 (1972) 64-81

von Rad, Gerhard, *Deuteronomy*, Westminster Press, 1966

von Rad, Gerhard, *Genesis*, Westminster Press, 1961

Wellhausen, J., *Prolegomena to the History of Israel*, Adam & Charles Black, Edinburgh, 1885

Whitelam, Keith W., *Israel's Traditions of Origin: Reclaiming the Land*, JSOT 44, 19-42, 1989

Wooley, C. L., and Lawrence, T. E., *The Wilderness of Zin*, Palestine Exploration Fund, London, 1915

Yadim, Yigael, *Hazor: Rediscovery of a Great Citadel of the Bible*, Random House, New York, 1975

Yardley, Michael, *T. E. Lawrence, A Biography*, Stein & Day, New York, 1985

Young, Gordon, Editor, *Mari in Retrospect*, Eisenbrauns, Winona Lake, Illinois, 1992

INDEX

A

B

C

G

H

I

J

K

L

O

P

R

S

T

U

W

Y

Z

ACKNOWLEDGMENTS

Although thanks should be extended to all of the authors whose works are listed in the Bibliography, special notice should be taken of Emil Kautzsch's *An Outline of the History of the Literature of the Old Testament*, S. R. Driver's *An Introduction to the Literature of the Old Testament*, Richard Elliott Friedman's *Who Wrote The Bible?*, Robert Alter's *The David Story: A Translation With Commentary of I and II Samuel*, Stefan Heym's *The King David Report*, Baruch Halpern's *David's Secret Demons*, Harold Bloom's *The Book of J*, Robert Coote's *In Defense of Revolution, the Elohist History*, Israel Finkelstein and Neil Asher Silberman's *The Bible Unearthed*, Amihai Mazar's *Archaeology of the Land of the Bible – 10,000-586 BCE*, and S. David Sperling's *The Original Torah, The Political Intent of the Bible's Writers*.

We acknowledge the contributions of the following publishers in particular: Fortress Press, Harcourt, Inc., Harper Collins, Alfred A. Knopf, New York University Press, W. W. Norton, Oxford University Press, University of Chicago Press, University of Sheffield Press and the firm of George Weidenfeld and Nicolson.

Credit for the physical appearance of the book—artwork, typography, and more—goes to Dale Murphy of Nuts-n-Bolts Graphics of San Francisco who worked under often very trying conditions—a manuscript which changed sometimes hourly. We acknowledge with gratitude the many hours that Jean O'Brien of the Old Monterey Book

Company and Dr. Paul McEvoy spent devising better ways to express ideas that had not then been clearly expressed. Special thanks go to Frank Field, my friend of over forty years, for his detailed commentaries on the content and form of the entire text.

Most importantly, credit for seeing this project through, from my first vague description of the book to its actual printing, goes to Van C. V. Francisco who has collaborated with me on wildly varying projects over the past thirty odd years.

Printed in the United States
56881LVS00001B/4-54